SECRET SOCIETIES OF THE MIDDLE AGES

SECRET SOCIETIES *of the* MIDDLE AGES

The Assassins,
the Templars &
the Secret Tribunals
of Westphalia

THOMAS KEIGHTLEY
introduction by JAMES WASSERMAN

WEISERBOOKS
Boston, MA/York Beach, ME

This edition first published in 2005 by
Red Wheel/Weiser, LLC
York Beach, ME
With offices at:
368 Congress Street
Boston, MA 02210
www.redwheelweiser.com

Cover art is a detail from the Bayeux Tapestry, 11th century. Used by special
permission of the City of Bayeux, France. The two horsemen that appear on
the cover are in reverse orientation from the original tapestry.

Library of Congress Cataloging-in-Publication Data available upon request

Introduction typeset in AGaramond by Kathryn Sky-Peck
Printed in Canada
TCP

12 11 10 09 08 07 06
8 7 6 5 4 3 2

INTRODUCTION TO THE 2005 EDITION

Thomas Keightley (1789–1872) was an extraordinarily prolific Irish-born scholar and writer who could read twenty different languages. He attended Trinity College in Dublin, but because of ill health, he did not join the Irish bar. He moved to London in 1824 to begin his literary career. His first solo work, *Fairy Mythology*, originally published anonymously in 1828 (and still in print), is said to have been praised by Jacob Grimm. *Secret Societies of the Middle Ages* was first published in 1837 anonymously and, according to the *Dictionary of National Biography*, "against his will."[1] It was reprinted at least three times over the next ten years.

I discovered Keightley only after I wrote *The Templars and the Assassins: The Militia of Heaven*. I was surprised indeed to find how similar in structure our books were. While many works on secret societies include short essays on the medieval Muslim Assassins and the Christian Knights Templar, both Keightley and I study and compare the two orders in greater detail.

Keightley's sophistication and erudition are unique for his day. His was virtually the first book in English to discuss a full history of the Assassins. A primary reference for him

---

1 The article on Thomas Keightley appears in volume 10 of *The Dictionary of National Biography* (London: Oxford University Press, 1917, reprinted 1959-1960).

was Joseph von Hammer-Purgstall (1774–1856) whose book *The History of the Assassins* (1818) had been solely available in German. (Keightley mentions here that an English translation, published in 1835, was released just as he was finishing his book.) Hammer-Purgstall is impossibly hostile to both the Assassins and the Templars. That Keightley could rise above the judgmental cultural attitude of his time is remarkable. He was clearly a man of vast learning and deep reflection, ahead of his time as a historian.

Further proof of this is the contemporary relevance of this classic work. Today we are engaged in what I believe may accurately be described as the modern-day Crusades. That war of cultures between Christianity and Islam that shook the world a thousand years ago—when Christian battled Muslim for possession and control of the holy sites on which both their religions were founded—has re-emerged as the central theme of modern life for millions, if not billions, of people worldwide. This book helps shed light on the roots of that conflict.

The Assassins and the Templars were mirror images of one another. The Templars were unique to Christianity. Parallels might be drawn to King David's battle with Goliath. In this case, the forces of darkness represented by Goliath and the Philistines arose to threaten the forces of light represented by David and the Israelis. Young David killed in service to a higher religious ideal. He could be accused of breaking the sixth Commandment, "Thou shalt not kill," yet he killed for the Lord. David's slaying of Goliath was an act of holy obedience. While he may have broken the Commandment, he obeyed his God. On this type of reasoning did the overall military campaign of the Crusades depend.

St. Bernard of Clairvaux (1090–1153) acted as the spiritual guide of the Knights Templar Order and promoted it to widespread acceptance. He was the most powerful Catholic cleric of his age and has been called the "Conscience of Christendom." Advisor to popes and kings, that which Bernard supported thrived, that which he opposed did not. In 1135, he wrote his famous letter of spiritual instruction to the knight-monks of the fledgling Order, In Praise of the New Knighthood, addressed to Templar founder Hughes de Payens. This powerful proclamation laid out the conceptual basis of the spiritual ideal of the warrior-monk. St. Bernard wrote of the Templar warrior vowed to the service of the Church: "If he kills malicious men, he is not a murderer under these circumstances, I say that he is murderer of wickedness and a champion of Christ."

The "average" Crusader was a secular knight doing good deeds for the salvation of his soul in service to the visions of his spiritual guide, the Pope. He could, in every other way, be a worldly individual—prone to drinking, bragging, treachery, lechery, and general unruliness. In the case of the Templar knight, the situation was completely different. The Templars were monks who exercised their religious devotion through force of arms. They were holy warriors, substituting the rigors of simplicity and poverty for the trumpery and ostentatiousness of the silk-clad, jewel-bedecked, secular knight whose lust for his Lady was often dressed in the romanticized idealism of chivalry.

The medieval chivalric ideal of the Divine Feminine represented a cultural watershed. Celebrated in the songs and poems of troubadours and embodied by the mounted, armored knight, chivalry exalted women in Christian

culture for the first time since the birth of the religion
from its male-oriented Jewish parent. It was a welcome
advance indeed. However, the Templars took the idealiza-
tion of the feminine to a higher realm altogether. The
Patroness of the Order was the Virgin Mary, Queen of
Heaven, Mother of God. Service to this ideal called forth
a physical chastity from the Templar warrior-monk, lest he
lose his greater focus and be distracted by an illusion of
that higher love, to waste his devotion on a lesser reflection
of the ultimate feminine archetype to whom he aspired.

The Assassins were a less foreign idea for Islam than the
Templars were to Christianity. *Jihad*, the principle of spiritual battle, was an established concept; in fact it has been
called the Sixth Pillar of Islam. The Prophet spread the
religion of Islam through the power of the sword. War
was a part of religious duty, especially for the early
Muslim. The Assassins, however, were the first monastic
military Order within Islam. Their use of the dagger in
service to the higher welfare of their community was a
departure from the idea that the campaign against the
infidels exempted Islam from battles between Muslims.
The Assassins declared themselves apart from all,
Muslims included. Their mission was to spread their
teaching both outside of and within Islam. All who did
not accept the doctrine of the Imamate of Nizar were
unbelievers, the infidels against whom Jihad might properly be waged. (The Assassins are more properly known as
the Nizari Ismailis.) To an Assassin, an observant Muslim
could be an unbeliever.

Their use of assassination as a technique was also
unique. The Assassins have been called the world's first
terrorists. Their strategy was to selectively target those

individuals who threatened their community—for example, hostile political rulers, noble advisors who counseled policies against the community, generals and other high-ranking military commanders who attacked them, or religious and educational leaders who publicly preached against or taught against the sect. They quite successfully created widespread fear among those who opposed them.

In view of our modern experience with terrorism, however, it should be noted that the Assassins were not the indiscriminate mass murderers targeting civilians with whom we are only too familiar today. I contend that as a religious brotherhood, even though they were killers like King David and the Knights Templar, the Assassins showed a basic respect for human life far different than we see in the militant Islamist movement of today. You may note that Hasan-i-Sabah, founder of the Assassins, killed one of his sons for violating Islamic law by drinking wine. Contrast this with reports that several of the September 11, 2001 killers spent their last nights on earth drinking alcohol at strip clubs.

The goal of the medieval Assassins was to carve out a territory for themselves in an otherwise hostile region where they might practice their religion undisturbed and to pursue their missionary activities among those receptive to their message. Assassination was one of the techniques they perfected to accomplish this goal. As Keightley points out, they were also adept at negotiation, fortress building, and agriculture.

One of the great services rendered by Keightley is his reporting of the vast repertoire of legends about the Assassins. Some of these I read for the first time in this book, despite my rather wide acquaintance with Assassin literature. While not all of them are historically accurate, the catalog presented here is instructive.

There is considerable documented historical interaction between the Templars and the Assassins. They occupied castles within several miles of each other, negotiated treaties together, paid ransoms and tributes to each other, arranged visits between themselves for the purpose of discussing religion, and even occasionally allied themselves militarily against common enemies. Within this historical context, it is likely that spiritual relationships were formed between Assassin adepts and certain Templar knights—philosophically motivated men who sought mysteries beyond the superstitions and dogmas offered by their own faith.

During the centuries-long rise of Christianity, the Pagan wisdom that had spiritually dominated the Mediterranean region for millennia was continuously displaced. As Christianity seized more political power, especially under Constantine in the fourth century, the older faiths were declared illegal in the Roman Empire. By the sixth century, the Roman Emperor Justinian closed the last Neo-Platonic academy in the West.

Pagan scholars, monks, and mystics fled eastward, welcomed by the ruling Sassanian dynasty of Persia. Thus, by the time of the founding of Islam in the seventh century, there was a flourishing wisdom tradition in the area. The Gnostic Neo-Platonism that had evolved from the Egyptian roots of classical Greece had been successfully transplanted to the soil of the Near East. These doctrines and practices, continuously interacting with the vibrancy of the new Muslim faith, would become the parent of the Sufi mysteries, as well as those of the Assassins.

Many scholars and occultists believe the interaction between the Assassins and Templars was instrumental in re-introducing the lost higher wisdom to the West. The Crusades began at the very end of the European Dark Ages—a period lasting some four centuries, characterized by a brutality of life, failed social conditions, and a dearth of spiritual values. Two centuries later, at the beginning of the fourteenth century, although defeated militarily, European culture was uplifted by its contact with the Muslim world. By the fifteenth century, this creative evolution began to flower into the Renaissance and the intense classical Pagan revival that was the motivating spiritual force of the Renaissance. Did returning Templars in fact carry the Wisdom teachings back to Europe? Is this perhaps the true identity of the legendary Templar treasure?

Keightley's informative treatment on the Holy Vehm (Fehm) is the most detailed I have read on this fascinating subject. The modern reader cannot help but draw parallels between the medieval system of the Holy Vehm and the modern FISA courts (established by the Foreign Intelligence Surveillance Act of 1978), the secret warrants authorized by the U.S. Patriot Act of 2001, and the military tribunals of the "War on Terror." A word of caution to the overly anxious reader: please pay attention to Keightley's characterization of the Vehm courts as a necessary corrective to the lawless times in which they initially operated. Of course what began as a useful system in the case of the Holy Vehm broke down and became corrupt. Americans, in particular, must exercise diligence to prevent the more offensive legal structures erected to deal with the very real threats of the post September 11 world from evolving into degenerate tools of tyranny as the threat subsides.

One of Keightley's statements with which I must vigorously disagree is in his brief conclusion. I was a bit surprised by his expression of relief at the lack of secret-society activity during the third and fourth decades of the nineteenth century. This was hardly the case. Revolutionary secret societies were in fact quite active when Keightley wrote. Many drew ideological inspiration from the Bavarian Illuminati (1776–1785), a secret society long considered to have influenced the French Revolution in 1787 through their infiltration of much of the existing Freemasonic Lodge network. From that bloodbath against Church and State emerged social revolutionaries like Gracchus Babeuf, Nicholas Bonneville, and Filippo Buonarroti, the ideological godparents of Karl Marx and Vladimir Lenin. The Italian Carbonari, an early nineteenth-century nationalist secret society became a trans-European revolutionary force, estimated at half a million strong before it was suppressed ca. 1820. It was revived soon after by Guiseppe Mazzini who fanned the flames of revolution establishing secret societies throughout continental Europe.

Indeed secret associations did not disappear in a quaint medieval past. Nor did they cease their activities after the nineteenth century. They are as active today as they have ever been. Spiritual secret societies that seek higher wisdom find that the confines of their closed membership provide an excellent forum to pursue their shared interests and disciplines with minimal distractions. Criminal organizations, such as the Mafia, will ever find secrecy, oaths of loyalty, and the bonds of criminal acts to be a guarantee of silence, loyalty, and common purpose. Those who seek political power over others continue to pursue their manipulative agendas in the heavily guarded mansions, palatial resorts, think-tank offices, global governance agencies, and foundation headquarters of the West, while their Islamofascist adversaries—in secret societies such as al-Qaeda—continue to fashion their equally obnoxious plans in the caves, mosques, and palaces of the Muslim world.

We are fortunate to have this timely book available again after nearly a century and a half. Many excellent works are available on the Templars and the Assassins. If this is your first such book, you are in for an exciting journey. If you are already familiar with some of the literature on these seminal secret societies, you will not be disappointed by Thomas Keightley's contribution.

—JAMES WASSERMAN
Fall Equinox 2004
New York City

SECRET SOCIETIES OF THE MIDDLE AGES

CONTENTS.

CONTENTS.

CHAPTER IV.

CHAPTER V.

CHAPTER VI.

CHAPTER VII.

CHAPTER VIII.

CHAPTER IX.

CONTENTS.

THE TEMPLARS.

CHAPTER I.

CHAPTER II.

CONTENTS.

CONTENTS.

Page

CHAPTER VII.

(fficers of the Order—The Master—Mode of Election—
His Rights and Privileges—Restraints on him—The
Seneschal—The Marshal—The Treasurer—The Draper
—The Turcopilar—Great-Priors —Commanders—Visi-
tors—Sub-Marshal—Standard-bearer .   .   . 253

CHAPTER VIII.

Chapters—Mode of holding them—Templars' Mode of
Living—Amusements—Conduct in War   .   . 266

CHAPTER IX.

Molay elected Master—Last attempt of the Christians in
Syria—Conduct of the Three Military Orders—Philip
the Fair and Pope Boniface VIII.—Seizure of the
Pope—Election of Clement V.—The Papal See removed
to France—Causes of Philip's enmity to the Templars
—Arrival of Molay in France—His interviews with the
Pope—Charges made against the Templars—Seizure
of the Knights—Proceedings in England—Nature of
the Charges against the Order   .   .   . 276

CHAPTER X.

Examination of the captive Knights—Different kinds of
Torture—Causes of Confession—What Confessions
were made—Templars brought before the Pope—Their
Declarations—Papal Commission—Molay brought before it—Ponsard de Gisi—Defenders of the Order—
Act of Accusation—Heads of Defence—Witnesses
against the Order—Fifty-four Templars committed to
the Flames at Paris—Remarkable words of Aymeric
de Villars-le-Duc—Templars burnt in other places—
Further Examinations—The Head worshipped by the
Templars—John de Pollincourt—Peter de la Palu   . 293

CHAPTER XI.

Examinations in England—Germany—Spain—Italy—
Naples and Provence—Sicily—Cyprus—Meeting of the

CONTENTS.

THE

SECRET TRIBUNALS OF WESTPHALIA.

CHAPTER I.

CHAPTER II.

CHAPTER III.

CHAPTER IV.

CHAPTER V.

CONTENTS.

SECRET SOCIETIES

OF

THE MIDDLE AGES.

INTRODUCTION.

IF we had the means of investigating historically the origin of Secret Societies, we should probably find that they began to be formed almost as soon as any knowledge had been accumulated by particular individuals beyond what constituted the common stock. The same thing has happened to knowledge that has happened to all other human possessions,—its actual holders have striven to keep it to themselves. It is true that in this case the possessor of the advantage does not seem to have the same reason for being averse to share it with others which naturally operates in regard to many good things of a different kind; he does not, by imparting it to those around him, diminish his own store. This is true, in so far as regards the possession of knowledge considered in its character of a real good; the owner of the treasure does not impoverish himself by giving it away, as he would by giving away his money, but remains as rich as ever, even after he has made ever so many others as rich as himself. But still there is one thing that he loses, and a thing upon which the human mind is apt to set a very high value; he loses the distinction which he derived from his knowledge. This distinction really serves, in many respects, the same purpose that money itself does. Like money, it brings observation and worship. Like money, it is the dearest of all things, power. Knowledge, however held, is indeed essentially power; to *ken*, that is, to know, is the same word and the same thing with to *can*, that is, to be able. But there is an additional and a different species of power conferred by knowledge when it exists as the distinction of a few individuals in the midst of general ignorance. Here it is power not only to do those things the methods of doing which it teaches; it is, besides, the power of governing other men through your comparative strength and their weakness.

So strong is the motive thus prompting the possessor of knowledge to the exclusive retention of his acquisitions, that unless it had been met by another motive appealing in like manner directly to our self-interest, it appears probable that scarcely any general dissemination of knowledge would ever have taken place. The powerful counteracting motive in question is derived from the consideration that in most cases one of the most effective ways which the possessor of knowledge can take of exciting the admiration of others, is to communicate what he knows. The light must give itself forth, and illuminate the world, even that it may be itself seen and admired. In the very darkest times, the scholar or philosopher may find his ambition sufficiently gratified by the mere reputation of superior attainments, and the stupid wonder, or it may be superstitious terror, of the uninquiring multitude. But as soon as any thing like a spirit of intelligence or of curiosity has sprung up in the general mind, all who aspire to fame or consideration from their learning, their discoveries, or their intellectual powers, address themselves to awaken the admiration of their fellow-men, not by concealing, but by displaying their knowledge—not by sealing up the precious fountain, but by allowing its waters to flow freely forth, that all who choose may drink of them. From this time science ceases almost to have any secrets; and, all the influences to which it is exposed acting in the same direction, the tendency of knowledge becomes wholly diffusive.

But in the preceding state of things the case was altogether the reverse. Then there was little or no inducement to the communication of knowledge, and every motive for those who were in possession of it to keep it to themselves. There was not intelligence enough abroad to appreciate, or even to understand, the truths of philosophy if they had been announced in their simplicity, and explained according to their principles; all that was cared for, all that was capable of arousing the vulgar attention, was some display, made as surprising and mysterious as possible, of their practical application. It would even have been attended with danger in many cases to attempt to teach true philosophy openly, or to make open profession of it; it was too much in opposition to some of the strongest prejudices which everywhere held sway. It is not, then, to be wondered at, that its cultivators should have sought to guard and preserve it by means of secret associations, which, besides excluding the multitude from a participation in the thing thus fenced round and hidden, answered also divers other convenient purposes. They afforded opportunities of free conference, which could not otherwise have been obtained. There was much in the very forms of mystery and concealment thus adopted calculated to impress the popular imagination, and to excite its reverence and awe. Finally, the veil which they drew around their proceedings enabled the members of these secret societies to combine their efforts, and arrange their plans, in security and without interruption, whenever they cherished any designs of political innovation, or other projects, the open avowal and prosecution of which the established authorities would not have tolerated.

The facilities afforded by the system of secret association, and it may even be said the temptations which it presents, to the pursuit of political objects forbidden by the laws, are so great as to justify all governments in prohibiting it, under whatever pretence it may be attempted to be introduced. It is nothing to the purpose to argue that under bad governments valuable political reforms have sometimes been effected by such secret associations which would not otherwise have been attained. The same mode of proceeding, in the nature of the thing, is equally efficacious for the overthrow of a good government. Bad men are as likely to combine in the dark for their objects as good men are for theirs. In any circumstances, a secret association is an *imperium in imperio*, a power separate from, and independent of, that which is recognized as the supreme power in the state, and therefore something essentially disorganizing, and which it is contrary to the first principles of all government for any state to tolerate. In the case of a bad government, indeed, all means are fairly available for its overthrow which are not morally objectionable, the simple rule for their application being that it shall be directed by considerations of prudence and discretion. In such a case a secret association of the friends of reform may sometimes be found to supply the most effective means for accomplishing the desired end; but that end, however desirable it may be, is not one which the constitution of the state itself can rationally contemplate. The constitution cannot be founded upon the supposition that even necessary alterations of it are to be brought about through agencies out of itself, and forming no part of its regular mechanism. Whenever such agencies are successfully brought into operation, there is a revolution, and the constitution is at an end. Even the amendment of the constitution so effected is its destruction.

Yet most of the more remarkable secret associations which have existed in different ages and countries have probably either been originally formed to accomplish some political end, or have come to contemplate such an object as their chief design. Even when nothing more than a reformation of the national religion has been, as far as can be discovered, the direct aim of the association, it may still be fairly considered as of a political character, from the manner in which religion has been mixed up in almost every country with the civil institutions of the state. The effect which it was desired to produce upon the government may in many cases have been very far from extending to its complete abolition, and the substitution of another form of polity; an alteration in some one particular may have been all that was sought, or the object of the association may even have been to support some original principle of the constitution against the influence of circumstances which threatened its subversion or modification. Whether directed to the alteration or to the maintenance of the existing order of things, the irregular and dangerous action of secret combinations is, as we have said, a species of force which no state can reasonably be expected to recognize. But it may nevertheless have happened at particular emergencies, and during times of very imperfect civilization, that valuable service has been rendered by such combinations to some of the most important interests of society, and that they have to a considerable extent supplied the defects of the rude and imperfect arrangements of the ordinary government.

The system of secret association is, indeed, the natural resource of the friends of political reform, in times when the general mind is not sufficiently enlightened to appreciate or to support their schemes for the improvement of the existing institutions and order of things. To proclaim their views openly in such circumstances would be of no more use than haranguing to the desert. They might even expose themselves to destruction by the attempt. But, united in a secret association, and availing themselves of all the advantages at once of their superior knowledge and intelligence, and of their opportunities of acting in concert, a very few individuals may work with an effect altogether out of proportion to their number. They may force in a wedge which in time shall even split and shiver into fragments the strength of the existing social system, no matter by how many ages of barbarism it may be consolidated. Or, in the absence of a more regular law and police, they may maintain the empire of justice by stretching forth the arm of their own authority in substitution for that of the state, which lies paralysed and powerless, and turning to account even the superstitions and terrors of the popular imagination by making these, as excited by their dark organization and mysterious forms of procedure, the chain whereby to secure the popular obedience.

On the whole, the system of secret association for political objects, even when there is no dispute about the desirableness of the ends sought to be accomplished, may be pronounced to be a corrective of which good men will avail themselves only in times of general ignorance, or under governments that sin against the first principles of all good government, by endeavouring to put a stop to the advancement of society through the prohibition of the open expression of opinion; but, in countries where the liberty of discussion exists, and where the public mind is tolerably enlightened, as entirely unsuited to the circumstances of the case as it is opposed to the rules and maxims on which every government must take its stand that would provide for its own preservation. In these happier circumstances the course for the friends of social improvement to follow is to come forward into the full light of day as the only place worthy of their mission, and to seek the realization of their views by directly appealing to the understandings of their fellow-citizens.

One evil to which secret societies are always exposed is the chance of the objects and principles of their members being misrepresented by those interested in resisting their power and influence. As the wakeful eyes of the government, and of those concerned in the maintenance of the actual system, will be ever upon them, they must strictly confine the knowledge of their real views and proceedings to the initiated, and as their meetings must for the same reason be held in retired places, and frequently by night, an opportunity, which is rarely neglected, is afforded to their enemies of spreading the most calumnious reports of their secret practices, which, though conscious of innocence, they may not venture openly to confute. By arts of this kind the suspicions and aversion of the people are excited, and they are often thus made to persecute their best friends, and still to bow beneath the yoke of their real foes. The similarity of the accusations made against secret associations in all parts of the world is a sufficient proof of their falsehood, and we should always listen to them with the utmost suspicion, recollecting the quarter from which they proceed. Of the spotless purity of the Christian religion when first promulgated through the Roman world no one can entertain a doubt; yet when persecution obliged its

professors to form as it were a secret society, the
same charges of Thyestian banquets, and of the pro-
miscuous intercourse of the sexes, were made against
them, which they themselves afterwards brought, and
with probably as little truth, against the various sects
of the Gnostic heresy.   Wherever there is secrecy
there will be suspicion, and charges of something
unable to bear the light of day will be made.

The ancient world presents one secret society of a
professedly political character—that of the Pythagoreans. Of religious ones it might be expected to yield
a rich harvest to the inquirer, when we call to mind
all that has been written in ancient and modern times
concerning the celebrated mysteries. But the original Grecian mysteries, such as those of Eleusis, appear
to have been nothing more than public services of
the gods, with some peculiar ceremonies performed at
the charge of the state, and presided over by the magistrates, in which there were no secrets communicated
to the initiated, no revelation of knowledge beyond
that which was generally attainable.   The *private*
mysteries, namely, the Orphic, Isiac, and Mithraic,
which were introduced from the East, were merely
modes employed by cunning and profligate impostors
for taking advantage of the weakness and credulity
of the sinful and the superstitious, by persuading
them that by secret and peculiar rites, and the invocation of strange deities, the apprehended punishment of sin might be averted.   The nocturnal assemblies for the celebration of these mysteries were
but too often scenes of vice and debauchery, and they
were discountenanced by all good governments.   It
is to these last, and not to the Eleusinian mysteries,
that the severe strictures of the fathers of the church
apply*.

The history of Pythagoras and his doctrines is

* See Lobeck's excellent work " Aglaophamus.''

extremely obscure. The accounts of this sage which have come down to us were not written till **many** centuries after his death, and but little reliance is to be placed on their details. Pythagoras was a Samian by birth ; he flourished in the sixth century before Christ, at the time when Egypt exercised so much influence over Greece, and its sages sought the banks of the Nile in search of wisdom. There is, therefore, no improbability in the tradition of Pythagoras also having visited that land of mystery, and perhaps other parts of the East, and marked the tranquil order of things where those who were esteemed the wise ruled over the ignorant people. He may therefore have conceived the idea of uniting this sacerdotal system with the rigid morals and aristocratic constitution of the Dorian states of Greece. His native isle, which was then under the tyranny of Polycrates, not appearing to him suited for the introduction of his new system of government, he turned his eyes to the towns of Magna Græcia, or Southern Italy, which were at that time in a highly flourishing condition, whose inhabitants were eager in the pursuit of knowledge, and some of which already possessed written codes of law. He fixed his view on Croton, one of the wealthiest and most distinguished of those towns.

Aristocracy was the soul of the Dorian political constitutions, and the towns of Magna Græcia were all Dorian colonies ; but in consequence of their extensive commerce the tendency of the people was at that time towards democracy. To preserve the aristocratic principle was the object of Pythagoras; but he wished to make the aristocracy not merely one of birth; he desired that, like the sacerdotal castes of the East, it should also have the supremacy in knowledge. As his system was contrary to the general feeling, Pythagoras saw that it was only by gaining

the veneration of the people that he could carry it
into effect; and by his personal advantages of beauty
of form, skill in gymnastic exercises, eloquence, and
dignity, he drew to himself the popular favour by
casting the mantle of mystery over his doctrines. He
thus at once inspired the people with awe for them,
and the nobles with zeal to become initiated in his
secrets.

The most perfect success, we are told, attended
the project of the philosopher. A total change of
manners took place in Croton; the constitution became nearly Spartan; a body of 300 nobles, rendered
by the lessons of the sage as superior to the people in
knowledge of every kind as they were in birth, ruled
over it. The nobles of the other states flocked to Croton to learn how to govern by wisdom; Pythagorean
missionaries went about everywhere preaching the
new political creed; they inculcated on the people
religion, humility, and obedience; such of the nobles
as were deemed capable were initiated in the wisdom
of the order, and taught its maxims and principles; a golden age, in which power was united with
wisdom and virtue, seemed to have begun upon
earth.

But, like every thing which struggles against the
spirit of the age, such a political system was not
fated to endure. While Croton was the chief seat of
Pythagoreanism, luxury had fixed her throne in the
neighbouring city of Sybaris. The towns were rivals.
one or the other must fall. It was little more than
thirty years after the arrival of Pythagoras in Croton
that a furious war broke out between them. Led by
Milo and other Pythagoreans, who were as expert
in military affairs as skilled in philosophy, the Cro-
toniates utterly annihilated the power of their rivals,
and Sybaris sank to rise no more. But with her
sank the power of the Pythagoreans. They judged

it inexpedient to give a large share of the booty to the people; the popular discontent rose; Cylon, a man who had been refused admittance into the order, took advantage of it, and urged the people on; the Pythagoreans were all massacred, and a democracy established. All the other towns took example by Croton, a general persecution of the order commenced, and Pythagoras himself was obliged to seek safety in flight, and died far away from the town which once had received him as a prophet. The Pythagoreans never made any further attempts at attaining political power, but became a mere sect of mystic philosophers, distinguished by peculiarities of food and dress.

Ancient times present us with no other society of any importance to which we can properly apply the term *secret*.

The different sects of the Gnostics, who are by the fathers of the church styled heretics, were to a certain extent secret societies, as they did not propound their doctrines openly and publicly; but their history is so scanty, and so devoid of interest, that an examination of it would offer little to detain ordinary readers.

The present volume is devoted to the history of three celebrated societies which flourished during the middle ages, and of which, as far as we know, no full and satisfactory account is to be found in English literature. These are the Assassins, or Ismaïlites, of the East, whose name has become in all the languages of Europe synonymous with murderer, who *were* a secret society, and of whom we have in general such vague and indistinct conceptions; the military order of the Knights Templars, who were most barbarously persecuted under the pretext of their holding a secret doctrine, and against whom the charge has been renewed at the present day; and, finally, the Secret Tribunals of Westphalia, in Germany, concerning which all our information has hitherto been derived from the incorrect statements of dramatists and romancers*.

It is the simplicity of truth, and not the excitement of romance, that the reader is to expect to find in the following pages,—pictures of manners and modes of thinking different from our own,—knowledge, not *mere* entertainment, yet as large an infusion of the latter as is consistent with truth and instruction.

* Since the present work was prepared, a translation of Von Hammer's History of the Assassins has been published by Dr. Oswald Charles Wood.

THE ASSASSINS*.

CHAPTER I.

State of the World in the 7th Century—Western Empire—Eastern Empire—Persia—Arabia—Mohammed—His probable Motives—Character of his Religion—The Koran.

AT the commencement of the 7th century of the Christian era a new character was about to be impressed on a large portion of the world. During the two centuries which preceded, the Goths, Vandals, Huns, and other martial tribes of the Germanic race, had succeeded in beating down the barriers opposed to them, and in conquering and dismembering the Western Empire. They brought with them and retained their love of freedom and spirit of dauntless valour, but abandoned their ancient and ferocious superstitions, and embraced the corrupt system which then degraded the name of Christianity. This system, hardened, as it were, by ideas retained and transferred from the original faith of its new disciples, which ideas were fostered by those passages of the books of the Hebrew Scriptures which accorded with their natural sentiments, afterwards, when allied with feudalism, engendered the spirit which poured the hosts of Western Europe over the mountains and plains of Asia for the conquest of the Holy Land.

* Hammer's *Geschichte der Assassinen* (History of the Assassins), and the same writer's *Fundgruben des Orients* (Mines of the East), M. Jourdain's *Extrait de l'Ouvrage de Mirkhond sur la Dynastie des Ismaelites*, and Malcolm's History of Persia, are the principal authorities for the following account of the Assassins.

A different picture was at this time presented by the empire of the East. It still retained the extent assigned to it by Theodosius; and all the countries from the Danube, round the east and south coasts of the Mediterranean, to the straits of Gades, yielded a more or less perfect obedience to the successors of Constantine. But a despotism more degrading, though less ferocious, than those of Asia paralyzed the patriotism and the energy of their subjects; and the acuteness, the contentiousness, and the imagination of the Greeks, combined with mysticism and the wild fancy of the Asiatics to transform the simplicity of the religion of Christ into a revolting system of intricate metaphysics and gross idolatry, which aided the influence of their political condition in chilling the martial ardour of the people. The various provinces of the empire were held together by the loosest and feeblest connexion, and it was apparent that a vigorous shock would suffice to dissolve the union.

The mountains of Armenia and the course of the Euphrates separated the Eastern Empire from that of Persia. This country had been under the dominion of the people named Parthians at the time when the eagles of the Roman republic first appeared on the Euphrates, and defeat had more than once attended the Roman armies which attempted to enter their confines. Like every dominion not founded on the freedom of the people, that of the Arsacides (the Parthian royal line) grew feeble with time, and after a continuance of nearly five centuries the sceptre of Arsaces passed from the weak hand of the last monarch of his line to that of Ardeshir Babegan (that is the son of Babec), a valiant officer of the royal army, and a pretended descendant of the ancient monarchs of Persia. Ardeshir, to accomplish this revolution, availed himself of the religious prejudices of the Persian people. The Parthian monarchs had inclined to the manners and the religion of the Greeks, and the Light-religion—the original faith of Persia, and one of the purest and most spiritual of those to which a divine origin may not be assigned—had been held in slight estimation, and its priests unvisited by royal favour. It was the pride and the policy of Ardeshir to restore the ancient religion to the dignity which it had enjoyed under the descendants of Cyrus, and Religion, in return, lent her powerful aid to his plans of restoring the royal dignity to its pristine vigour, and of infusing into the breast of the people the love of country and the ardour for extending the Persian dominion to what it had been of old ; and for 400 years the Sassanides* were the most formidable enemies of the Roman empire. But their dominion had, at the period of which we write, nearly attained the greatest limit allotted to Oriental dynasties ; and though Noosheerwan the Just had attained great warlike fame, and governed with a vigour and justice that have made his name proverbial in the East, and Khoosroo Purveez displayed a magnificence which is still the theme of Persian poetry and romance, and carried his victorious arms over Syria and Egypt, and further along the African coast than even those of Darius I. had been able to advance, yet defeat from the gallant Emperor Heraclius clouded his latter days, and the thirteenth year after his death, by showing the Persian armies in flight, and the palladium of the empire, the jewel-set apron of the blacksmith Kawah, in the hands of the rovers of the deserts, revealed the secret that her strength

* The name given to the dynasty founded by Ardeshir, from his pretended ancestor Sassan, a grandson of Isfundear, a hero greatly celebrated in the ancient history of Persia. Isfundear was the son of Gushtasp, who is supposed to be the Darius Hystaspes of the Greek historians. Sir John Malcolm has endeavoured to identify Isfundear with the Xerxes of the Greeks.

was departed from Persia. The brilliancy of the
early part of the reign of Khoosroo Purveez had been
but the flash before death which at times is displayed in empires as in individuals. The vigour was
gone which was requisite to stem the torrent of
fanatic valour about to burst forth from the wilds of
Arabia.

It is the boast of Arabia that it has never been
conquered. This immunity from subjugation has,
however, been only partial, and is owing to the
nature of the country; for although the barren sands
of the Hejaz and Nejed have always baffled the
efforts of hostile armies, yet the more inviting region
of Yemen, the Happy Arabia of the ancients, has
more than once allured a conqueror, and submitted
to his sway. The inhabitants of this country have
been the same in blood and in manners from the
dawn of history. Brave, but not sanguinary, robbers, but kind and hospitable, of lively and acute
intellect, we find the Arabs, from the days of Abraham to the present times, leading the pastoral and
nomadic life in the desert, agriculturists in Yemen,
traders on the coasts and on the confines of Syria and
Egypt. Their foreign military operations had
hitherto been confined to plundering expeditions
into the last-mentioned countries, unless they were
the Hycsos, or Shepherd Kings, who, according to
tradition, once made the conquest of Egypt. Arabia
forming a kind of world in itself, its various tribes
were in ceaseless hostility with each other; but it was
apparent that if its brave and skilful horsemen could
be united under one head, and animated by motives
which would inspire constancy and rouse valour,
they might present a force capable of giving a fatal
shock to the empires of Persia and of Rome.

It is impossible, on taking a survey of the history
of the world, not to recognize a great predisposing

cause, which appoints the time and circumstances of every event which is to produce any considerable change in the state of human affairs. The agency of this overruling providence is nowhere more perceptible than in the present instance. The time was come for the Arabs to leave their deserts and march to the conquest of the world, and the man was born who was to inspire them with the necessary motives.

Mohammed (*Illustrious**) was the son of Abd-Allah (*Servant of God*), a noble Arab of the tribe of Koreish, which had the guardianship of the Kaaba (*Square House of Mecca*), the *Black Stone* contained in which (probably an aerolite) had been for ages an object of religious veneration to the tribes of Arabia. His mother was Amineh, the daughter of a chief of princely rank. He was early left an orphan, with the slender patrimony of five camels and a female Æthiopian slave. His uncle, Aboo Talib, brought him up. At an early age the young Mohammed accompanied his uncle to the fair of Bozra, on the verge of Syria, and in his 18th year he signalized his valour in an engagement between the Koreish and a hostile tribe. At the age of 25 he entered the service of Khadijah, a wealthy widow, with whose merchandise he visited one of the great fairs of Syria. Mohammed, though poor, was noble, handsome, acute, and brave; Khadijah, who was fifteen years his senior, was inspired with love; her passion was returned; and the

* The Oriental proper names being mostly all significant, we shall translate them when we first employ them. As, however, it is not always that it can be discovered what the original Arabic characters are of an eastern word which we meet in Roman letters, we shall be sometimes obliged to leave names unexplained, and at other times to hazard conjectural explanations. In the last case, we shall affix a mark of doubt.

gift of her hand and wealth gave the nephew of Aboo Talib affluence and consideration.

Mohammed's original turn of mind appears to have been serious, and it is not unlikely that the great truth of the Unity of the Deity had been early impressed on his mind by his mother or his Jewish kindred. The Koreish and the rest of his country-men were idolaters; Christianity was now corrupted by the intermixture of many superstitions; the fire-worship of the Persians was a worshipping of the Deity under a material form; the Mosaic religion had been debased by the dreams and absurd distinctions of the Rabbis. A simpler form than any of these seemed wanted for man. God, moreover, was believed to have at sundry times sent prophets into the world for its reformation, and might do so again; the Jews still looked for their promised Messiah; many Christians held that the Paraclete was yet to come. Who can take upon him to assert that Mohammed may not have believed him-self to be set apart to the service of God, and appointed by the divine decree to be the preacher of a purer faith than any which he then saw existing? Who will say that in his annual seclusions of fifteen days in the cave of Hira he may not have fallen into ecstatic visions, and that in one of these waking dreams the angel Gabriel may not have appeared to his distempered fancy to descend to nominate him to the office of a prophet of God, and present to him, in a visible form, that portion of his future law which had probably already passed through his mind*?

* The Kubla Khan of Coleridge (Poetical Works, vol. i. p. 266) is a fine instance of this power of the mind, withdrawn from the contemplation of material objects. The reader will probably recollect the sign given from heaven to Lord Herbert of Cherbury, on the occasion of his work written against re-

A certain portion of self-delusion is always mingled with successful imposture; the impostor, as it were, makes his first experiment on himself. It is much more reasonable to conclude that Mohammed had at first no other object than the dissemination of truth by persuasion, and that he may have beguiled himself into a belief of his being the instrument selected for that purpose, than that the citizen of a town in the secluded region of Arabia beheld in ambitious vision from his mountain-cave his victorious banners waving on the banks of the Oxus and the Ebro, and his name saluted as that of the Prophet of God by a fourth part of the human race. Still we must not pass by another, and perhaps a truer supposition, namely, that, in the mind of Mohammed, as in that of so many others, the end justified the means, and that he deemed it lawful to feign a vision and a commission from God in order to procure from men a hearing for the truth.

Whatever the ideas and projects of Mohammed may originally have been, he waited till he had attained his fortieth year (the age at which Moses showed himself first to the Israelites), and then revealed his divine commission to his wife Khadijah, his slave Zeid, his cousin Ali, the son of Aboo Talib, and his friend, the virtuous and wealthy Aboo Bekr. It is difficult to conceive any motive but conviction to have operated on the minds of these

vealed religion. The writer has lately heard an instance of a lady of fortune, to whom, as she reclined one day on a sofa, a voice seemed to come from heaven, announcing to her that she was selected as the instrument for accomplishing a great work in the hands of God; and giving, as a sign, that, for a certain number of months, she should be unable to leave the sofa on which she was lying. Such is the power of imagination, that the supposed intimation in regard to the sign actually took effect; she believed herself to have lost the power of motion, and therefore did in reality lose it.

different persons, who at once acknowledged his
claim to the prophetic office; and it speaks not a
little for the purity of the previous life of the new
Prophet, that he could venture to claim the faith
of those who were most intimately acquainted with
him.   The voice of wisdom has assured us that
a prophet has no honour in his own country and
among his own kindred, and the example of Mohammed testified the truth of the declaration.
During thirteen years the new religion made but
slow and painful progress in the town of Mecca;
but the people of Yathreb, a town afterwards dignified with the appellation of the City of the Prophet
(*Medinat-en-Nabi*), were more susceptive of faith ;
and when, on the death of Aboo Talib, who pro-
tected his nephew, though he rejected his claims, his
celebrated Flight (*Hejra*) brought him to Yathreb,
the people of that town took arms in his defence
against the Koreish.   It was probably now that new
views opened to the mind of the Prophet.   Prince
of Yathreb, he might hope to extend his sway over
the ungrateful Mecca; and those who had scoffed at
his arguments and persuasions might be taught
lessons of wisdom by the sword.   These anticipa-
tions were correct, and in less than ten years after
the battle of Bedr (the first he fought) he saw his
temporal power and his prophetic character acknowledged by the whole of the Arabian peninsula.

It commonly happens that, when a new form of
religion is proposed for the acceptance of mankind,
it surpasses in purity that which it is intended to
supersede.   The Arabs of the days of Mohammed
were idolaters; 300 is said to have been the number
of the images which claimed their adoration in the
Caaba.   A gross licentiousness prevailed among
hem ; their polygamy had no limits assigned to it*.

* See, in Sir J. Malcolm's History of Persia, the dialogue

For this the Prophet substituted the worship of One God, and placed a check on the sensual propensities of his people. His religion contained descriptions of the future state of rewards and punishments, by which he allured to obedience and terrified from contumacy or opposition. The pains of hell which he menaced were such as were most offensive to the body and its organs; the joys of Paradise were verdant meads, shady trees, murmuring brooks, gentle airs, precious wines in cups of gold and silver, stately tents, and splendid sofas; the melody of the songs of angels was to ravish the souls of the blessed; the black-eyed Hoories were to be the ever-blooming brides of the faithful servants of God. Yet, though sensual bliss was to be his ultimate reward, the votary was taught that its attainment demanded self-denial on earth; and it has been justly observed that " a devout Mussulman exhibits more of the Stoical than of the Epicurean character*." As the Prophet had resolved that the sword should be unsparingly employed for the diffusion of the truth, the highest degree of the future bliss was pronounced to be the portion of the martyrs, *i. e.*, of those who fell in the holy wars waged for the dissemination of the faith. " Paradise," says the Prophet, " is beneath the shadow of swords." At the

between the Persian king Yezdijird and the Arab envoy. " Whatever," said the latter, " thou hast said regarding the former condition of the Arabs is true. Their food was green lizards; they buried their infant daughters alive; nay, some of them feasted on dead carcasses and drank blood, while others slew their relations, and thought themselves great and valiant when, by such an act, they became possessed of more property. They were clothed with hair garments, knew not good from evil, and made no distinction between that which is lawful and that which is unlawful. Such was our state. But God in his mercy has sent us by a holy prophet a sacred volume, which teaches us the true faith," &c.

* Hallam, Middle Ages, ii. 165.

day of judgment the wounds of the fallen warrior were to be resplendent as vermilion, and odoriferous as musk; and the wings of angels were to supply the loss of limbs. The religion of Mohammed was entitled Islam (*resignation*), whence its votaries were called by the Arabs Moslems, and in Persian Mussulmans. Its articles of belief were five—belief in God, in his angels, in his Prophet, in the last day, and in predestination. Its positive duties were also five—purification, prayer, fasting, alms, and the pilgrimage to Mecca. Various rites and observances which the Arabs had hitherto practised were retained by the Prophet, either out of regard for the prejudices of his followers, or because he did not, or could not, divest his own mind of respect for usages in which he had been reared up from infancy.

Such is a slight sketch of the religion which Mohammed substituted for the idolatry of Arabia. It contained little that was original; all its details of the future state were borrowed from Judaism or from the Magian system of Persia. The book which contains it, entitled the Koran (*reading*), was composed in detached pieces, during a long series of years, by the *illiterate* Prophet, and taken down from his lips by his scribes. His own account of its origin was that each Sura, or revelation, was brought to him from heaven by the angel Gabriel. It is regarded by the Mohammedan East, and by most European Orientalists, as the masterpiece of Arabian literature; and when we make due allowance for the difference of European and Arabian models and taste, and consider that the rhyme* which in prose is insufferable to the former, may to the latter sound grateful, we may allow that the praises lavished on it are not

---

* The Hebrews, as appears from the poetic parts of the Scriptures, had the same delight in the clang of rhyme as the Arabs. See particularly Isaiah in the original.

unmerited. Though tedious and often childish legends, and long and tiresome civil regulations, occupy the greater part of it, it is pervaded by a fine strain of fervid piety and humble resignation to the will of God, not unworthy of the inspired seers of Israel; and the sublime doctrine of the Unity of God runs like a vein of pure gold through each portion of the mass, giving lustre and dignity to all. Might we not venture to say that Christianity itself has derived advantage from the imposture of Mohammed, and that the clear and open profession of the Divine Unity by their Mohammedan enemies kept the Christians of the dark ages from smothering it beneath the mass of superstition and fable by which they corrupted and deformed so much of the majestic simplicity of the Gospel? No one, certainly, would dream of comparing the son of Abd-Allah with the Son of God, of setting darkness by the side of light; but still we may confess him to have been an agent in the hands of the Almighty, and admit that his assumption of the prophetic office was productive of good as well as of evil.

The Mohammedan religion is so intimately connected with history, law, manners, and opinions, in the part of the East of which we are about to write, that this brief view of its origin and nature was indispensable. We now proceed to our history.

CHAPTER II.

Origin of the Khalifat—The first Khalifs—Extent of the
Arabian Empire—Schism among the Mohammedans—
Soonees and Sheähs—Sects of the latter—The Keissanee—
The Zeidites—The Ghoollat—The Imamee—Sects of the
Imamee—Their political Character—The Carmathites—
Origin of the Fatimite Khalifs—Secret Society at Cairo—
Doctrines taught in it—Its Decline.

THE civil and ecclesiastical dignities were united in
the person of Mohammed. As Emir (*prince*) he administered justice and led his followers to battle ; as
Imam (*director*) he on every Friday (the Mohammedan sabbath) taught the principles and duties of
religion from his pulpit. Though his wives were
numerous, the Prophet had no male issue surviving
at the time when he felt the approaches of death ;
but his daughter Fatima was married to his cousin
Ali, his early and faithful disciple, and it was naturally to be expected that the expiring voice of the
Prophet would nominate him as his Khalif (*successor*)
over the followers of his faith. But Ayesha, the
daughter of Aboo Bekr, Mohammed's youthful and
best beloved wife, was vehemently hostile to the son
of Aboo Talib, and she may have exerted all the influence of a revengeful woman over the mind of the
dying Prophet. Or perhaps Mohammed, like Alexander, perplexed with the extent of dominion to
which he had attained, and aware that only a vigour
of character similar to his own would avail to retain
and enlarge it, and, it may be, thinking himself an-

swerable to God for the choice he should make, deemed it the safest course to leave the matter to the free decision of his surviving followers. His appointing Aboo Bekr, a few days before his death, to officiate in his pulpit, might seem to indicate an intention of conferring the khalifat on him; and he is said to have at one time declared that the strength of character displayed by his distinguished follower, Omar, evinced his possession of the virtues of a prophet and a khalif. Tradition records no equally strong declaration respecting the mild and virtuous Ali.

At all events the Prophet expired without having named a successor, and the choice devolving on his companions dissension was ready to break out, when Omar, abandoning his own claims, gave his voice for Aboo Bekr. All opposition was thus silenced, and the father of Ayesha reigned for two years over the faithful. Ali at first refused obedience, but he finally acknowledged the successor of the Prophet. When dying, Aboo Bekr bequeathed the sceptre to Omar, as the worthiest, and when, twelve years afterwards, Omar perished by the dagger of an assassin, six electors conferred the vacant dignity on Othman, who had been the secretary of the Prophet. Age having enfeebled the powers of Othman, the reins of authority were slackened, and a spirit of discord pervaded all Arabia, illustrative of the Prophet's declaration of vigour being essential to a khalif. A numerous body of rebels besieged the aged Othman in Medina, and he was slain, holding the Koran in his lap, by a band of murderers, headed by the brother of Ayesha, who, the firebrand of Islam, it is probable had been secretly active in exciting the rebellion.

The popular choice now fell upon Ali, but the implacable Ayesha stimulated to revolt against his au-

thority two powerful Arab chiefs, named Telha and
Zobeir, who raised their standards in the province of
Arabian Irak. Ayesha, mounted on a camel, appeared in the thickest of the battle, in which the rebel
chiefs were defeated and slain. The generous Ali
sent her to dwell at the tomb of the Prophet, where
she passed in tranquillity the remainder of her days.
The khalif himself was less fortunate. Moawiya,
the Governor of Syria, son of Aboo Sofian, the most
violent of the opponents of the Prophet, assumed
the office of the avenger of Othman, whose death he
charged on Ali and his party, and, declaring himself
to be the rightful khalif, roused Syria to arms against
the Prophet's son-in-law. In the war success was on
the side of Ali, till the superstition of his troops
obliged him to agree to a treaty; and shortly afterwards he was murdered by a fanatic in the mosk
of Coofa. His son Hassan was induced by Moawiya
to resign his claims and retire to the city of Medina;
but his more high-spirited brother, Hussein, took
arms against the khalif Yezid, the son of Moawiya;
and the narrative of his death is one of the most pathetic and best related incidents of Oriental history*.
The sisters and children of Hussein were spared by
the clemency of the victorious Yezid, and from them
descend a numerous race, glorying in the blood of
Ali and the Prophet.

The Arabian empire was now of immense extent.
Egypt, Syria, and Persia had been conquered in the
reign of Omar. Under the first khalifs of the
dynasty of the Ommiades (so called from Ommiyah,
the great-grandfather of Moawiya), the conquest of
Africa and Spain was achieved, and the later princes
of this family ruled over the most extensive empire
of the world.

* See Ockley's History of the Saracens.

The great schism of the Mohammedan church (we must be permitted to employ this term, the only one our language affords) commences with the accession of the house of Ommiyah. The Mohammedans have, as is generally known, been from that time to the present day divided into two great sects, the Soonees and the Sheähs, the orthodox and the dissenters, as we might venture to call them, whose opposite doctrines, like those of the Catholics and the Protestants of the Christian church, are each the established faith of great and independent nations. The Ottoman and the Usbeg Turks hold the Soonee faith ; the Persians are violent Sheähs ; and national and religious animosity concur in making them the determined and inveterate foes of each other.

The Soonees hold that the first four khalifs were all legitimate successors of the Prophet; but as their order was determined by their degree of sanctity, they assign the lowest rank to Ali. The Sheähs, on the contrary, maintain that the dignity of the Prophet rightfully descended to the son of his uncle and the husband of his daughter. They therefore regard Aboo Bekr, Omar, and Othman, as usurpers, and curse and revile their memory, more especially that of the rigid Omar, whose murderer they venerate as a saint. It must be steadily kept in mind, in every discussion respecting the Mohammedan religion, that Mohammed and his successors succeeded in establishing what the lofty and capacious mind of Gregory VII. attempted in vain—the union of the civil and ecclesiastical powers in the same person. Unlike the schisms of the eastern and western, of the Catholic and Protestant churches, which originated in difference of opinion on points of discipline or matters of doctrine, that of the Mohammedans arose solely from ambition and the struggle for temporal power. The sceptre of the greatest empire of the world was to be the reward of the party who could gain the greatest number of believers in his right to grasp the staff and ascend the pulpit of the Prophet of God. Afterwards, when the learning of the Greeks and the Persians became familiar to the Arabs, theological and metaphysical niceties and distinctions were introduced, and the two great stems of religion threw out numerous sectarian branches. The Soonees are divided into four main sects, all of which are, however, regarded as orthodox, for they agree in the main points, though they differ in subordinate ones. The division of the Sheähs is also into four sects, the point of agreement being the assertion of the right of Ali and his descendants to the imamat, or supreme ecclesiastical dignity; the point of difference being the nature of the proof on which his rights are founded, and the order of succession among his descendants. These four sects and their opinions are as follows:—

I. The first and most innocuous of the sects which maintained the rights of the family of Ali were the Keissanee, so named from Keissan, one of his freedmen. These, who were subdivided into several branches, held that Ali's rights descended, not to Hassan or Hussein, but to their brother, Mohammed-ben-Hanfee. One of these branch-sects maintained that the imamat *remained* [*] in the person of this Mohammed, who had never died, but had since appeared, from time to time, on earth, under various names. Another branch, named the Hashemites, held that the imamat descended from Mohammed-ben-Hanfee to his son Aboo-Hashem, who transmitted it to Mohammed, of the family of Abbas, from whom it descended to Saffah, the founder of the Abbasside dynasty of khalifs[†]. It is quite evident

---

[*] Hence they were named the Standing (*Wakfiyah*).

[†] Abbas, the ancestor of this family, was one of the uncles

that the object of this sect was to give a colour to
the claims of the family of Abbas, who stigmatized
the family of Ommiyah as usurpers, and insisted
that the khalifat belonged of right to themselves.
Aboo-Moslem, the great general who first gave dominion to the family of Abbas, was a real or pretended maintainer of the tenets of this sect, the only
branch, by the way, of the Sheähs which supported
the house of Abbas.

II. A second branch of the Sheähs was named
Zeidites. These held that the imamat descended
through Hassan and Hussein to Zein-al-Abedeen, the
son of this last, and thence passed to Zeid (whence
their name), the son of Zein ; whereas most other
Sheähs regarded Mohammed Bakir, the brother of
Zeid, as the lawful imam. The Zeidites differed
from the other Sheähs in acknowledging the three
first khalifs to have been legitimate successors of the
Prophet. Edris, who wrested a part of Africa from
the Abbasside khalifs, and founded the kingdom of
Fez, was a real or pretended descendant of Zeid.

III. The Ghoollat (*Ultras*), so named from the
extravagance of their doctrines, which, passing all
bounds of common sense, were held in equal abomination by the other Sheähs and by the Soonees.
This sect is said to have existed as early as the time
of Ali himself, who is related to have burnt some of
them on account of their impious and extravagant

of the Prophet. They obtained possession of the khalifat
A.D. 750, and retained it through an hereditary succession of
princes for 500 years. Al-Mansoor, the second khalif of this
dynasty, transferred the royal residence from Damascus, where
the Ommiades had dwelt, to Bagdad, which he founded on
the banks of the Tigris. This city, also named the City of
Peace, the Vale of Peace, the House of Peace, has acquired,
beyond what any other town can claim, a degree of romantic
celebrity by means of the inimitable Thousand and One
Nights. Such is the ennobling power of genius!

opinions. They held, as we are told, that there was
but one imam, and they ascribed the qualities of
divinity to Ali. Some maintained that there were
two natures (the divine and the human) in him,
others that the last alone was his. Some again said
that this perfect nature of Ali passed by transmigration
through his descendants, and would continue so to
do till the end of all things; others that the transmission stopped with Mohammed Bakir, the son of
Zein-al-Abedeen, who still abode on earth, but un-
seen, like Khizer, the Guardian of the Well of Life,
according to the beautiful eastern legend*. Others,
still more bold, denied the transmission, and asserted
that the divine Ali sat enthroned in the clouds, where
the thunder was the voice and the lightning the
scourge wherewith he terrified and chastised the
wicked. This sect presents the first (though a very
early) instance of the introduction into Islam of that
mysticism which appears to have had its original

---

* Khizer, by some supposed, but perhaps erroneously, to
be the prophet Elias, is regarded by the Mohammedans in
the light of a beneficent genius. He is the giver of youth to
the animal and the vegetable world. He is clad in garments
of the most brilliant green, and he stands as keeper of the
Well of Life in the Land of Darkness. According to the
romances of the East, Iskander, that is, Alexander the Great,
resolved to march into the West, to the Land of Darkness, that
he might drink of the water of immortality. During seven
entire days he and his followers journeyed through dark and
dismal deserts. At length they faintly discerned in the distance the green light which shone from the raiment of Khizer.
As they advanced it became more and more resplendent, like
the brightest and purest emeralds. As the monarch approached, Khizer dipped a cup in the verdant Water of Life,
and reached it to him; but the impatience of Iskander was so
great that he spilt the contents of the cup, and the law of fate
did not permit the guardian of the fount to fill it for him
again. The moral of this tale is evident. Its historic foundation is the journey of the Macedonian to the temple of
Ammon.

birth-place in the dreamy groves of India. As a political party the Ghoollat never seem to have been formidable.

IV. Such, however, was not the case with the Imamee, the most dangerous enemies of the house of Abbas. Agreeing with the Ghoollat in the doctrine of an *invisible* imam, they maintained that there had been a series of *visible* imams antecedent to him, who had vanished. One branch of this sect (thence called the Seveners—*Sebiïn*) closed the series with Ismaïl, the grandson of Mohammed Bakir, the *seventh* imam, reckoning Ali himself the first. These were also called Ismaïlites, from Ismaïl. The other branch, called Imamites, continued the series from Ismaïl, through his brother Moosa Casim, down to Askeree, the twelfth imam. These were hence called the Twelvers (*Esnaashree*). They believed that the imam Askeree had vanished in a cavern at Hilla, on the banks of the Euphrates, where he would remain invisible till the end of the world, when he would again appear under the name of the Guide (*Mehdee*) to lead mankind into the truth. The Imamee, wherever they might stop in the series of the visible imams, saw that, for their political purposes, it was necessary to acknowledge a kind of *locum tenentes* imams; but, while the Zeidites, who agreed with them in this point, required in these princes the royal virtues of valour, generosity, justice, knowledge, the Imamee declared themselves satisfied if they possessed the saintly ones of the practice of prayer, fasting, and alms-giving. Hence artful and ambitious men could set up any puppet who was said to be descended from the last of the visible imams, and aspire to govern the Mohammedan world in his name.

The Twelvers were very near obtaining possession of the khalifat in the time of the first Abbassides;

for the celebrated Haroon Er-Rasheed's son, Al-
Mamoon, the eighth khalif of that house, moved
either by the strength or preponderance which
the Sheäh party had arrived at, or, as the eastern
historians tell us, yielding to the suggestions of his
vizir, who was devoted to that sect, named Ali Riza,
the eighth imam, to be his successor on the throne.
He even laid aside the black habiliments peculiar to
his family, and wore green, the colour of Ali and
the Prophet. But the family of Abbas, which now
numbered 30,000 persons, refused their assent to
this renunciation of the rights of their line. They
rose in arms, and proclaimed as khalif Al-Mamoon's
uncle Ibrahim. The obnoxious vizir perished, and
the opportune death of Ali Riza (by poison, as was
said) relieved the son of Haroon Er-Rasheed from
embarrassment. Ali Riza was interred at Meshed,
in the province of Khorasan ; and his tomb is, to the
present day, a place of pilgrimage for devout Persians*.

The Ismaïlites were more successful in their attempts at obtaining temporal power; and, as we
shall presently see, a considerable portion of their
dominions was wrested from the house of Abbas.

Religion has, in all ages, and in all parts of the
world, been made the mask of ambition, for which
its powerful influence over the minds of the ignorant
so well qualifies it. But the political influence of
religion among the calmer and more reasoning nations of Europe is slight compared with its power
over the more ardent and susceptible natives of Asia.
Owing to the effects of this principle the despotism
of the East has never been of that still, undisturbed
nature which we might suppose to be its character.
To say nothing of the bloody wars and massacres
which have taken place under the pretext of religion

* See Frazer's Khorasān.

in the countries from Japan to the Indus, the Mohammedan portion of the East has been, almost without ceasing, the theatre of sanguinary dramas, where ambition, under the disguise of religion, sought for empire ; and our own days have seen, in the case of the Wahabees, a bold though unsuccessful attempt of fanaticism to achieve a revolution in a part of the Ottoman empire. It was this union of religion with policy which placed the Suffavee family on the throne of Persia in the fifteenth century; and it was this also which, at a much earlier period, established the dominion of the Fatimite khalifs of Egypt. The progress of this last event is thus traced by oriental historians* :—

The encouragement given to literature and science by the enlightened Al-Mamoon had diffused a degree of boldness of speculation and inquiry hitherto unknown in the empire of the Arabs. The subtile philosophy of the Greeks was now brought into contact with the sublime but corrupted theology of the Persians, and the mysticism of India secretly mingled itself with the mass of knowledge. We are not, perhaps, to give credit to the assertion of the Arab historian that it was the secret and settled plan of the Persians to undermine and corrupt the religion, and thus sap the empire, of those who had overcome them in the field; but it is not a little remarkable that, as the transformation of the Mosaic religion into Judaism may be traced to Persia, and as the same country sent forth the monstrous opinions which corrupted the simplicity of the Gospel, so it is in Persia that we find the origin of most of the sects which have sprung up in Islam. Without agreeing with those who would derive all knowledge from India, it may be held not improbable that the

* Lari and Macrisi, quoted by Hammer.

intricate metaphysics and mysticism of that country
have been the source of much of the corruption of
the various religions which have prevailed in Cis-
Indian Asia. It is at least remarkable that the
north-east of Persia, the part nearest to India, has
been the place where many of the impostors who
pretended to intercourse with the Deity made their
appearance. It was here that Mani (*Manes*), the
head of the Manichæans, displayed his arts, and
it was in Khorasan (*Sun-land*) that Hakem,
who gave himself out for an incarnation of the
Deity, raised the standard of revolt against the
house of Abbas. But, be this as it may, on sur-
veying the early centuries of Islam, we may observe that all the rebellions which agitated the
empire of the khalifs arose from a union of the claims
of the family of Ali with the philosophical doctrines
current in Persia.

We are told that, in the ninth century of the Christian era, Abdallah, a man of Persian lineage, residing
at Ahwaz, in the south of Persia, conceived the design
of overturning the empire of the khalifs by secretly
introducing into Islam a system of atheism and
impiety. Not to shock deep-rooted prejudices in
favour of the established religion and government,
he resolved to communicate his doctrines gradually,
and he fixed on the mystic number seven as that of
the degrees through which his disciples should pass
to the grand revelation of the vanity of all religions
and the indifference of all actions. The political
cloak of his system was the assertion of the claims
of the descendants of Mohammed, the son of Ismaïl,
to the imamat, and his missionaries (*dais*) engaged
with activity in the task of making proselytes throughout the empire of the khalifs. Abdallah afterwards
removed to Syria, where he died. His son and

grandsons followed up his plans, and in their time a convert was made who speedily brought the system into active operation*.

The name of this person was Carmath, a native of the district of Koofa, and from him the sect was called Carmathites. He made great alterations in the original system of Abdallah; and as the sect was now grown numerous and powerful, he resolved to venture on putting the claims of the descendants of Ismaïl to the test of the sword. He maintained that the indefeasible right to earthly dominion lay with what he styled the imam Maässoom (*spotless*), a sort of ideal of a perfect prince, like the wise man of the Stoics; consequently all the reigning princes were usurpers, by reason of their vices and imperfections; and the warriors of the perfect prince were to precipitate them all, without distinction, from their thrones. Carmath also taught his disciples to understand the precepts and observances of Islam in a figurative sense. Prayer signified obedience to the imam Maässoom, alms-giving was paying the tithe due to him (that is, augmenting the funds of the society), fasting was keeping the political secrets relating to the imam and his service. It was not the tenseel, or outward word of the Koran, which was to be attended to; the taweel, or exposition, was alone worthy of note. Like those of Mokanna, and other opponents of the house of Abbas, the followers of Carmath distinguished themselves by wearing white raiment to mark their hostility to the reigning khalifs, whose garments and standards retained the black hue which they had displayed against the white banners of the house of Ommiyah. A bloody war was renewed at various periods during

* Macrisi is Hammer's authority for the preceding account of Abdallah. It is to be observed that this Abdallah is unnoticed by Herbelot.

an entire century between the followers of Carmath and the troops of the khalifs, with varying success. In the course of this war the holy city of Mecca was taken by the sectaries (as it has been of late years by the Wahabees), after the fall of 30,000 Moslems in its defence. The celebrated black stone was taken and conveyed in triumph to Hajar, where it remained for two-and-twenty years, till it was redeemed for 50,000 ducats by the emir of Irak, and replaced in its original seat. Finally, like so many of their predecessors, the Carmathites were vanquished by the yet vigorous power of the empire, and their name, though not their principles, was extinguished.

During this period of contest between the house of Abbas and the Carmathites, a dai (*missionary*) of the latter, named Abdallah, contrived to liberate from the prison into which he had been thrown by the khalif Motadhad a real or pretended descendant of Fatima, named Obeid-Allah*, whom he conveyed to Africa, and, proclaiming him to be the promised Mehdi (*guide*), succeeded in establishing for him a dominion on the north coast of that country. The gratitude of Obeid-Allah was shown by his putting to death him to whom he was indebted for his power; but talent and valour can exist without the presence of virtue, and Obeid-Allah and his two next descendants extended their sway to the shores of the Atlantic. Moez-ladin-Allah, his great-grandson, having achieved the conquest of Egypt and Syria, wisely abandoned his former more distant dominions along the coast of the Mediterranean, his eye being fixed on the more valuable Asiatic empire of he Abbassides. This dynasty of Fatimite khalifs,

---

* The genuineness of the descent of Obeid-Allah has been a great subject of dispute among the eastern historians and jurists. Those in the interests of the house of Abbas strained very nerve to make him out an impostor.

as they were called, reigned during two centuries at
Cairo, on the Nile, the foes and rivals of those who
sat in Bagdad, on the banks of the Tigris. Like
every other eastern dynasty, they gradually sank into
impotence and imbecility, and their throne was
finally occupied by the renowned Koord Saladin.

Obeid-Allah derived his pedigree from Ismaïl, the
seventh imam. His house, therefore, looked to the
support of the whole sect of the Seveners, or Ismaïlites, in their projects for extending their sway over
the Mohammedan world; and it was evidently their
interest to increase the numbers and power of that
sect as much as possible. We are accordingly justified in giving credit to the assurances of the eastern
historians, that there was a secret institution at Cairo,
at the head of which was the Fatimite khalif, and of
which the object was the dissemination of the doctrines of the sect of the Ismaïlites, though we may
be allowed to hesitate as to the correctness of some
of the details.

This society, we are told, comprised both men
and women, who met in separate assemblies, for the
common supposition of the insignificance of the
latter sex in the east is erroneous. It was presided
over by the chief missionary (*Dai-al-Doat**), who
was always a person of importance in the state,
and not unfrequently supreme judge (*Kadhi-al-
kodhat†*). Their assemblies, called Societies of
Wisdom (*Mejalis-al-hicmet*), were held twice a-week,
on Mondays and Wednesdays. All the members
appeared clad in white. The president, having first
waited on the khalif, and read to him the intended
lecture, or, if that could not be done, having gotten
his signature on the back of it, proceeded to the
assembly and delivered a written discourse. At the

* That is, *Missionary of Missionaries.*
† *Cadhi of Cadhis.*

D

conclusion of it those present kissed his hand and reverently touched with their forehead the hand-writing of the khalif.   In this state the society con-tinued till the reign of that extraordinary madman the khalif Hakem-bi-emr-illah (*Judge by the com-mand of God*), who determined to place it on a splendid footing.   He erected for it a stately edifice, styled the House of Wisdom (*Dar-al-hicmet*), abundantly furnished with books and mathematical instruments.   Its doors were open to all, and paper, pens, and ink were profusely supplied for the use of those who chose to frequent it.   Professors of law, mathematics, logic, and medicine were appointed to give instructions; and at the learned disputations which were frequently held in presence of the khalif, these professors appeared in their state caftans (*Khalaä*), which, it is said, exactly resembled the robes worn at the English universities.   The income assigned to this establishment, by the mu-nificence of the khalif, was 257,000 ducats annually, arising from the tenths paid to the crown.

The course of instruction in this university pro-ceeded, according to Macrisi, by the following nine degrees:—1. The object of the first, which was long and tedious, was to infuse doubts and difficulties into the mind of the aspirant, and to lead him to repose a blind confidence in the knowledge and wis-dom of his teacher.   To this end he was perplexed with captious questions; the absurdities of the literal sense of the Koran, and its repugnance to reason, were studiously pointed out, and dark hints were given that beneath this shell lay a kernel sweet to the taste and nutritive to the soul.   But all further information was most rigorously withheld till he had consented to bind himself by a most solemn oath to absolute faith and blind obedience to his instructor. 2. When he had taken the oath he was admitted to the second degree, which inculcated the acknowledgment of the imams appointed by God as the sources of all knowledge. 3. The third degree informed him what was the number of these blessed and holy imams; and this was the mystic seven; for, as God had made seven heavens, seven earths, seas, planets, metals, tones, and colours, so seven was the number of these noblest of God's creatures. 4. In the fourth degree the pupil learned that God had sent *seven* lawgivers into the world, each of whom was commissioned to alter and improve the system of his predecessor; that each of these had *seven* helpers, who appeared in the interval between him and his successor; these helpers, as they did not appear as public teachers, were called the mute (*samit*), in contradistinction to the *speaking* lawgivers. The seven lawgivers were Adam, Noah, Abraham, Moses, Jesus, Mohammed, and Ismaïl, the son of Jaaffer; the seven principal helpers, called Seats (*soos*), were Seth, Shem, Ishmael (the son of Abraham), Aaron, Simon, Ali, and Mohammed, the son of Ismaïl. It is justly observed* that, as this last personage was not more than a century dead, the teacher had it in his power to fix on whom he would as the mute prophet of the present time, and inculcate the belief in, and obedience to, him of all who had not got beyond this degree. 5. The fifth degree taught that each of the seven mute prophets had twelve apostles for the dissemination of his faith. The suitableness of this number was also proved by analogy. There are twelve signs of the zodiac, twelve months, twelve tribes of Israel, twelve joints in the four fingers of each hand, and so forth. 6. The pupil being led thus far, and having shown no symptoms of restiveness, the precepts of the Koran were once more brought under consideration, and he was told that all the positive portions of

* Hammer, p. 54.

religion must be subordinate to philosophy. He
was consequently instructed in the systems of Plato
and Aristotle during a long space of time; and (7),
when esteemed fully qualified, he was admitted to
the seventh degree, when instruction was communicated in that mystic Pantheism which is held and
taught by the sect of the Soofees. 8. The positive
precepts of religion were again considered, the veil
was torn from the eyes of the aspirant, all that had
preceded was now declared to have been merely
scaffolding to raise the edifice of knowledge, and
was to be flung down. Prophets and teachers,
heaven and hell, all were nothing; future bliss and
misery were idle dreams; all actions were permitted.
9. The ninth degree had only to inculcate that nought
was to be believed, everything might be done*.

In perusing the accounts of secret societies, their
rules, regulations, degrees, and the quantity or
nature of the knowledge communicated in them, a
difficulty must always present itself. Secrecy being
of the very essence of everything connected with
them, what means had writers, who were generally
hostile to them, of learning their internal constitution
and the exact nature of their maxims and tenets?
In the present case our authority for this account of
a society which chiefly flourished in the tenth and
eleventh centuries is Macrisi, a writer of the fifteenth
century. His authorities were doubtless of more
ancient date, but we know not who they were or
whence they derived their information. Perhaps our

---

* Mr. De Sacy (*Journal des Savans*, an 1818) is of opinion
that the Arabic words *Taleel* and *Ibahat* will not bear the
strong sense which Hammer gives them. The former, he
says, only signifies that Deism which regards the Deity as
merely a speculative being, and annihilates the moral relations
between him and the creature ; the latter only denotes eman-
cipation from the positive precepts of laws, such as fasting
prayer, &c., but not from moral obligations.

safest course in this, as in similar cases, would be to admit the general truth of the statement, but to suffer our minds to remain in a certain degree of suspense as to the accuracy of the details. We can thus at once assent to the fact of the existence of the college at Cairo, and of the mystic tenets of Soofeeism being taught in it, as also to that of the rights of the Fatimites to the khalifat being inculcated on the minds of the pupils, and missionaries being thence sent over the east, without yielding implicit credence to the tale of the nine degrees through which the aspirant had to pass, or admitting that the course of instruction terminated in a doctrine subversive of all religion and of all morality.

As we have seen, the Dai-al-doat, or chief missionary, resided at Cairo, to direct the operations of the society, while the subordinate dais pervaded all parts of the dominions of the house of Abbas, making converts to the claims of Ali. The dais were attended by companions (*Refeek*), who were persons who had been instructed up to a certain point in the secret doctrines, but who were neither to presume to teach nor to seek to make converts, that honour being reserved to the dais. By the activity of the dais the society spread so widely that in the year 1058 the emir Bessassiri, who belonged to it, made himself master of Bagdad, and kept possession of it during an entire year, and had money struck, and prayer made, in the name of the Egyptian khalif. The emir, however, fell by the sword of Toghrul the Turk, whose aid the feeble Abbasside implored, and these two distinguishing acts of Mohammedan sovereignty were again performed by the house of Abbas. Soon afterwards the society at Cairo seems to have declined along with the power of the Fatimite khalifs. In 1123 the powerful vizir Afdhal, on occasion of some disturbance caused by them, shut up the Dar-al-hicmet, or, as it would appear, destroyed it. His successor Mamoon permitted the society to hold their meetings in a building erected in another situation, and it lingered on till the fall of the khalifat of Egypt. The policy of Afdhal is perhaps best to be explained by a reference to the state of the East at that time. The khalif of Bagdad was become a mere pageant devoid of all real power; the former dominions of the house of Abbas were in the hands of the Seljookian Turks; the Franks were masters of a great part of Syria, and threatened Egypt, where the khalifs were also fallen into incapacity, and the real power had passed to the vizir. As this last could aspire to nothing beyond preserving Egypt, a society instituted for the purpose of gaining partisans to the claims of the Fatimites must have been rather an impediment to him than otherwise. He must therefore have been inclined to suppress it, especially as the society of the Assassins, a branch of it, had now been instituted, which, heedless of the claims of the Fatimites, sought dominion for itself alone. To the history of that remarkable association we now proceed.

Chapter III.

Ali of Rei—His son Hassan Sabah—Hassan sent to study at
Nishaboor—Meets there Omar Khiam and Nizam-al-Moolk
—Agreement made by them—Hassan introduced by Nizam
to Sultan Malek Shah—Obliged to leave the Court—Anecdote of him—His own account of his Conversion—Goes to
Egypt—Returns to Persia—Makes himself Master of Alamoot.

THERE was a man named Ali, who resided in the
city of Rei, in Persia. He was a strenuous Sheäh,
and maintained that his family had originally come
from Koofa, in Arabia ; but the people of Khorasan
asserted that his family had always dwelt in one of
the villages near Toos, in that province, and that
consequently his pretensions to an Arabian extraction were false. Ali, it would appear, was anxious
to conceal his opinions, and employed the strongest
asseverations to convince the governor of the province, a rigid Soonite, of his orthodoxy, and finally
retired into a monastery to pass the remainder of his
days in meditation. As a further means of clearing
himself from the charge of heresy he sent his only
son Hassan Sabah* to Nishaboor to be instructed by
the celebrated imam Mowafek, who resided at that
place. What lessons he may have given the young
Hassan previously to parting with him, and what
communication he may have afterwards kept up with
him, are points on which history is silent.

The fame of the imam Mowafek was great over
all Persia, and it was currently believed that those

* Or Hassan-ben-Sabah (*son of Sabah*), so named from
Sabah Homairi, one of his pretended Arabian ancestors.

who had the good fortune to study the Koran and
the Soonna* under him were secure of their fortune
in after-life. His school was consequently thronged
by youths ambitious of knowledge and future distinction; and here Hassan met, and formed a strict
intimacy with, Omar Khiam, afterwards so distinguished as a poet and an astronomer, and with
Nizam-al-Moolk (*Regulation of the Realm*), who
became vizir to the monarchs of the house of Seljook.
This last, in a history which he wrote of himself and
his times, relates the following instance of the early
development of the ambition of Hassan. As these
three, who were the most distinguished pupils of the
imam, were one day together, "It is the general
opinion," said Hassan, "that the pupils of the imam
are certain of being fortunate. This opinion may be
verified in one of us. So come, let us pledge ourselves to one another that he who shall be successful
will make the other two sharers in his good fortune."
His two companions readily assented, and the promise was mutually given and received.

Nizam-al-Moolk entered the path of politics, where
his talents and his noble qualities had free course,
and he rose through the various gradations of office,
till at length he attained the highest post in the
realm, the viziriate, under Alp Arslan (*Strong Lion*),
the second monarch of the house of Seljook. When
thus exalted he forgot not his former friends ; and
calling to mind the promise which he had made, he
received with great kindness Omar Khiam, who
waited on him to congratulate him on his elevation ;
and he offered at once to employ all his interest to
procure him a post under the government. But
Omar, who was devoted to Epicurean indulgences,
and averse from toil and care, thanking his friend,

* The Soonna is the body of traditions, answering to the
Mishna of the Jews, held by the orthodox Mussulmans.

declined his proffered services; and all that the vizir could prevail on him to accept was an annual pension of 1,200 ducats on the revenues of Nishaboor, whither he retired to spend his days in ease and tranquillity. The case was different with Hassan. During the ten years' reign of Alp Arslan he kept aloof from the vizir, living in obscurity, and probably maturing his plans for the future. But when the young prince Malek Shah (*King King*) mounted the throne he saw that his time was come. He suddenly appeared at the court of the new monarch, and waited on the powerful vizir. The story is thus told by the vizir himself in his work entitled Wasaya (*Political Institutes*), whence it is given by Mirkhond.

" He came to me at Nishaboor in the year that Malek Shah, having got rid of Kaward, had quieted the troubles which his rebellion had caused. I received him with the greatest honours, and performed, on my part, all that could be expected from a man who is a faithful observer of his oaths, and a slave to the engagements which he has contracted. Each day I gave him a new proof of my friendship, and I endeavoured to satisfy his desires. He said to me once, ' Khojah (*master*), you are of the number of the learned and the virtuous; you know that the goods of this world are but an enjoyment of little duration. Do you then think that you will be permitted to fail in your engagements by letting yourself be seduced by the attractions of greatness and the love of the world? and will you be of the number of *those who violate the contract made with God?*' 'Heaven keep me from it!' replied I. ' Though you heap honours upon me,' continued he, ' and though you pour upon me benefits without number, you cannot be ignorant that that is not the way to perform what we once pledged ourselves to respecting each other.' 'You are right,' said I; ' and I

D 5.

am ready to satisfy you in what I promised. All
that I possess of honour and power, received from
my fathers or acquired by myself, belongs to you in
common with me.' I then introduced him into the
society of the sultan, I assigned him a rank and suitable titles, and I related to the prince all that had
formerly passed between him and me. I spoke in
terms of such praise of the extent of his knowledge,
of his excellent qualities, and his good morals, that
he obtained the rank of minister and of a confidential
man. But he was, like his father, an impostor, a
hypocrite, one who knew how to impose, and a
wretch. He so well possessed the art of covering
himself with an exterior of probity and virtue that
in a little time he completely gained the mind of the
sultan, and inspired him with such confidence that
that prince blindly followed his advice in most of
those affairs of a greater and more important nature
which required good faith and sincerity, and he was
always decided by his opinion. I have said all this
to let it be seen that it was I who had raised him to
this fortune, and yet, by an effect of his bad character,
there came quarrels between the sultan and me, the
unpleasant result of which had like to have been that
the good reputation and favour which I had enjoyed
for so many years were near going into dust and
being annihilated; for at last his malignity broke
out on a sudden, and the effects of his jealousy
showed themselves in the most terrible manner in
his actions and in his words."

In fact, Hassan played the part of a treacherous
friend. Everything that occurred in the divan was
carefully reported to the sultan, and the worst construction put upon it, and hints of the incapacity and
dishonesty of the vizir were thrown out on the fitting
occasions. The vizir himself has left us an account
of what he considered the worst trick which his old

schoolfellow attempted to play him. The sultan, it seems, wishing to see a clear and regular balance-sheet of the revenues and expenditure of his empire, directed Nizam-al-Moolk to prepare it. The vizir required a space of more than a year for the accomplishment of the task. Hassan deemed this a good opportunity for distinguishing himself, and boldly offered to do what the sultan demanded in forty days, not more than one-tenth of the time required by the vizir. All the clerks in the finance department were immediately placed at the disposal of Hassan; and the vizir himself confesses that at the end of the forty days the accounts were ready to be laid before the sultan. But, just when we might expect to see Hassan in triumph, and enjoying the highest favour of the monarch, we find him leaving the court in disgrace and vowing revenge on the sultan and his minister. This circumstance is left unexplained by the Ornament of the Realm, who however acknowledges, with great *naïveté*, that, if Hassan had not been obliged to fly, he should have left the court himself. But other historians inform us that the vizir, apprehensive of the consequences, had recourse to art, and contrived to have some of Hassan's papers stolen, so that, when tne latter presented himself before the sultan, full of hope and pride, and commenced his statement, he found himself obliged to stop for want of some of his most important documents. As he could not account for this confusion, the sultan became enraged at the apparent attempt to deceive him, and Hassan was forthwith obliged to retire from court with precipitation.

Nizam-al-Moolk determined to keep no measures with a man who had thus sought his ruin, and he resolved to destroy him. Hassan fled to Rei, but, not thinking himsel safe there, he went further south, and took refuge with his friend the reis* Aboo-'l-Fazl (*Father of Excellence*), at Isfahan. What his plans may have hitherto been is uncertain; but now they seem to have assumed a definite form, and he unceasingly meditated on the means of avenging himself on the sultan and his minister. In consultation one day with Aboo-'l-Fazl, who appears to have adopted his speculative tenets, after he had poured out his complaints against the vizir and his master, he concluded by passionately saying, " Oh that I had but two faithful friends at my devotion! soon should I overthrow the Turk and the peasant," meaning the sultan and the vizir. Aboo-'l-Fazl, who was one of the most clear-headed men of his time, and who still did not comprehend the long-sighted views of Hassan, began to fancy that disappointment had deranged the intellect of his friend, and, believing that reasoning would in such a case be useless, commenced giving him at his meals aromatic drinks and dishes prepared with saffron, in order to relieve his brain. Hassan perceived what his kind host was about, and resolved to leave him. Aboo-'l-Fazl in vain employed all his eloquence to induce him to prolong his visit; Hassan departed, and shortly afterwards set out for Egypt.

Twenty years afterwards, when Hassan had accomplished all he had projected, when the sultan and the vizir were both dead, and the society of the Assassins was fully organized, the reis Aboo-'l-Fazl, who was one of his most zealous partisans, visited him at his hill-fort of Alamoot. " Well, reis," said Hassan,

---

* *Reis*, from the Arabic Râs (*the head*), answers in some respects to *captain*, a word of similar origin. Thus the master of a ship is called the Reis. Sir John Malcolm says, " it is equivalent to *esquire*, as it was originally understood. It implies in Persia the possession of landed estates and some magisterial power. The reis is in general the hereditary head of a village."

"which of us was the madman? did you or I stand most in need of the aromatic drinks and the dishes prepared with saffron which you used to have served up at Isfahan? You see that I kept my word as soon as I had found two trusty friends."

When Hassan left Isfahan, in the year 1078, the khalif Mostanser, a man of some energy, occupied the throne of Egypt, and considerable exertions were made by the missionaries of the society at Cairo to gain proselytes throughout Asia. Among these proselytes was Hassan Sabah, and the following account of his conversion, which has fortunately been preserved in his own words, is interesting, as affording a proof that, like Cromwell, and, as we have supposed, Mohammed, and all who have attained to temporal power by means of religion, he commenced in sincerity, and was deceived himself before he deceived others.

"From my childhood," says he, "even from the age of seven years, my sole endeavour was to acquire knowledge and capacity. I had been reared up, like my fathers, in the doctrine of the twelve imams, and I made acquaintance with an Ismaïlite companion (*Refeek*), named Emir Dhareb, with whom I knit fast the bonds of friendship. My opinion was that the tenets of the Ismaïlites resembled those of the Philosophers, and that the ruler of Egypt was a man who was initiated in them. As often, therefore, as Emir said anything in favour of these doctrines I fell into strife with him, and many controversies on points of faith ensued between him and me. I gave not in to anything that Emir said in disparagement of our sect, though it left a strong impression on my mind. Meanwhile Emir parted from me, and I fell into a severe fit of sickness, during which I reproached myself, saying, that the doctrine of the Ismaïlites was assuredly the true one, and that yet out of obstinacy I had not gone over to it, and that

should death (which God avert!) overtake me, I
should die without having attained to the truth. At
length I recovered of that sickness, and I now met
with another Ismaïlite, named Aboo Nejm Zaraj, of
whom I inquired touching the truth of his doctrine.
Aboo Nejm explained it to me in the fullest manner,
so that I saw quite through the depths of it. Finally
I met a dai, named Moomin, to whom the sheikh
Abd-al-Melik (*Servant of the King*, i. e. *of God*) Ben
Attash, the director of the missions of Irak, had given
permission to exercise this office. I besought that he
would accept my homage (in the name of the Fatimite khalif), but this he at the first refused to do,
because I had been in higher dignities than he; but
when I pressed him thereto beyond all measure, he
yielded his consent. When now the sheikh Abd-
al-Melik came to Rei, and through intercourse learned
to know me, my behaviour was pleasing unto him,
and he bestowed on me the office of a dai. He said
unto me, ' Thou must go unto Egypt, to be a sharer
in the felicity of serving the imam Mostander.' When
the sheikh Abd-al-Melik went from Rei to Isfahan
I set forth for Egypt*."

There is something highly interesting in this account of his thoughts and feelings given by Hassan
Sabah, particularly when we recollect that this was
the man who afterwards organized the society of the
Assassins, so long the scourge of the East. We here
find him, according to his own statement, dreading
the idea of dying without having openly made profession of the truth, yet afterwards, if we are to credit
the Oriental historians, he inculcated the doctrine of
the indifference of all human actions. Unfortunately
this declension from virtue to vice has been too often
exhibited to allow of our doubting that it may have
happened in the case of Hassan Sabah. A further re-

* Mirkhond.

flection which presents itself is this : Can anything be
more absurd than those points which have split the
Moslems into sects? and yet how deeply has conscience been engaged in them, and with what sincerity have they not been embraced and maintained !
Will not this apply in some measure to the dissensions
among Christians, who divide into parties, not for
the essential doctrines of their religion, but for some
merely accessory parts?

Hassan, on his arrival in Egypt, whither his fame
had preceded him, was received with every demon-
stration of respect. His known talents, and the
knowledge of the high favour and consideration which
he had enjoyed at the court of Malek Shah, made
the khalif esteem him a most important acquisition
to the cause of the Ismaïlites, and no means were
omitted to soothe and flatter him. He was met on
the frontiers by the **Dai-al-Doat**, the sherif Taher
Casvini, and several other persons of high consideration; the great officers of state and court waïted on
him as soon as he had entered Cairo, where the
khalif assigned him a suitable abode, and loaded
him with honours and tokens of favour. But such
was the state of seclusion which the Fatimite khalifs
had adopted, that during the eighteen months which
Hassan is said to have passed at Cairo he never once
beheld the face of Mostanser, though that monarch
always evinced the utmost solicitude about him, and
never spoke of him but in terms of the highest praise.

While Hassan abode in Egypt the question of the
succession to the throne (always a matter of dispute
in Oriental monarchies) became a subject of dissension and angry debate at court. The khalif had
declared his eldest son, Nesar, to be his legitimate
successor; but Bedr-al-Jemali, the Emir-al-Juyoosh,
or commander-in-chief of the army, who enjoyed
almost unlimited power under the Fatimites, asserted

the superior right of Musteäli, the khalif's second
son, which right his power afterwards made good.
Hassan Sabah, not very wisely, as it would seem, took
the side of Prince Nesar, and thereby drew on himself
the hostility of Bedr-al-Jemali, who resolved on his
destruction.   In vain the reluctant khalif struggled
against the might of the powerful Emir-al-Juyoosh ;
he was obliged to surrender Hassan to his vengeance,
and to issue an order for committing him to close
custody in the castle of Damietta.

While Hassan lay in confinement at Damietta one
of the towers of that city fell down without any apparent cause.   This being looked upon in the light
of a miracle by the partisans of Hassan and the
khalif, his enemies, to prevent his deriving any advantage from it, hurried him on board of a ship
which was on the point of sailing for Africa. Scarcely
had the vessel put to sea when a violent tempest came
on.   The sea rolled mountains high, the thunder
roared, and the lightning flamed.   Terror laid hold
on all who were aboard, save Hassan Sabah, who
looked calm and undisturbed on the commotion of
the elements, while others gazed with agony on the
prospect of instant death.   On being asked the cause
of his tranquillity he made answer, in imitation probably of St. Paul, " Our Lord (*Seydna*) has promised
me that no evil shall befall me."   Shortly afterwards
the storm fell and the sea grew calm.   The crew and
passengers now regarded him as a man under the
especial favour of Heaven, and when a strong west
wind sprung up, and drove them to the coast of
Syria, they offered no opposition to his leaving the
vessel and going on shore.

Hassan proceeded to Aleppo, where he staid
some time, and thence directed his course to Bagdad.
Leaving that city he entered Persia, traversed the
province of Khuzistan, and, visiting the cities of

Isfahan and Yezd, went on to the eastern province of Kerman, everywhere making proselytes to his opinions. He then returned to Isfahan, where he made a stay of four months. He next spent three months in Khuzistan. Having fixed his view on Damaghan and the surrounding country in Irak as a district well calculated to be the seat of the power which he meditated establishing, he devoted three entire years to the task of gaining disciples among its inhabitants. For this purpose he employed the most eloquent dais he could find, and directed them to win over by all means the inhabitants of the numerous hill-forts which were in that region. While his dais were thus engaged he himself traversed the more northerly districts of Jorjan and Dilem, and when he deemed the time fit returned to the province of Irak, where Hussein Kaïni, one of the most zealous of his missionaries, had been long since engaged in persuading the people of the strong hill-fort of Alamoot to swear obedience to the khalif Mostanser. The arguments of the dai had proved convincing to the great majority of the inhabitants, but the governor, Ali Mehdi, an upright and worthy man, whose ancestors had built the fort, remained, with a few others, faithful to his duty, and would acknowledge no spiritual head but the Abbasside khalif of Bagdad; no temporal chief but the Seljookian Malek Shah. Mehdi, when he first-perceived the progress of Ismaïlism among his people, expelled those who had embraced it, but afterwards permitted them to return. Sure of the aid of a strong party within the fort, Hassan is said to have employed against the governor the same artifice by which Dido is related to have deceived the Lybians*. He

---

* Sir J. Malcolm says that the person with whom he read this portion of history in Persia observed to him that the English were well acquainted with this stratagem, as it was by means of it that they got Calcutta from the poor Emperor of Delhi.

offered him 3,000 ducats for as much ground as he could compass with an ox-hide. The guileless Mehdi consented, and Hassan instantly cutting the hide into thongs surrounded with it the fortress of Alamoot. Mehdi, seeing himself thus tricked, refused to stand to the agreement. Hassan appealed to justice, and to the arms of his partisans within the fortress, and by their aid compelled the governor to depart from Alamoot. As Mehdi was setting out for Damaghan, whither he proposed to retire, Hassan placed in his hand an order on the reis Mozaffer, the governor of the castle of Kirdkoo, couched in these terms : " Let the reis Mozaffer pay to Mehdi, the descendant of Ali, 3,000 ducats, as the price of the fortress of Alamoot. Peace be upon the Prophet and his family ! God, the best of directors, sufficeth us." Mehdi could hardly believe that a man of the consequence of the reis Mozaffer, who held an important government under the Seljookian sultans, would pay the slightest attention to the order of a mere adventurer like Hassan Sabah ; he, however, resolved, out of curiosity, or rather, as we are told, pressed by his want of the money, to try how he would act. He accordingly presented the order, and, to his infinite surprise, was forthwith paid the 3,000 ducats. The reis had in fact been long in secret one of the most zealous disciples of Hassan Sabah.

Historians are careful to inform us that it was on the night of Wednesday, the sixth of the month Rejeb, in the 483d year of the Hejra, that Hassan Sabah made himself master of Alamoot, which was to become the chief seat of the power of the sect of the Ismaïlites. This year answers to the year 1090 of the Christian era, and thus the dominion of the Assassins was founded only nine years before the Christians of the west established their empire in the Holy Land.

Hill Fort.

Chapter IV.

Description of Alamoot—Fruitless Attempts to recover it—
Extension of the Ismaïlite Power—The Ismaïlites in Syria
—Attempt on the Life of Aboo-Hard Issa—Treaty made
with Sultan Sanjar—Death of Hassan—His Character.

ALAMOOT, a name so famous in the history of the
East, signifies the Vulture's Nest, an appellation derived from its lofty site.   It was built in the year
860, on the summit of a hill, which bears a fancied
resemblance to a lion couching with his nose to the
ground, situated, according to Hammer, in 50½° E.
long. and 36° N. lat. It was regarded as the strongest
of 50 fortresses of the same kind, which were scattered over the district of Roodbar (*River-land*), the
mountainous region which forms the border between
Persian Irak and the more northerly provinces of
Dilem and Taberistan, and is watered by the stream
called the King's River (*Shahrood*).   As soon as
Hassan saw himself master of this important place
he directed his thoughts to the means of increasing
its strength.   He repaired the original walls, and
added new ones; he sunk wells, and dug a canal,
which conveyed water from a considerable distance
to the foot of the fortress.   As the possession of
Alamoot made him master of the surrounding country, he learned to regard the inhabitants as his subjects, and he stimulated them to agriculture, and
made large plantations of fruit-trees around the
eminence on which the fortress stood.

But before Hassan had time to commence, much
less complete these plans of improvement, he saw

himself in danger of losing all the fruits of his toil. It was not to be expected that the emir, on whom the sultan had bestowed the province of Roodbar, would calmly view its strongest fort in the possession of the foe of the house of Seljook. Hassan, therefore, had not had time to collect stores and provisions when he found all access to the place cut off by the troops of the emir. The inhabitants were about to quit Alamoot, but Hassan exerted the usual influence of a commanding spirit over their minds, and confidently assured them that that was the place in which fortune would favour them. They yielded faith to his words and staid; and at length their perseverance wore out the patience of the emir, and Alamoot thence obtained the title of the Abode of Fortune. The sultan, who had at first viewed the progress of his ex-minister with contempt, began soon to grow apprehensive of his ultimate designs, and in 1092 he issued orders to the emir Arslantash (*Lion-stone*) to destroy Hassan and his adherents. Arslantash advanced against Alamoot. Hassan, though he had but 70 men with him, and was scantily supplied with provisions, defended himself courageously till Aboo Ali, the governor of Casveen, who was in secret one of his dais, sent 300 men to his aid. These fell suddenly, during the night, on the troops of the emir; the little garrison made at the same time a sortie; the sultan's troops took to flight, and Alamoot remained in the possession of the Ismaïlites. Much about the same time Malek Shah sent troops against Hussein Kaini, who was actively engaged in the cause of Hassan Sabah in Kuhistan. Hussein threw himself into Moominabad, a fortress nearly as strong as that of Alamoot, and the troops of the sultan assailed him in vain. It was now that Hassan began to display the system which we shall presently unveil. The aged vizir, the great and good Nizam-al-Moolk, perished by the daggers of his emissaries, and the sultan himself speedily followed his minister to the tomb, not without suspicion of poison.

Circumstances were now particularly favourable to the plans of Hassan Sabah. On the death of sultan Malek Shah a civil war broke out among his sons for the succession. All the military chiefs and persons of eminence were engaged on one side or the other, and none had leisure or inclination to attend to the progress of the Ismaïlites. These, therefore, went on gradually extending their power, and fortress after fortress fell into their hands. In the course of ten years they saw themselves masters of the principal hill-forts of Persian Irak; they held that of Shahdorr* (*King's pearl*), and two other fortresses, close to Isfahan; that of Khalankhan, on the borders of Fars and Kuhistan; Damaghan, Kirdkoo, and Firoozkoo, in the district of Komis; and Lamseer and several others in Kuhistan. It was in vain that the most distinguished imams and doctors of the law issued their *fetuas* against the sect of the Ismaïlites, and condemned them to future perdition; in vain they called on the orthodox to employ the

---

* This castle was built by sultan Malek Shah. The following was its origin;—As Malek Shah, who was a great lover of the chase, was out one day a hunting, one of the hounds went astray on the nearly inaccessible rock on which the castle was afterwards erected. The ambassador of the Byzantine emperor, who was of the party, observed to the sultan, that in his master's dominions so advantageous a situation would not be left unoccupied, but would long since have been crowned with a castle. The sultan followed the ambassador's advice, and erected the castle of the King's Pearl on this lofty rock. When the castle fell into the hands of the Ismaïlites, pious Moslems remarked that it could not have better luck, since its site had been pointed out by a dog (an unclean beast in their eyes), and its erection advised by an infidel.

sword of justice in freeing the earth from this godless and abominable race. The sect, strong in its secret bond of unity and determination of purpose, went on and prospered; the dagger avenged the fate of those who perished by the sword, and, as the Oriental-ized European historian of the society expresses it[*], "heads fell like an abundant harvest beneath the twofold sickle of the sword of justice and the dagger of murder."

The appearance of the Ismaïlites, under their new form of organization, in Syria, happened at the same time with that of the crusaders in the Holy Land. The Siljookian Turks had made the conquest of that country, and the different chiefs who ruled Damascus, Aleppo, and the other towns and their districts, some of whom were of Turkish, others of Syrian extraction, were in a constant state of enmity with each other. Such powerful auxiliaries as the followers of Hassan Sabah were not to be neglected; Risvan, Prince of Aleppo, so celebrated in the history of the crusades, was their declared favourer and protector, and an Ismaïlite agent always resided with him. The first who occupied this post was an astrologer, and on his death the office fell to a Persian goldsmith, named Aboo Taher Essaigh. The enemies of Risvan felt the effects of his alliance with the Ismaïlites. The Prince of Emessa, for example, fell by their daggers, as he was about to relieve the castle of the Koords, to which Raymond, Count of Toulouse, had laid siege.

Risvan put the strong castle of Sarmin, which lay about a day's journey south of Aleppo, into the hands of Aboo-'l-Fettah, the nephew of Hassan Sabah, and his Dai-el-Kebir (*Great Missionary*) for the province of Syria. The governor of this fortress was Aboo Taher Essaigh. A few years afterwards (1107) the people of Apamea invoked the aid of Aboo Taher

* Hammer, 97.

against Khalaf, their Egyptian governor. Aboo
Taher took possession of the town in the name of
Risvan, but Tancred, who was at war with that
prince, having come and attacked it, it was forced to
surrender. Aboo Taher stipulated for free egress
for himself; but Tancred, in violation of the treaty,
brought him to Antioch, where he remained till his
ransom was paid. Aboo-'l-Fettah and the other
Ismaïlites were given up to the vengeance of the sons
of Khalaf. Tancred took from them at the same
time another strong fortress, named Kefrlana. This
is to be noted as the first collision between the
Crusaders and the Assassins, as we shall now begin
to call them. The origin of this name shall presently
be explained.

On the return of Aboo Taher to Aleppo a very
remarkable attempt at assassination took place.
There was a wealthy merchant, named Aboo-Hard
Issa*, a sworn foe to the Ismaïlites, and who
had spent large sums of money in his efforts
to injure them. He was now arrived from the
borders of Toorkistan with a richly laden caravan
of 500 camels. An Ismaïlite, named Ahmed,
a native of Rei, had secretly accompanied him
from the time he left Khorasan, with the design of
avenging the death of his father, who had fallen
under the blows of Aboo-Hard's people. The Ismaïlite, on arriving at Aleppo, immediately communicated with Aboo Taher and Risvan. Revenge,
and the hope of gaining the wealth of the hostile
merchant, made them yield assent at once to the
project of assassination. Aboo Taher gave Ahmed

---

* That is, Jesus. It may be here observed that the proper
names of the Old Testament are still used in the East. Ibrahim, Ismael, Yahya, Joossuf, Moossa, Daood, Suleiman, Issa,
are Abraham, Ishmael, Jacob, Joseph, Moses, David, Solomon,
and Joshua, or Jesus.

a sufficient number of assistants; Risvan promised the aid of his guards; and one day, as the merchant was in the midst of his slaves, counting his camels, the murderers fell on him. But the faithful slaves valiantly defended their master, and the Ismaïlites expiated their guilt with their lives. The princes of Syria heaped reproaches on Risvan for this scandalous violation of the rights of hospitality, and he vainly endeavoured to justify himself by pretending ignorance of the fact. Aboo Taher, as the increasing hatred of the people of Aleppo to the sect made that town an unsafe abode, returned to Persia, his native country, leaving his son, Aboo-'l-Fettah, to manage the affairs of the society in his stead.

The acquisition of castles and other places of strength was now the open and avowed object of the society, whose aim was evidently at the empire of Asia, and no mean was left unemployed for the effecting of this design. In the year 1108 they made a bold attempt at making themselves masters of the strong castle of Khizar, also in Syria, which belonged to the family of Monkad. The festival of Easter being come, when the Mussulman garrison was in the habit of going down into the town to partake in the festivities of the Christians, during their absence the Ismaïlites entered the castle, and barred the gates. When the garrison returned towards night, they found themselves excluded; but the Ismaïlites, in their reliance on the strength of the place, being negligent, the women drew up their husbands by cords at the windows, and the intruders were speedily expelled.

In the year 1113, as Mevdood, Prince of Mosul, was walking up and down, on a festival day, in the mosk of Damascus, with the celebrated Togteghin, he was fallen on and slain by an Ismaïlite. The murderer was cut to pieces on the spot.

E

This year was, however, near proving fatal to the society in Syria. Risvan, their great protector, died; and the eunuch Looloo, the guardian of his young son, was their sworn enemy. An order for their indiscriminate destruction was forthwith issued, and, in consequence, more than 300 men, women, and children were massacred, while 200 more were thrown into prison. Aboo-'l-Fettah was put to death with torture; his body was cut to pieces and burnt at the gate looking towards Irak, and his head sent through all Syria. They did not, however, fall totally unavenged; the daggers of the society were directed against the governors and men in power, many of whom became their victims. Thus, in the year 1115, as the Attabeg Togteghin was receiving an audience at the court of the khalif of Bagdad, the governor of Khorasan was fallen upon by three Ismaïlites, who probably mistook him for the Attabeg, and he and they perished. In 1119 as Bedii, the governor of Aleppo, was journeying with his sons to the court of the emir Il-Ghazi, they were fallen upon by two assassins; Bedii and one of his sons fell by their blows; his other sons cut the murderers down; but a third then sprang forth, and gave the finishing stroke to one of the young men, who was already wounded. The murderer was taken, and brought before Togteghin and Il-Ghazi, who only ordered him to be put in prison; but he drowned himself to escape their vengeance, from which he had, perhaps, nothing to apprehend.

In fact at this time the dread of the followers of Hassan Sabah had sunk deep into the hearts of all the princes of the East, for there was no security against their daggers. Accordingly, when the next year (1120) Aboo Mohammed, the head of them at Aleppo, where they had re-established themselves, sent to the powerful Il-Ghazi to demand of him pos-

session of the castle of Sherif, near that town, he
feared to refuse; but the people of Aleppo, at the
persuasion of one of their fellow-citizens (who speedily
paid for his advice with his blood), rose *en masse*,
levelled the walls, filled up the ditches, and united
the castle to the town. Even the great Noor-ed-deen
(*Lamp of Religion*) was some years afterwards
obliged to have recourse to the same artifice to save
the castle of Beitlaha from becoming one of their
strong-holds.

The same system was pursued in Persia, where
sultan Sanjar, the son of Malek Shah, had united
under his sceptre the greater part of the dominions
of his father and Fakhr-al-Moolk (*Fame of the
Realm*). The son and successor of Nizam-al-Moolk
and Chakar Beg, the great uncle of the sultan, perished by the daggers of the emissaries of Hassan
Sabah. Sultan Sanjar was himself on his march,
intending to lay siege to Alamoot, and the other
strong-holds of the Ismaïlites, when one morning, on
awaking, he found a dagger struck in the ground
close to his pillow. The sultan was dismayed, but
he concealed his terror, and a few days afterwards
there came a brief note from Alamoot, containing
these words : " Were we not well affected towards the
sultan, the dagger had been struck in his bosom,
not in the ground." Sanjar recollected that his brother Mohammed, who had laid siege to the castles of
Lamseer and Alamoot, had died suddenly just as
they were on the point of surrendering—an event so
opportune for the society, that it was but natural to
ascribe it to their agency—and he deemed it the safest
course to proceed gently with such dangerous opponents. He accordingly hearkened to proposals of
peace, which was concluded on the following conditions : 1. That the Ismaïlites should add no new
works to their castles; 2. That they should purchase

no arms or military machines; 3. That they should make no more proselytes. The sultan, on his part, released the Ismaïlites from all tolls and taxes in the district of Kirdkoh, and assigned them a part of the revenue of the territory of Komis by way of annual pension. To apprehend clearly what the power of the society was, we must recollect that sultan Sanjar was the most powerful monarch of the East, that his mandate was obeyed from Cashgar to Antioch, from the Caspian to the Straits of Bab-el-Mandeb.

Thirty-four years had now elapsed since the acquisition of Alamoot, and the first establishment of the power of Hassan Sabah. In all that time he had never been seen out of the castle of Alamoot, and had been even known but twice to leave his chamber, and to make his appearance on the terrace. In silence and in solitude he pondered the means of extending the power of the society of which he was the head, and he drew up, with his own hand, the rules and precepts which were to govern it. He had outlived most of his old companions and early disciples, and he was now childless, for he had put to death his two only sons, the elder for having been concerned in the murder of his faithful adherent Hussein Kaini; the younger for having violated the precept of the Koran against drinking wine. Feeling the approaches of death, he summoned to Alamoot Keäh Buzoorg Oomeid (*Keäh of Good Hope*), who was residing at Lamseer, which he had conquered twenty years before, and Aboo Ali, of Casveen, and committed the direction of the society to them, appointing the former to be its proper spiritual head and director, and placing in the hands of the latter the administration of the civil and external affairs. He then calmly expired, apparently unconscious of or indifferent to the fact of having, by the organization of his pernicious society, rendered his name an object of execration, a by-word and a proverb among the nations.

Dimly as we may discern the character of Hassan Sabah through the medium of prejudice and hatred through which the scanty notices of it have reached us, we cannot refuse him a place among the higher order of minds. The founder of an empire or of a powerful society is almost always a great man; but Hassan seems to have had this advantage over Loyola and other founders of societies, that he saw clearly from the commencement what might be done, and formed all his plans with a view to one ultimate object. He surely had no ordinary mind who could ask but two devoted adherents to shake the throne of the house of Seljook, then at the acmé of its power.

CHAPTER V.

Organization of the Society—Names given to the Ismaïlites
—Origin of the name Assassin—Marco Polo's description of
the Paradise of the Old Man of the Mountain—Description
of it given by Arabian writers—Instances of the obedience
of the Fedavee.

HAVING traced thus far the history of this celebrated
society, having shown its origin, and how it grew
out of the claims of the descendants of Ali to the
khalifat, mixed with the mystic tenets which seem
to have been ultimately derived from India, we proceed to describe its organization, and its secret doctrines, as they are related by oriental historians.

Hassan Sabah clearly perceived that the plan of
the society at Cairo was defective as a mean of acquiring temporal power. The Dais might exert
themselves, and proselytes might be gained; but till
possession was obtained of some strongholds, and a
mode of striking terror into princes devised, nothing
effectual could be achieved. He first, therefore, as
we have seen, made himself master of Alamoot and
the other strong places, and then added to the Dais
and the Refeek another class, named Fedavee (*Devoted*), whose task it was to yield implicit obedience
to the mandate of their chief, and, without inquiry or
hesitation, plunge their daggers into the bosom of
whatever victim was pointed out to them, even
though their own lives should be the immediate
sacrifice. The ordinary dress of the Fedavee was
(like that of all the sects opposed to the house of
Abbas) white; their caps, girdles, or boots, were
red. Hence they were named the White (*Mubei-*

yazah), and the Red (*Muhammeré**); but they could with ease assume any guise, even that of the Christian monk, to accomplish their murderous designs.

The gradations in the society were these. At the head of it stood Hassan himself and his successors, with the title of Seydna, or Sidna † (*Our Lord*), and Sheikh-al-Jebal (*Mountain Chief*), a name derived from that of the territory which was the chief seat of the power of the society. This last, owing to the ambiguity of the word *sheikh* (which, like *seigneur* and *signore*, signifies either an *elder* or *chief*), has been ridiculously translated by the early European historians *Old Man of the Mountain*. Under him were the Dai-'l-Kebir (*Great Missionaries*), of which there were three, for the three provinces of Jebal, Kuhistan and Syria‡. Then came the Dais, next the Refeek, then the Fedavee, and lastly the Lazik, or aspirants.

Hassan was perfectly aware that without the compressing power of positive religion no society can well be held together. Whatever, therefore, his private opinions may have been, he resolved to impose on the bulk of his followers the most rigid obedience to the positive precepts of Islam, and, as we have seen, actually put his own son to death for a breach of one of them.

Hassan is said to have rejected two of the degrees of the Ismaïlite society at Cairo, and to have reduced them to seven, the original number in the plan of Abdallah Maimoon, the first projector of this secret society. Besides these seven degrees, through which the aspirants gradually rose to knowledge, Hassan,

---

* Ahmar, fem. Hamra, is *red* in Arabic; hence the cele‑brated Moorish palace at Granada was called Alhambra (*Al Hamra*), *i. e.* the Red.

† Hence the Spanish *Cid*.　　‡ Hammer, book ii.

in what Hammer terms the breviary of the order, drew up seven regulations or rules for the conduct of the teachers in his society. 1. The first of these, named Ashinai-Risk (*Knowledge of duty*), inculcated the requisite knowledge of human nature for selecting fit persons for admission. To this belonged the proverbial expressions said to have been current among the Dais, similar to those used by the ancient Pythagoreans, such as *Sow not on barren ground* (that is, Waste not your labour on incapable persons). *Speak not in a house where there is a lamp*, (that is, Be silent in the presence of a lawyer). 2. The second rule was called Teënis (*Gaining of confidence*), and taught to win the candidates by flattering their passions and inclinations. 3. The third, of which the name is not given, taught to involve them in doubts and difficulties by pointing out the absurdities of the Koran, and of positive religion. 4. When the aspirant had gone thus far, the solemn oath of silence and obedience, and of communicating his doubts to his teacher alone, was to be imposed on the disciple; and then (5.) he was to be informed that the doctrines and opinions of the society were those of the greatest men in church and state. 6. The Tessees (*Confirmation*) directed to put the pupil again through all he had learned, and to confirm him in it. And, (7.) finally, the Teëvil (*Instruction in allegory*) gave the allegorical mode of interpreting the Koran, and drawing whatever sense might suit their purposes from its pages. Any one who had gone through this course of instruction, and was thus become perfectly imbued with the spirit of the society, was regarded as an accomplished Dai, and employed in the important office of making proselytes and extending its influence.

We must again express our opinion that the minute accounts which are given to us by some writers, respecting the rules and doctrines of secret associations, should be received with a considerable degree of hesitation, owing to the character and the means of information of those from whom we receive them. In the present case our authority is a very suspicious one. We are told that when Alamoot was taken by Hoolekoo Khan, the Mongol prince, he gave his vizir, the learned Ata-Melek (*King's father*) Jowani, permission to examine the library, and to select such books as were worthy of being preserved. The vizir took out the Korans and some other books of value in his eyes ; the rest, among which are said to have been the archives and the secret rules and doctrines of the society, he committed, after looking cursorily through them, to the flames. In an historical work of his own he gave the result of his discoveries in those books, and he is the authority from which Mirkhond and other writers have derived the accounts which they have transmitted to us. It is quite clear, therefore, that the vizir of Hoolakoo was at liberty to invent what atrocities he pleased of the sect which was destroyed by his master, and that his testimony is consequently to be received with suspicion. On the other hand it receives some confirmation from its agreement with the account of the society at Cairo given by Macrisi, and is not repugnant to the spirit of Soofeïsm.

This last doctrine, which is a kind of mystic Pantheism, viewing God in all and all in God, may produce, like fatalism, piety or its opposite. In the eyes of one who thus views God, all the distinctions between vice and virtue become fleeting and uncertain, and crime may gradually lose its atrocity, and be regarded as only a mean for the production of a good end. That the Ismaïlite Fedavee murdered innocent persons without compunction, when ordered so to do by his superiors, is an undoubted fact, and there is no absurdity in supposing that he and they may have

thought that in so doing they were acting right, and
promoting the cause of truth.   Such sanctifying of
crime is not confined to the East; the maxim that
the end sanctions the means is of too convenient a
nature not to have prevailed in all parts of the world;
and the assassins of Henry III. and Henry IV. of
France displayed all the sincerity and constancy of
the Ismaïlite Fedavees.   Without, therefore, regarding the heads of the Ismaïlites, with Hammer,
mere ruthless and impious murderers, who trampled
under foot religion and morals with all their obligations, we may assent to the opinion of their leading
doctrine being Soofeïsm carried to its worst consequences.

The followers of Hassan Sabah were called the
Eastern Ismaïlites, to distinguish them from those of
Africa.   They were also named the Batiniyeh (*Internal or Secret*), from the secret meaning which they
drew from the text of the Koran, and Moolhad, or Moolahid (*Impious*) on account of the imputed impiety of
their doctrines,—names common to them with most of
the preceding sects.   It is under this last appellation
that they were known to Marco Polo, the Venetian
traveller.   The name, however, by which they are
best known in Europe, and which we shall henceforth
chiefly employ, is that of Assassins.   This name is
very generally derived from that of the founder of
their society; but M. De Sacy has made it probable
that the oriental term Hashisheen, of which the
Crusaders made Assassins, comes from Hashish,
a species of hemp, from which intoxicating opiates
were made, which the Fedavee were in the habit of
taking previously to engaging in their daring enter-
prises, or employed as a medium of procuring delicious
visions of the paradise promised to them by the
Sheikh-al-Jebal.

It is a curious question how Hassan Sabah contrived to infuse into the Fedavee the recklessness of life, joined with the spirit of implicit obedience to the commands of their superiors, which they so invariably displayed. We are told* that the system adopted for this purpose was to obtain, by purchase or otherwise, from their parents, stout and healthy children. These were reared up in implicit obedience to the will of the Sheikh, and, to fit them for their future office, carefully instructed in various languages. The most agreeable spots were selected for their abode, they were indulged in the gratification of their senses, and, in the midst of their enjoyments, some persons were directed to inflame their imaginations by glowing descriptions of the far superior delights laid up in the celestial paradise for those who should be admitted to repose in its bowers; a happiness only to be attained by a glorious death met in obedience to the commands of the Sheikh. When such ideas had been impressed on their minds, the glorious visions ever floated before their eyes, the impression was kept up by the use of the opiate above-mentioned, and the young enthusiast panted for the hour when death, obtained in obeying the order of the Sheikh, should open to him the gates of paradise to admit him to the enjoyment of bliss never to end.

The celebrated Venetian, Marco Polo, who traversed the most remote parts of the East in the 13th century, gave on his return to Europe an account of the regions which he had visited, which filled the minds of men with wonder and amazement. As is usual in such cases this was followed or accompanied by unbelief, and it is only by the inquiries and discoveries of modern travellers that the veracity of Marco Polo, like that of Herodotus, has been established and placed beyond doubt.

Among other wonderful narratives which we meet

* Wilken, Geschichte der Kreuzzüge, vol. ii

in the travels of Marco Polo is the account which he gives of the people whom he calls Mulehetites (that is, Moolahid), and their prince the Old Man of the Mountain. He describes correctly the nature of this society, and gives the following romantic narrative of the mode employed by that prince to infuse the principle of implicit obedience into the minds of his followers*.

" In a beautiful valley," says he, " enclosed between two lofty mountains, he had formed a luxurious garden, stored with every delicious fruit and every fragrant shrub that could be procured. Palaces of various sizes and forms were erected in different parts of the grounds, ornamented with works of gold, with paintings, and with furniture of rich silks. By means of small conduits contained in these buildings streams of wine, milk, honey, and some of pure water, were seen to flow in every direction. The inhabitants of these palaces were elegant and beautiful damsels, accomplished in the arts of singing, playing upon all sorts of musical instruments, dancing, and especially those of dalliance and amorous allurement. Clothed in rich dresses, they were seen continually sporting and amusing themselves in the garden and pavilions, their female guardians being confined within doors, and never suffered to appear. The object which the chief had in view in forming a garden of this fascinating kind was this : that Mahomet having promised to those who should obey his will the enjoyments of paradise, where every species of sensual gratification should be found in the society of beautiful nymphs, he was desirous of its being understood by his followers that he also was a prophet, and a compeer of Mahomet, and had the power of admitting to paradise such as he should choose to favour. In order that none without his licence should find their way into this delicious valley, he caused a strong and inexpugnable

* Marsden's Translation.

castle to be erected at the opening of it, through which the entry was by a secret passage. At his court, likewise, this chief entertained a number of youths, from the age of twelve to twenty years, selected from the inhabitants of the surrounding mountains, who showed a disposition for martial exercises, and appeared to possess the quality of daring courage. To them he was in the daily practice of discoursing on the subject of the paradise announced by the Prophet and of his own, of granting admission, and at certain times he caused draughts of a soporific nature to be administered to ten or a dozen of the youths, and when half dead with sleep he had them conveyed to the several apartments of the palaces in the garden. Upon awakening from this state of lethargy their senses were struck with all the delightful objects that have been described, and each perceived himself surrounded by lovely damsels, singing, playing, and attracting his regards by the most fascinating caresses, serving him also with delicious viands and exquisite wines, until, intoxicated with excess of enjoyment, amidst actual rivers of milk and wine, he believed himself assuredly in paradise, and felt an unwillingness to relinquish its delights. When four or five days had thus been passed, they were thrown once more into a state of somnolency and carried out of the garden. Upon their being introduced to his presence, and questioned by him as to where they had been, their answer was, 'In paradise, through the favour of your highness;' and then, before the whole court, who listened to them with eager curiosity and astonishment, they gave a circumstantial account of the scenes to which they had been witnesses. The chief thereupon addressing them said, 'We have the assurance of our Prophet that he who defends his lord shall inherit paradise, and if you show yourselves devoted to the obedience of my orders, that happy lot

awaits you.' Animated to enthusiasm by words of
this nature all deemed themselves happy to receive
the commands of their master, and were forward to
die in his service."

This romantic narrative, more suited to a place
among the wonders of the "Thousand and One
Nights" than to admission into sober history, has
been very generally rejected by judicious inquirers
such as De Sacy and Wilkin, the able historians
of the Crusades; but it has found credence with
Hammer, to whose work we are indebted for the far
greater part of the present details on the subject of
the Assassins. This industrious scholar has, as he
thinks, found a proof of its truth in the circumstance
of similar narratives occurring in the works of some
Arabian writers which treat of the settlements of the
society in Syria, forgetting that a fabulous legend is
often more widely diffused than sober truth. All,
therefore, that can be safely inferred from this collection of authorities is that the same marvellous tale
which the Venetian traveller heard in the north of
Persia was also current in Syria and Egypt. Its truth
must be established by a different species of proof.

In the Siret-al-Hakem (*Memoirs of Hakem*), a
species of Arabian historic romance, the following account of the gardens at Massyat, the chief seat of
the Assassins in Syria, was discovered by Hammer* :—

" Our narrative now returns to Ismaïl the chief of
the Ismaïlites. He took with him his people laden
with gold, silver, pearls, and other effects, taken away
from the inhabitants of the coasts, and which he had
received in the island of Cyprus, and on the part of
the king of Egypt, Dhaher, the son of Hakem-
biëmr-Illah. Having bidden farewell to the sultan
of Egypt at Tripolis, they proceeded to Massyat, when

* Fundgruben des Orients, vol.i ii.

the inhabitants of the castles and fortresses assembled to enjoy themselves, along with the chief Ismail and his people. They put on the rich dresses with which the sultan had supplied them, and adorned the castle of Massyat with everything that was good and fine. Ismaïl made his entry into Massyat with the Devoted (*Fedavee*), as no one has ever done at Massyat before him or after him. He stopped there some time to take into his service some more persons whom he might make Devoted both in heart and body.

" With this view he had caused to be made a vast garden, into which he had water conducted. In the middle of this garden he built a kiosk raised to the height of four stories. On each of the four sides were richly-ornamented windows joined by four arches, in which were painted stars of gold and silver. He put into it roses, porcelain, glasses, and drinking-vessels of gold and silver. He had with him Mamlooks (*i. e.* slaves), ten males and ten females, who were come with him from the region of the Nile, and who had scarcely attained the age of puberty. He clothed them in silks and in the finest stuffs, and he gave unto them bracelets of gold and of silver. The columns were overlaid with musk and with amber, and in the four arches of the windows he set four caskets, in which was the purest musk. The columns were polished, and this place was the retreat of the slaves. He divided the garden into four parts. In the first of these were pear-trees, apple-trees, vines, cherries, mulberries, plums, and other kinds of fruit-trees. In the second were oranges, lemons, olives, pomegranates, and other fruits. In the third were cucumbers, melons, leguminous plants, &c. In the fourth were roses, jessamine, tamarinds, narcissi, violets, lilies, anemonies, &c. &c.

"The garden was divided by canals of water, and the kiosk was surrounded with ponds and reservoirs. There were groves in which were seen antelopes, ostriches, asses, and wild cows. Issuing from the ponds, one met ducks, geese, partridges, quails, hares, foxes, and other animals. Around the kiosk the chief Ismaïl planted walks of tall trees, terminating in the different parts of the garden. He built there a great house, divided into two apartments, the upper and the lower. From the latter covered walks led out into the garden, which was all enclosed with walls, so that no one could see into it, for these walks and buildings were all void of inhabitants. He made a gallery of coolness, which ran from this apartment to the cellar, which was behind. This apartment served as a place of assembly for the men. Having placed himself on a sofa there opposite the door, the chief made his men sit down, and gave them to eat and to drink during the whole length of the day until evening. At nightfall he looked around him, and, selecting those whose firmness pleased him, said to them, 'Ho! such-a-one, come and seat thyself near me.' It is thus that Ismaïl made those whom he had chosen sit near him on the sofa and drink. He then spoke to them of the great and excellent qualities of the imam Ali, of his bravery, his nobleness, and his generosity, until they fell asleep, overcome by the power of the *benjeh** which he had given them, and which never failed to produce its effects in less than a quarter of an hour, so that they fell down as if they were inanimate. As soon as the man had fallen the chief Ismaïl arose, and, taking him up, brought him into a dormitory, and then, shutting the

* The Arabic name of the hyoscyamus, or henbane. Hammer conjectures that the word *benge*, or, with the Coptic article in the plural, *ni-benje*, is the same with the nepenthe of the ancients.—Fundgruben des Orients, iii. 202.

door, carried him on his shoulders into the gallery ot coolness, which was in the garden, and thence into the kiosk, where he committed him to the care of the male and female slaves, directing them to comply with all the desires of the candidate, on whom they flung vinegar till he awoke. When he was come to himself the youths and maidens said to him, ' We are only waiting for thy death, for this place is destined for thee. This is one of the pavilions of paradise, and we are the hoories and the children of paradise. If thou wert dead thou wouldest be for ever with us, but thou art only dreaming, and wilt soon awake.' Meanwhile the chief Ismaïl had returned to the company as soon as he had witnessed the awakening of the candidate, who now perceived nothing but youths and maidens of the greatest beauty, and adorned in the most magnificent manner.

" He looked round the place, inhaled the fragrance of musk and frankincense, and drew near to the garden, where he saw the beasts and the birds, the running water, and the trees. He gazed on the beauty of the kiosk, and the vases of gold and silver, while the youths and maidens kept him in converse. In this way he remained confounded, not knowing whether he was awake or only dreaming. When two hours of the night had gone by, the chief Ismaïl returned to the dormitory, closed to the door, and thence proceeded to the garden, where his slaves came around him and rose before him. When the candidate perceived him he said unto him, ' O chief Ismaïl, do I dream, or am I awake?' The chief Ismaïl then made answer to him, ' O such-a-one, beware of relating this vision to any one who is a stranger to this place ! Know that the Lord Ali has shown thee the place which is destined for thee in paradise. Know that at this moment the Lord Ali and I have been sitting together in the regions of the empyrean.

So do not hesitate a moment in the service of the imam who has given thee to know his felicity.' Then the chief Ismaïl ordered supper to be served. It was brought in vessels of gold and of silver, and consisted of boiled meats and roast meats, with other dishes. While the candidate ate he was sprinkled with rose-water; when he called for drink there were brought to him vessels of gold and silver filled with delicious liquors, in which also had been mingled some *benjeh*. When he had fallen asleep, Ismaïl carried him through the gallery back to the dormitory, and, leaving him there, returned to his company. After a little time he went, back, threw vinegar on his face, and then, bringing him out, ordered one of the Mamlooks to shake him. On awaking, and finding himself in the same place among the guests, he said, 'There is no god but God, and Mohammed is the Prophet of God!' The chief Ismaïl then drew near and caressed him, and he remained, as it were, immersed in intoxication, wholly devoted to the service of the chief, who then said unto him, 'O such-a-one, know that what thou hast seen was not a dream, but one of the miracles of the imam Ali. Know that he has written thy name among those of his friends. If thou keep the secret thou art certain of thy felicity, but if thou speak of it thou wilt incur the resentment of the imam. If thou die thou art a martyr; but beware of relating this to any person whatever. Thou hast entered by one of the gates to the friendship of the imam, and art become one of his family; but if thou betray the secret, thou wilt become one of his enemies, and be driven from his house.' Thus this man became one of the servants of the chief Ismaïl, who in this manner surrounded himself with trusty men, until his reputation was established. This is what is related of the chief Ismaïl and his Devoted."

To these romantic tales of the paradise of the Old

Man of the Mountain we must add a third of a still more juggling character, furnished by the learned and venerable Sheikh Abd-ur-Rahman (*Servant of the Compassionate*, i. e., *of God*) Ben Ebubekr Al-Jeriri of Damascus, in the twenty-fourth chapter of his work entitled "A Choice Book for discovering the Secrets of the Art of Imposture*."

After giving some account of Sinan, the chief of the Syrian Assassins, whom we shall presently have occasion to mention, the sheikh proceeds to narrate the artifice which he employed to deceive his followers :—

" There was near the sofa on which he sat a hole in the ground sufficiently deep for a man to sit down in it. This he covered with a thin piece of wood, leaving only so much of it open as would contain the neck of a man. He placed on this cover of wood a disk of bronze with a hole in the middle of it, and put in it two doors. Then taking one of his disciples, to whom he had given a considerable sum of money to obtain his consent, he placed the perforated disk round his neck, and kept it down by weights, so that nothing appeared but the neck of the man ; and he put warm blood upon it, so that it looked as if he had just cut off his head. He then called in his companions, and showed them the plate, on which they beheld the head of their comrade. 'Tell thy comrades,' said the master to the head, 'what thou hast seen, and what has been said unto thee.' The man then answered as he had been previously instructed. 'Which wouldest thou prefer,' said the master, ' to return to the world and thy friends, or to dwell in paradise?' ' What need have I,' replied the head, 'to return to the world after having seen my pavilion in paradise, and the hoories, and all that God has prepared for me ? Comrades, salute

* Fundgruben des Orients, vol. iv.

my family, and take care not to disobey this prophet, who is the lord of the prophets in the state of time, as God has said unto me. Farewell.' These words strengthened the faith of the others; but when they were gone the master took the man up out of the hole, and cut off his head in right earnest. It was by such means as this that he made himself obeyed by his people."

The preceding accounts, whatever may be thought of their truth, serve to testify a general belief throughout the East of some extraordinary means being employed by the mountain chief to acquire the power which he was known to possess over the minds of his Fedavee. And, in fact, there is no great improbability in the supposition of some artifice of that nature having been occasionally employed by him; for, when we recollect that an Asiatic imagination is coarse, especially among the lower orders, and that in the East men rarely see any females but those of their own family, the chief might find no great difficulty in persuading a youth, whom he had transported in a state of stupor into an apartment filled with young girls, of his having been in the actual paradise promised to the faithful.

But, laying aside supposition, we may observe that the very power over the minds of their followers ascribed to Hassan Sabah and his successors has been actually exercised in our own days by the chief of the Wahabees. Sir John Malcolm* informs us, from a Persian manuscript, that a few years ago one of that sect, who had stabbed an Arab chief near Bussora, when taken, not only refused to do anything towards saving his life, but, on the contrary, seemed anxiously to court death. He was observed to grasp something firmly in his hand, which he appeared to prize beyond life itself. On its being taken from him and exa-

* History of Persia, vol. i.

mined, it proved to be an order from the Wahabee chief for an emerald palace and a number of beautiful female slaves in the blissful paradise of the Prophet. This story, however, it must be confessed, appears to be little consistent with the principles of the sect of the Wahabees, and we may suspect that it has originated in some misapprehension.

The following instance of the implicit obedience of the Fedavee to the orders of Hassan Sabah is given by a respectable oriental historian*. An ambassador from the Sultan Malek Shah having come to Alamoot to demand the submission and obedience of the sheikh, Hassan received him in a hall in which he had assembled several of his followers. Making a sign to one youth, he said, " Kill thyself!" Instantly the young man's dagger was plunged into his own bosom, and he lay a corpse upon the ground. To another he said, " Fling thyself down from the wall." In an instant his shattered limbs were lying in the castle ditch. Then turning to the terrified envoy, " I have seventy thousand followers who obey me after this fashion. This be my answer to thy master."

Very nearly the same tale is told of the Assassins of Syria by a western writer†. As Henry Count of Champagne was journeying, in the year 1194, from Palestine to Armenia‡, his road lay through the confines of the territory of the Ismaïlites. The chief sent some persons to salute him, and to beg that, on his return, he would stop at, and partake of the hospitality of his castle. The count accepted the invitation. As he returned the Dai-al-Kebir advanced to meet him, showed him every mark of honour, and led him to view his castles and fortresses. Having

* Elmacin, Historia Saracenica, l. iii. p. 286.
† Marinus Sanutus, l. iii. p. x. c. 8.
‡ This was the Armenia in Cilicia.

passed through several, they came at length to one the towers of which rose to an exceeding height. On each tower stood two sentinels clad in white. "These," said the chief, pointing to them, "obey me far better than the subjects of you Christians obey their lords;" and at a given signal two of them flung themselves down, and were dashed to pieces. "If you wish," said he to the astonished count, "all my white ones shall do the same." The benevolent count shrank from the proposal, and candidly avowed that no Christian prince could presume to look for such obedience from his subjects. When he was departing, with many valuable presents, the chief said to him significantly, "By means of these trusty servants I get rid of the enemies of our society."

In oriental, and also in occidental history, the same anecdote is often told of different persons, a circumstance which might induce us to doubt of its truth altogether, or at least of its truth in any particular case. The present anecdote, for instance, with a slight variation in the details, is told of Aboo Taher, a celebrated leader of the Carmathites. This chief, after his expedition to Mecca, in which he had slain 30,000 of the inhabitants, filled the hallowed well Zemzem with the bodies of dead men, and carried off the sacred black stone in triumph, had the hardihood to approach Bagdad, the residence of the khalif, with only 500 horsemen. The pontiff of Islam, enraged at the insult, ordered his general Aboo Saj to take 30,000 men, and make him a prisoner. The latter, having collected his forces, sent a man off to Aboo Taher to tell him on his part that out of regard for him, who had been his old friend, he advised him, as he had so few troops with him, either to yield himself at once to the khalif or to see about making his escape. Aboo Taher asked of the envoy how many men Aboo Saj had with him. The envoy replied, " Thirty thousand." " He still wants three like mine," said Aboo Taher; and calling to him three of his men, he ordered one of them to stab himself, another to throw himself into the Tigris, a third to fling himself down from a precipice. His commands were at once obeyed. Then turning to the envoy, " He who has such troops fears not the number of his enemies. I give thyself quarter; but know that I shall soon let thee see thy general Aboo Saj chained among my dogs." In fact, that very night he attacked and routed the troops of the khalif, and Aboo Saj, happening to fall into his hands, soon appeared chained among the mastiffs of the Car-mathite chief*.

The preceding details on the paradise of the Sheikh-al-Jebal, and his power over the minds of his followers, will at least help to illustrate the manners and modes of thinking of the orientals. We now resume the thread of our narrative, and proceed to narrate the deeds of the Assassins, as we shall henceforth designate them.

* D'Herbelot, titre Carmath.

CHAPTER VI.

Keäh Buzoorg Oomeid—Affairs of the Society in Persia—
They acquire the Castle of Banias, in Syria—Attempt to
betray Damascus to the Crusaders—Murders committed
during the reign of Keäh Buzoorg.

KEAH BUZOORG OOMEID trod faithfully in the foot-
prints of his predecessor. He built the strong fortress
of Maimoondees, and he made the enemies of the
society feel that it was still animated by the spirit of
Hassan Sabah. Sultan Sanjar, who, on account of
the favourable terms on which he had made peace
with the Assassins, was regarded by the rigidly orthodox as a secret follower of their doctrine, declared
himself once more their open enemy, and sent an
army to ravage Kirdkoh. These troops were defeated by those which Keäh sent against them; but
the following year Sanjar put to the sword a great
number of the members of the sect. The dagger, as
usual, retaliated. Mahmood, the successor of Sanjar,
having first tried in vain the effect of arms, sent his
grand falconer Berenkesh to Alamoot, to desire that
an envoy might be sent to him to treat of peace. The
Khojah (*Master*) Mohammed Nassihi accompanied
Berenkesh back to court, and kissed the hand of the
sultan, who spoke to him a few words about the
peace; but as the Khojah was going out of the palace,
he and his followers were fallen upon and massacred
by the people.

When the sultan sent an ambassador to Alamoot
to exculpate himself from the guilt of participation in
this violation of the laws of nations, Keäh made

answer, " Go back to the sultan, and tell him, in
my name, Mohammed Nassihi trusted to your perfidious assurances, and repaired to your court; if you
speak truly, deliver up the murderers to justice ; if not,
expect my vengeance." On the refusal of the sultan
to surrender the murderers, a corps of Assassins appeared at the gates of Casveen, slew 400 men, and led
away 3,000 sheep, 200 horses, and 200 oxen. Next
year the sultan took, and retained for a short time, the
fortress of Alamoot; but a body of 2,000 men which he
sent against Lamseer fled, without drawing a sword,
when they heard that the Refeek (*Companions*) of the
society were marching against them. Shortly afterwards the sultan died, and the Assassins made another incursion into the district of Casveen, where
they carried off booty and prisoners.

The mountain chief would tolerate no rival near
his throne. Hearing that one Aboo Hashem, a
descendant of Ali, had arrogated to himself the dignity of imam in the province of Ghilan, which lies
north of Kuhistan, and had issued letters calling on
the people to acknowledge him, Keäh wrote to him
to desist from his pretensions. The self-appointed
imam only replied by reviling the odious tenets of
the Ismaïlites. The sheikh forthwith sent a body of
his troops against him, took him prisoner, and, after
trying him by a court-martial, committed him to the
flames.

Though, as we have seen, the settlements of the
Assassins were in the mountainous region of Irak, in
the north-west of Persia, their power was of such a
nature that no distance was a security against it. A
Fedavee could speedily traverse the intervening regions
to plant his dagger in the bosom of any prince or
minister who had incurred the vengeance of the
Sheikh-al-Jebal. Accordingly we find the shah
(*King*) of Khaurism, between which and Irak lies

the extensive province of Khorasan, coming to
Sultan Massood, the successor of Mahmood, to concert with him a plan for the destruction of these formidable foes to princes. The shah of Khaurism
had been formerly rather disposed to favour the Ismaïlites, but his eyes were now opened, and he was
become their most inveterate enemy. Sultan Massood, we know not for what reason, bestowed on him
the lands which Berenkesh, the grand falconer, had
held of the sultan. Berenkesh, mortally offended at
this unworthy treatment, retired, with his family, to
the territory of the Ismaïlites, and sought the protection of Keäh, whose open enemy he had hitherto
been. Policy, or a regard to good faith and humanity, made the Assassin prince grant the protection
which was required; and when the shah of Khaurism
wrote, reminding Keäh of his own former friendship,
and the bitter hostility of Berenkesh, and requesting
him, on that plea, to give up the fugitive, the sheikh
replied, "The shah of Khaurism speaks true, but we
will never give up our suppliants." Long and bloody
enmity between the sheikh and the shah was the
consequence of this refusal to violate the rights of
hospitality.

The Syrian branch of the society begins at this
time to attract rather more attention than that of
Persia, chiefly on account of its connexion with the
Crusaders, who had succeeded in establishing an
empire extending from the frontiers of Egypt to those
of Armenia. A Persian Ismaïlite, named Behram
of Astrabad, who is said to have commenced his
career by the murder of his own father, gained the
confidence of the vizir of the prince of Damascus,
who gave him the castle of Banias, or Panias (the
ancient Balanea), for the use of the society. This
place, which became the nucleus of the power of
the Assassins in Syria, lies in a fertile, well-watered

plain, about 4,000 paces from the sea. The valley
whence the numerous streams which fructify it issue
is called the Wadi-al-Jinn (*Valley of Demons*),
" a place," observes Hammer, whom no casual
coincidence escapes, " from its very name worthy
of becoming a settlement of the Assassins." From
Banias they extended their power over the neighbouring castles and fortresses, until, twelve years
afterwards, the seat of dominion was transferred
thence to Massyat.

Behram fell shortly afterwards in an engagement
against the people of the valley of Taïm, the brother
of whose chief had perished by the daggers of the
Assassins. His successor was Ismaïl, a Persian, who
continued the bond of amity with the vizir of Damascus, whither he sent, by way of resident, a man
named, rather inappropriately as it would appear,
Aboo-'l-Wefa (*Father of Fidelity*). This man so
won the favour of the vizir and prince that he was
appointed to the office of Hakem, or supreme judge ;
and having thus acquired power and influence, he
immediately turned his thoughts to the best mode of
employing them for the advantage of the society, an
object always near the heart of a true Ismaïlite. A
place of strength on the sea-coast would, he conceived, be of the utmost importance to them; so he
fixed his eyes upon Tyre, and fell upon the following
expedient to obtain possession of it.

The Franks had been now upwards of thirty years
established in the East. Their daring and enthu-
siastic valour was at once the dread and the admiration of their Mussulman foes, and feats almost sur-
passing the fables of the romances of chivalry had
been performed by their gallant warriors. These
were the auxiliaries to whom Aboo-'l-Wefa directed
his attention; for we are to observe that as yet the
fanatic spirit had not united all the Moslems in en

mity against the followers of the Cross, and the princes of Aleppo, Damascus, and the other districts of Syria, had been more than once in alliance with the Christian realms of Jerusalem and Antioch. Aboo-'l-Wefa sent therefore and concluded a secret treaty with Baldwin II., king of Jerusalem, in which he engaged, if the Christian warriors would secretly march and appear before Damascus on a Friday, when the emir and his officers would be at the mosk, to give them possession of the gates of the town. The king was in return to put Tyre into the hands of the Ismaïlites.

The Christian army was assembled; all the barons of the kingdom appeared in arms; the king in person led the host; the newly-formed military order of the Templars displayed for the first time in the field their striped banner *Beauséant,* afterwards so well known in many a bloody fray. Prince Bernard of Antioch, Count Pontius of Tripolis, the brave Joscelin of Edessa, led their knights and footmen to share in the capture of the wealthy city of Damascus. The mountains which environ Lake Tiberias were left behind, and the host joyfully emerged into the plain watered by the streams Abana and Pharpar. But here defeat awaited them. Taj-al-Molook (*Diadem of Kings*) Boozi, the emir of Damascus, had in time discovered the plot of his hakem. He had put him and the vizir to death, and had ordered a general massacre of the Ismaïlites in the city*. The Christian army was now at a place named Marj Safar, and the footmen had begun to plunder the villages for food, when a small body of gallant Damascene warriors rushed from the town and fell upon them. The defenceless Christians sank beneath their blows, incapable of resistance. The rest of the army advanced to aid or avenge their brethren, when sud-

* The number slain was 6,000.

denly* the sky became overcast, thick darkness enveloped all objects, the thunder roared, the lightning flashed, the rain poured down in torrents, and, by a rapid transition, peculiar to Eastern climates, the rain and waters turned into snow and ice, and augmented the horrors of the day. The superstitious and conscience-stricken Crusaders viewed in this awful phenomenon the immediate agency of heaven, and deemed it to be sent as a punishment for their sins; and, recollecting that on that very spot but four years before King Baldwin had gained, with a handful of men, a victory over an army of the Damascenes, they were plunged into grief and humiliation. The only advantage which they derived from this expedition was the acquisition of the castle of Banias, which the Ismaïlite governor put into their hands, that under their protection he might escape the fate of his brethren.

Banias was given up to the Christians in the same year in which Alamoot was taken by the Seljookian sultan, and thus the power of the Assassins seemed to be almost gone. But it had in it a conservative principle, and, hydra-like, it grew by its wounds. Alamoot was speedily recovered, and three years afterwards Banias was once more the seat of a Daï-al-Kebir. At the same time the dagger raged with unwonted fury against all of whom the society stood in apprehension, and the annals of the reign of Keäh Buzoorg Oomeid furnish a list of illustrious victims.

The first of these was the celebrated Aksunkur, Prince of Mossul, a warrior equally dreaded by the Christians and by the Assassins. As this prince, on his return from Maärra Mesrin, where the Moslem and Christian hosts had parted without venturing to engage, entered the mosk at Mossul to perform his

* It was the month of December.

devotions, he was attacked at the moment when he was about to take his usual seat by eight assassins, disguised as dervishes.   Three of them fell beneath the blows of the valiant emir, but ere his people could come to his aid he had received his death-wound and expired.   The remainder of the murderers became victims to the vengeance of the people; one youth only escaped.   The Arabian historian, Kemal-ed-Deen, relates on this occasion a curious trait of the fanaticism and Spartan spirit which animated the members of the sect of the Ismaïlites.   When the mother of the youth above-mentioned heard that the formidable Aksunkur had been slain, she painted her face and put on her gayest raiment and ornaments, rejoicing that her son had been found worthy to die the glorious death of a martyr in the cause of the Imam.   But when she saw him return alive and unscathed, she cut off her hair and blackened her countenance, and would not be comforted.

In the following year (1127) fell Moin-ed-deen, the vizir of Sultan Sanjar.   In this case the Assassin had engaged himself as a groom in the service of the vizir.   As Moin-ed-deen went one day into the stable to look at his horses the Assassin appeared before him, stripped, and holding one of the horses by the bridle.   As the vizir, unsuspicious of danger, came near where he was, the false groom made the horse rear, and, under the pretence of soothing and pacifying the restive animal, he took out a small dagger which he had concealed in the horse's mane, and plunged it into the bosom of the vizir.

The slaughter of the Ismaïlites by the Prince of Damascus was not forgotten, and two years afterwards he received two dagger wounds, one of which proved mortal.   Their vengeance was not appeased by his blood, and his son and successor, Shems-al-Molook (*Sun of Kings*), perished by a conspiracy with the guilt of which the Assassins were charged. In the catalogue of the victims of this period appear also the names of the Judges of the East and of the West, of the Mufti of Casveen, of the Reis of Isfahan, and the Reis of Tebreez.

The East has been at all times prolific of crime; human life is not there held to be of the value at which it is estimated in Europe; and the dagger and poison are freely employed to remove objects of apprehension, to put obstacles out of the way of ambition, or to satiate the thirst of vengeance. We are not, therefore, lightly to give credit to every charge made against the Assassins, and to believe them guilty of murders from which they had no advantage to derive. Thus, when at this time the Fatimite Khalit Amir bi-ahkami-llah (*Commander of the observance of the laws of God*) fell by the hands of murderers, the probability is that he was not a victim to the vengeance of the Ismaïlite society, whom he had never injured, but rather to that of the family of the powerful vizir Afdal, who had been assassinated some time before by the khalif's order, as we have every reason to suppose.

With a greater show of reason may the murder ot Mostarshed, the Khalif of Bagdad, be imputed to the policy of the mountain chief. The Seljookian princes, the predecessors of Massood, had been satisfied to exercise all real power in the empire which had once obeyed the house of Abbas, leaving to that feeble *Shadow of God upon Earth* the unsubstantial privilege of having the coin of the realm struck and prayers offered on Friday in the mosk in his name. But Massood arrogated even these rights to himself. and the helpless successor of the Prophet was obliged to submit to the indignity which he could not pre vent. At length some discontented military chiefs passed with their troops over to the khalif, and per-

suaded him that by one bold effort he might overthrow the might of the Turkish sultan, and recover
all his rights. The khalif listened to their arguments, and, placing himself at the head of an army,
marched against Sultan Massood. But fortune
proved adverse to him. At the first shock the
greater part of the troops of Bagdad abandoned him,
and he remained a captive in the hands of the sultan,
who brought him with him a prisoner to Maragha.
Here a treaty was concluded between them, and the
khalif bound himself not to go any more outside of
the walls of Bagdad, and annually to pay a sum of
money. This treaty appears to have been displeasing
to the Assassins; and, watching their opportunity,
when Massood was gone to meet the ambassadors of
Sultan Sanjar, a party of them fell upon and massacred the khalif and his train. The lifeless body of
the Commander of the Faithful was mangled by
them in the most scandalous manner.

After a blood-stained reign of fourteen years and
three days Keäh Buzoorg Oomeid died. Departing from the maxims of Hassan Sabah, who it is
probable wished to imitate the conduct of the Prophet, and leave the supreme dignity elective, he appointed his own son, Keäh Mohammed, to be his
successor, induced either by paternal partiality, or
believing him to be the person best qualified for the
office.

CHAPTER VII.

Keäh Mohammed—Murder of the Khalif—Castles gained in Syria—Ismaïlite Confession of Faith—Mohammed's Son Hassan gives himself out for the promised Imam—His Followers punished—Succession of Hassan—He abolishes the Law—Pretends to be descended from the Prophet—Is murdered.

THE policy of the society underwent no alteration on the accession of Mohammed. The dagger still smote its enemies, and as each victim fell, the people who maintained the rights of Ismaïl, and who were kept in rigid obedience to the positive precepts of the Koran, beheld nothing but the right hand of Heaven made bare for the punishment of crime and usurpation. The new mountain prince had hardly taken the reins of government into his hands when Rasheed, the successor of the late khalif, eager to avenge the murder of his father, assembled an army and marched against Alamoot. He had reached Isfahan, but there his march terminated. Four Assassins, who had entered his service for the purpose, fell upon him in his tent and stabbed him. When the news was conveyed to Alamoot great rejoicings were made, and for seven days and seven nights the trumpets and kettle-drums resounded from the towers of the fortress, proclaiming the triumph of the dagger to the surrounding country.

The Syrian dominion of the Ismaïlites was at this time considerably extended. They purchased from Ibn Amroo, the r owner, the castles of Cadmos and Kahaf, and took by force that of Massyat from the

lords of Sheiser.   This castle, which was situated on
the west side of Mount Legam, opposite Antaradus,
became henceforth the chief seat of Ismaïlite power
in Syria.   The society had now a line of coast to the
north of Tripolis, and their possessions extended in-
land to the verge of the Hauran.

The reign of Mohammed presents few events to
illustrate the history of the Assassins.   It was probably in his time that the following confession of the
Ismaïlite faith was made to the persons whom Sultan
Sanjar sent to Alamoot to inquire into it*:

"This is our doctrine," said the heads of the society.   "We believe in the unity of God, and acknowledge as the true wisdom and right creed only that
which accords with the word of God and the commands of the Prophet.   We hold these as they are
delivered in the holy writ, the Koran, and believe in
all that the Prophet has taught of the creation, and
the last things, of rewards and punishments, of the
last judgment, and the resurrection.   To believe this
is necessary, and no one is authorized to judge of the
commands of God for himself, or to alter a single
letter in them.   These are the fundamental doctrines
of our sect, and if the sultan does not approve of
them, let him send hither one of his learned divines,
that we may argue the matter with him."

To this creed no orthodox Mussulman could well
make any objection.   The only question was, what
was the Ismaïlite system of interpretation, and what
other doctrines did they deduce from the sacred text;
and the active employment of the dagger of the Fedavee suggested in tolerably plain terms that there
were others, and that something not very compatible
with the peace and order of society lay behind the
veil.   Indeed the circumstance of the Ismaïlite chiefs

* As Sanjar lived to a great age he was contemporary with
several of the Ismaïlite sheikhs.

professing themselves to be only the ministers and
representatives of the invisible imam was in itself
highly suspicious; for what was to prevent their en-
joining any atrocity which might be for their interest,
in the name of their viewless master? They are
ignorant indeed of human nature who suppose that
a prompt obedience would not be yielded to all such
commands by the ignorant and bigoted members of
the sect.

The ill leaven of the secret doctrine displayed
itself before very long. Keäh Mohammed, who appears to have been a weak, inefficient man, was held
in little esteem by his followers. They began to
attach themselves to his son Hassan, who had the
reputation of being a man of prodigious knowledge,
learned in tradition and the text of the Koran,
versed in exposition, and well acquainted with the
sciences. Hassan, either through vanity or policy,
began secretly to disseminate the notion of his being
himself the imam whose appearance had been promised by Hassan Ben Sabah. Filled with this idea,
the more instructed members of the society vied with
each other in eagerness to fulfil his commands, and
Keäh Mohammed, seeing his power gradually slip-
ping from him, was at length roused to energy.
Assembling the people, he reprobated in strong terms
the prevailing heresy. "Hassan," said he, "is my
son, and I am not the imam, but only one of his
missionaries. Whoever maintains the contrary is an
infidel." Then, in true Assassin fashion, he gave
effect to his words by executing 250 of his son's adherents, and banishing an equal number from the
fortress. Hassan himself, in order to save his life,
was obliged publicly to curse those who held the new
opinions, and to write dissertations condemning their
tenets, and defending those of his father. By
these means he succeeded in removing suspicion

from the mind of the old chief; but, as he continued
to drink wine in private, and violated several of the
other positive precepts of the law, his adherents became only the more convinced of his being the imam,
at whose coming all the precepts of the law were to
cease to be of any force.

Hassan was obliged to be cautious and conceal
his opinions during the lifetime of his father; for,
whatever their opinion might be of the capacity and
intellectual power of the head of their sect, the Assassins believed themselves to be bound to obey his
orders, as proceeding from the visible representative
of the sacred invisible imam; and, high as their veneration for Hassan was, his blood would have flowed
on the ground the instant an order to that effect had
passed the lips of his father. But no sooner was
Keäh Mohammed dead, after a reign of twenty-four
years, and the supreme station was come to Hassan
himself, than he resolved to fling away the mask at
once, and not only to trample on the law himself, but
to authorize and encourage all his people to do the
same.

Accordingly, when the month Ramazan (the Mohammedan Lent) of the 559th year of the Hejra
(A. D. 1163) was come, he ordered all the inhabitants
of Roodbar to assemble on the place of prayer (Mo-
sella), or esplanade, before the castle of Alamoot.
Facing the direction of the Keblah* he caused a
pulpit to be erected, at whose four corners were displayed banners of the different hues familiar to Islam,
namely, a white, a red, a yellow, a green, colours
adverse to the black of the Abbassides.

On the 17th day of the month the people, in
obedience to his commands, appeared in great numbers beneath the walls of the fortress. After a little

* That is, the point towards which they turn in prayer,
namely, Mecca.

time Hassan came forth and ascended the pulpit. All voices were hushed; expectation waited on the words of the Sheikh-al-Jebal. He commenced his discourse by perplexing the minds of his auditors by enigmatical and obscure sentences. When he had thus deluded them for some time, he informed them that an envoy of the imam (that is, the phantom of a khalif who was still sitting on the throne at Cairo) had arrived, and had brought him a letter addressed to all Ismaïlites, whereby the fundamental tenets of the sect were renewed and confirmed. He proceeded to assure them that, by this letter, the gates of mercy and compassion had been opened for all who would follow and obey him; that they were the true elect; that they were freed from all obligations of the law, and delivered from the burden of all commands and prohibitions; that he had now conducted them to the day of the resurrection, that is, of the revelation of the imam. He then commenced in Arabic the Khootbeh, or public prayer, which he said he had received from the imam; and an interpreter, who stood at the foot of the pulpit, translated it for them to the following effect:—

" Hassan, the son of Mohammed, the son of Buzoorg Oomeid, is our khalif (*successor*), dai, and hoojet (*proof*). All who follow our doctrine must hearken to him in affairs of faith and of the world, and regard his commands as imperative, his words as impressive. They must not transgress his prohibitions, and they must regard his commands as ours. They should know that our lord has had compassion upon them, and has conducted them to the most high God."

When this proclamation was made known Hassan came down from the pulpit, directed tables to be spread, and commanded the people to break the fast, and to give themselves up, as on festival days, to all

G

kinds of enjoyment, with music, and various games and sports. "For this," cried he, "this is the day of the resurrection;" that is, according to the Ismaïlite mode of interpreting the Koran, the day of the manifestation of the imam.

What the orthodox had before only suspected was now confirmed. It was now manifest, beyond doubt, that the Ismaïlites were heretics who trampled under foot all the most plain and positive precepts of Islam; for, though they might pretend to justify their practice by their allegorical system of interpretation, it was clearly repugnant to common sense, and might be made the instrument of sanctioning, under the name of religion, every species of enormity. From this time the term Moolahid (*impious*) began to become the common and familiar appellation of the Ismaïlites in the mouths of the orthodox Moslems. As to the Ismaïlites themselves, they rejoiced in what they had done; they exulted like emancipated bondsmen in the liberty which they had acquired; and they even commenced a new era from the 17th (or, according to some authorities, the 7th) Ramazan of the 559th year, namely, the day of the manifestation of the imam. To the name of Hassan they henceforth affixed the formula " *On his memory be peace ;*" which formula, it would appear, was employed by itself to designate him; for the historian Mirkhond assures us that he had been informed by a credible person that over the door of the library in Alamoot was the following inscription :—

> " With the aid of God, the bonds
> Of the law he took away,
> The commander of the world,
> Upon whose name be peace."

The madness of Hassan now attained its climax. He disdained to be regarded, like his predecessors, as merely the representative of the imam on earth, but asserted himself to be the true and real imam, who was now at length made manifest to the world. He sent letters to all the settlements of the society, requiring them to acknowledge him in his new capacity. He was prudent enough, however, to show a regard for the dignity and power of his different lieutenants in these letters, as appears by the following specimen, being the letter which was sent to Kuhistan, where the reis Mozaffar commanded:—

" I Hassan say unto you that I am the representative of God upon earth, and mine in Kuhistan is the reis Mozaffar, whom the men of that country are to obey, and to receive his word as mine."

The reis erected a pulpit in the castle of Moominabad, the place of his residence, and read the letter aloud to the people, the greater part of whom listened to its contents with joy. The tables were covered before the pulpit, the wine was brought forth, the drums and kettle-drums resounded, the notes of the pipe and flute inspired joy, and the day of the abolition of the positive precepts of the law was devoted to mirth and festivity. Some few, who were sincere and upright in their obedience to Islam, quitted the region which they now regarded as the abode of infidelity, and went in search of other abodes; others, of a less decided character, remained, though shocked at what they were obliged every day to behold. The obedience to the commands of the *soi-disant* imam was, however, tolerably general, and, according to Hammer, who can scarcely, however, be supposed to regard the system of Hassan as really more licentious than he has elsewhere described that of Mahomet, " the banner of the freest infidelity, and of the most shameless immorality, now waved on all the castles of Roodbar and Kuhistan, as the standard of the new illumination ; and, instead of the name of the Egyptian khalif, resounded from all the pulpits that of Hassan as the true successor of the Prophet."

The latter point had presented some difficulty to Hassan; for, in order to satisfy the people on that head, it was necessary to prove a descent from the Prophet, and this was an honour to which it was well known the family from which he was sprung had never laid claim. He might take upon him to abolish the positive precepts of the law as he pleased, and the people, whose inclinations were thereby gratified, would not perhaps scan very narrowly the authority by which he acted; but the attempt to deprive the Fatimite khalif of the honour which he had so long enjoyed, and to assume the rank of God's vicegerent on earth in his room, was likely to give too great a shock to their prejudices, if not cautiously managed.

It was necessary, therefore, that he should prove himself to be of the blood of the Fatimites. He accordingly began to drop some dark hints respecting the truth of the received opinion of his being the son of Keäh Mohammed. Our readers will recollect that, when Hassan Sabah was in Egypt, a dispute had taken place respecting the succession to the throne, in which Hassan had nearly lost his life for opposing the powerful commander-in-chief (*Emir-al-Jooyoosh*), and Nezar, the prince for whom the khalif Mostanser had designed the succession, had been deprived of his right by the influence of that officer. The confidents of Hassan now began to give out that, in about a year after the death of the khalif Mostanser, a certain person named Aboo-'l-Zeide, who had been high in his confidence, had come to Alamoot, bearing with him a son of Nezar, whom he committed to the care of Hassan Sabah, who, grateful to the memory of the khalif and his son, had received the fugitive with great honour, and assigned a village at the foot of Alamoot for the residence of the young imam. When the youth was grown up he married and had a son, whom he named *On his Memory be Peace*. Just at the time when the imam's wife was confined in the village, the consort of Keäh Mohammed lay in at the castle; and, in order that the descendant of Fatima might come to the temporal power which was his right, a confidential woman undertook and succeeded in the task of secretly changing the children. Others went still further, and did not hesitate to assert that the young imam had intrigued with the wife of Keäh Mohammed, and that Hassan was the fruit of their adulterous intercourse. Like a true pupil of ambition, Hassan was willing to defame the memory of his mother, and acknowledge himself to be a bastard, provided he could succeed in persuading the people to believe him a descendant of the Prophet.

These pretensions of Hassan to a Fatimite pedigree gave rise to a further increase of the endless sects into which the votaries of Islam were divided. Those who acknowledged it got the name of Nezori, and by them Hassan was called the Lord of the Resurrection (*Kaim-al-Kiamet*), and they styled themselves the Sect of the Resurrection.

The reign of the vain, inconsiderate Hassan was but short. He had governed the society only four years when he was assassinated by his brother-in-law, Namver, a descendant, we are told, of the family of Buyah, which had governed the khalifs and their dominions before the power passed into the hands of the Turkish house of Seljook.

CHAPTER VIII.

Mohammed II.—Anecdote of the Imam Fakhr-ed-deen—
Noor-ed-deen—Conquest of Egypt—Attempt on the Life of
Saladin.

THE death of Hassan was amply avenged by his son
and successor, Mohammed II. Not only was the
murderer himself put to death; vengeance, in its
oriental form, extended itself to all his kindred of
both sexes, and men, women, and children bled beneath the sword of the executioner.   Mohammed,
who had been carefully trained up in the study of
philosophy and literature, was, like his father, puffed
up with vanity and ambition, and, far from receding
from any of his predecessor's pretensions to the
imamat, he carried them to even a still greater length
than he had done.   At the same time he maintained
a high character for knowledge and talent among
his literary contemporaries, who were numerous, for
his reign extended through a period of forty-six years,
and the modern Persian literature was now fast
approaching its climax. Not to mention other names,
less familiar to our readers, we shall remark, as a
proof of what we have said, that this was the period
in which Nizamee of Ghenj sang in harmonious
numbers the loves of Khosroo and Shireen, and of
Mujnoon and Leila (these last the Romeo and Juliet
of the east), the crown and flower of the romantic
poetry of Persia.   Then too flourished the great
panegyrist Enveree, and a crowd of historians, jurists,
and divines.

One of the most celebrated men of this time was

the imam Fakhr-ed-deen (*Glory of Religion*) Rasi, who gave public lectures on the law in his native city of Rei. It being slanderously reported that he was devoted in secret to the opinions of the Ismaïlites, and was even one of their missionaries, he adopted the ordinary expedient of abusing and reviling that sect, and each time he ascended the pulpit to preach he reprobated and cursed the *Impious* in no measured terms. Intelligence of what he was about was not long in reaching the eyrie of the Sheikh-al-Jebal, and a Fedavee received his instructions, and forthwith set out for Rei. He here entered himself as a student of the law, and sedulously attended the lectures of the learned imam. During seven months he watched in vain for an opportunity of executing his commission. At length he discovered one day that the attendants of the imam had left him to go to fetch him some food, and that·he was alone in his study. The Fedavee entered, fastened the doors, seized the imam, cast him on the ground, and directed his dagger at his bosom. "What is thy design?" said the astonished imam. " To rip up thy belly and breast." "And wherefore?" "Wherefore? Because thou hast spoken evil of the Ismaïlites in the pulpit." The imam implored and entreated, vowing that, if his life was spared, he would never more say aught to offend the sect of Ismaïl. " I cannot trust thee," cried the Assassin; " for when I am gone thou wilt return to thy old courses, and, by some ingenious shift or other, contrive to free thyself from the obligation of thy oath." The imam then, with a most solemn oath, abjured the idea of explaining away his words, or seeking absolution for perjury. The Assassin got up from over him, saying, " I had no order to slay thee, or I should have put thee to death without fail. Mohammed, the son of Hassan, greets thee, and invites thee to honour

him by a visit at his castle. Thou shalt there have
unlimited power, and we will all obey thee like trusty
servants. We despise, so saith the sheikh, the discourses of the rabble, which rebound from our ears
like nuts from a ball; but *you* should not revile us,
since your words impress themselves like the strokes
of the graver in the stone." The imam replied that
it was totally out of his power to go to Alamoot, but
that in future he should be most careful never to suffer
a word to pass his lips to the discredit of the mountain prince. Hereupon the Fedavee drew 300 pieces
of gold from his girdle, and, laying them down, said,
" See! here is thy annual pension; and, by a decree
of the divan, thou shalt every year receive an equal
sum through the reis Mozaffer. I also leave thee,
for thy attendants, two garments from Yemen, which
the Sheikh-al-Jebal has sent thee." So saying, the
Fedavee disappeared. The imam took the money
and the clothes, and for some years his pension was
paid regularly. A change in his language now became perceptible, for, whereas he was used before,
when, on treating of any controverted point, he
had occasion to mention the Ismaïlites, to express
himself thus, " Whatever the Ismaïlites, whom God
curse and destroy! may say,"—now that he was
pensioned he contented himself with merely saying, " Notwithstanding what the Ismaïlites may
say." When one of his scholars asked him the
cause of this change he made answer, " We cannot
curse the Ismaïlites, they employ such *sharp* and
convincing arguments." This anecdote is related by
several of the Persian historians, and it serves to
prove, like the case of sultan Sanjar, related above,
that the Ismaïlites were not so thoroughly ruthless
and bloodthirsty as not to prefer rendering an enemy
innocuous by gentle means to depriving him of life.

Historians record no other event connected with

the eastern establishment of the Ismaïlite society during the long reign of Mohammed II. We shall now, therefore, turn our view to the Syrian branch, which attracts attention by the illustrious names which appear in oriental history at that time, and with which the ruler of Massyat came into hostile or friendly relations. The names of Noor-ed-deen (*Light of Religion*), Salah-ed-deen (*Integrity of Religion*), the Noradin and Saladin of western writers, and the Lion-hearted king of England, will at once awake the attention of the reader.

The celebrated Emod-ed-deen (*Pillar of Religion*) Zengi, who gave the Christian power in the east its first shock by the conquest of Edessa, perished by the hand of a slave shortly after that achievement. His power and the title Atabeg fell to his son Noor-ed-deen, who carried on the war against the Christians with all the activity of his father, and with more of the gentleness and courtesies which shed a lustre on zeal and valour. Noor-ed-deen was one of the most accomplished characters which the East has exhibited. He was generous and just, and strict in the observance of all the duties of Islam. No pomp or magnificence surrounded him. He wore neither silk nor gold. With the fifth part of the booty, which was his share as prince, he provided for all his expenses. A zealous Moslem, he was evermore engaged in the combats of the Holy War,—either the *greater*, which was held to be fought against the world and its temptations by fasting and prayer, by study, and the daily practice of the virtues required of him who is placed in authority,—or the *lesser*, which was fought with natural weapons against the foes of Islam. From this union of piety and valour he acquired the titles of Gasi (*Victor*) and Sheheed (*Martyr*); for, though he did not fall in the defence of the faith, he was regarded as being entitled to all the future rewards attendant on actual martyrdom. Notwithstanding his being one of the most deadly foes that the Christians ever encountered, their historians did justice to the illustrious Noor-ed-deen, and the learned William, Archbishop of Tyre, says of him, " He was a prudent, moderate man, who feared God according to the faith of his people, fortunate, and an augmenter of his paternal inheritance."

The possession of Mossul and Aleppo made Noor-ed-deen master of northern Syria; the southern part of that country was under the Prince of Damascus. Twice did the atabeg lay siege, without effect, to that city ; at length the inhabitants, fearing the Crusaders, invited him to take possession of it, and the feeble prince was obliged to retire, accepting Emessa in exchange for the " Queen of Syria." The power of Noor-ed-deen now extended from the Euphrates to the Holy Land, and his thoughts were directed towards his grand object of expelling the Franks from the East, when an opportunity presented itself of bringing Egypt once more under the spiritual dominion of the house of Abbas.

Degeneracy is the inevitable lot of unlimited power. The Fatimite Commanders of the Faithful were now become mere puppets in the hands of their ministers, and the post of vizir was now, as was so often the case with the throne, contended for with arms. A civil war was at this time raging in Egypt between Shaver and Dhargam, rival candidates for the viziriate. The former came in person to Damascus, and offered the atabeg Noor-ed-deen a third of the revenues of Egypt if he would aid him to overcome his rival. Without hesitation Noor-ed-deen ordered Asad-ed-deen (*Lion of Religion*) Sheerkoh (*Mountain Lion*)*, a Koordish chief who commanded for him at Emessa, to assemble an army and march for

* The former of these names is Arabic, the latter Persian

Egypt. Sheerkoh obeyed, and sorely against his will, and only at the urgent command of Noor-ed-deen, did his nephew, the then little known, after-wards so justly famous, Saladin, quit the banquets and enjoyments of Damascus, and the other towns of Syria, to accompany his uncle to the toils and the perils of war. Dhargam was victorious in the first action, but he being murdered shortly afterwards by one of his slaves, Shaver obtained possession of the dignity which he sought. The new vizir then tried to get rid of his allies, but such was not the intention of Noor-ed-deen, and Sheerkoh took his post with his troops in the north-eastern part of the kingdom, where he occupied the frontier town of Belbeïs, on the most eastern branch of the Nile, under pretext of receiving the third part of the revenue which had been promised to Noor-ed-deen. Shaver, anxious to get rid of such dangerous guests, formed a secret league with Amalric, King of Jerusalem, and engaged to give him 60,000 ducats for his aid against them. Sheerkoh, who had been reinforced, advanced into Upper Egypt, and Saladin took the command of Alexandria, which he gallantly defended for three months against the combined forces of the Christians and Egyptians, and, after some fighting, peace was made on condition of Noor-ed-deen receiving 50,000 ducats, and double that sum being paid annually to the King of Jerusalem.

Shortly afterwards an unprincipled attempt was made on Egypt by Amalric, at the suggestion of the Master of the Hospitallers, and Shaver, in his distress, had once more recourse to Noor-ed-deen. The phantom-khalif joined in the supplication, and sent what is the greatest mark of need in the east—locks of the hair of his women, which is as much as to say, "Aid! aid! the foe is dragging the women forth by the hair." Belbeïs had now been conquered, and

Cairo was besieged by the Christians. Shaver had burnt the old town, and defended himself and the khalif in the new town, the proper Cairo. Sheerkoh appeared once more in Egypt with a larger army han before*, but, ere he reached the beleaguered town, Shaver and Amalric had entered into a composition, and the former had withdrawn on receiving a sum of 50,000 ducats. Sheerkoh however advanced, and pitched his tents before the walls of Cairo. The khalif Adhad and his principal nobles came forth to receive him, and that unhappy prince made his complaints of the tyranny and selfishness of Shaver, who had brought so much misery on him and his kingdom. He concluded by requesting the head of his vizir at the hand of the general of Noor-ed-deen. Shaver, aware of the danger which menaced him, invited Sheerkoh, his nephew, and the other chiefs of the army, to a banquet, with the intention of destroying them, but his plot was discovered, and his head cast at the feet of the khalif. Sheerkoh was forthwith appointed to the vacant dignity, with the honourable title of Melik-el-Mansoor (Victorious King), but he enjoyed it only for a short time, having been carried off by death in little more than two months after his elevation. He was succeeded in his rank, and in the

---

* He was accompanied by Saladin, who gives the following account of his own repugnance to the expedition:—"When Noor-ed-deen ordered me to go to Egypt with my uncle, after Sheerkoh had said to me in his presence, ' Come Yoossuf, make ready for the journey!' I replied, ' By God, if thou wert to give me the kingdom of Egypt I would not go, for I have endured in Alexandria what I shall not forget while I live.' But Sheerkoh said to Noor-ed-deen, ' It cannot be but that he should accompany me.' Whereupon Noor-ed-deen repeated his command, but I persisted in my refusal. As Noor-ed-deen also adhered to his determination, I excused myself by pleading the narrowness of my circumstances. Noor-ed-deen then gave me all that was requisite for my outfit, but I felt as if I was going to death."—*Abulfeda.*

command of the army, by his nephew Saladin, who now became in effect master of Egypt. Noor-ed-deen, thinking the time was come for establishing the spiritual sway of the house of Abbas, sent directions to Saladin to fill all the offices which had been occupied by the Sheähs with the orthodox, and hear prayer celebrated in the name of the Khalif of Bagdad; but this prudent chief, who knew that the great majority of the people of Egypt were firmly attached to the belief of the Fatimites being the rightful successors of the Prophet, hesitated to comply. At length the death of the Fatimite khalif occurred most opportunely to free him from embarrassment. Adhad-ladin-Allah, the last of the descendants of Moez-ladin-Allah, the founder of the dynasty, died suddenly—of disease, according to the oriental historians,—by the hand of Saladin, according to the rumour which went among the Christians*. All obstacles being now removed, public prayer was celebrated in the mosks of Egypt in the name of the Abbasside khalif, and the power of the western Ismaïlites, after a continuance of 200 years, brought completely to an end.

Noor-ed-deen, who saw that the power of his lieutenant was now too great to be controlled, adopted the prudent plan of soothing him by titles and marks of confidence. The khalif of Bagdad sent him a dress of honour and a letter of thanks for having reduced under his spiritual dominion a province which had been so long rebellious against his house. But the most important consequence of the timely death of the khalif to Saladin was the acquisition of the accumulated treasures of the Fatimites, which fell into his hands, and which he employed as the means of securing the fidelity of his officers and soldiers. As a specimen of oriental exaggeration, we shall give the list of these treasures as they are enumerated by

* William of Tyre xx. 12.

H

eastern writers.   There were, we are assured, no less
than 700 pearls, each of which was of a size that
rendered it inestimable, an emerald a span long,
and as thick as the finger, a library consisting of
2,600,000 books, and gold, both coined and in the
mass; aloes, amber, and military arms and weapons
past computation.   A large portion of this enormous
treasure was distributed by Saladin among his soldiers; the remainder was applied, during ten suc-
cessive years, to defray the expenses of his wars
and buildings.   As Saladin's name was Yoossuf
(Joseph), the same with that of the son of Jacob,
the minister of king Pharaoh, it is not an improbable
supposition that, in Egyptian tradition, the two
Josephs have been confounded, and the works of the
latter been ascribed to the former; for it is the character of popular tradition to leap over centuries, and
even thousands of years, and to form out of several
heroes one who is made to perform the actions of
them all.

As long as Noor-ed-deen lived, Saladin continued
to acknowledge his superiority; and when, on his
death, he left his dominions to his son Malek-es-
Saleh, the coins of Egypt bore the name of the
young prince.   As Malek-es-Saleh was a minor,
and entirely under the guidance of the eunuch
Kameshtegin, great discontent prevailed among
the emirs; and Seif-ed-deen (Sword of Religion),
the cousin of the young prince, who was at the
head of an army in Mesopotamia, prepared to wrest
the dominion from the young Malek-es-Saleh.   All
eyes were turned to Saladin, as the only person capable of preserving the country.   He left Egypt with
only 700 horsemen.   The governor and people of
Damascus cheerfully opened the gates to him.   Hems
and Hama followed the example of Damascus.   Saladin took the government under the modest title of

lieutenant of the young atabeg, whose rights he declared himself ready to maintain on all occasions. He advanced to Aleppo, where Malek-es-Saleh was residing; but the militia of that town, moved by the tears of the young prince, who was probably influenced by the eunuch Kameshtegin, who feared to lose his power, marched out and put to flight the small force with which Saladin had approached the town. Having collected a larger army, Saladin laid siege regularly to Aleppo, and Kameshtegin, despairing of force, resolved to have recourse to treachery. He sent accordingly to Sinan, the Sheikh of the Assassins, who resided at Massyat, representing to him how dangerous a foe to the Ismaïlites was the valiant Koord, who was so ardent in his zeal for the house of Abbas, and had put an end to the dynasty of the Fatimites, who had so long given lustre to the maintainers of the rights of Ismaïl by the possession of extensive temporal power and dignity. He reminded him that, if Saladin succeeded in his ambitious projects in Syria, he would, in all probability, turn his might against the Assassins, and destroy their power in that country. These arguments were enforced by gold, and the sheikh, readily yielding to them, despatched without delay three Fedavees, who fell on Saladin in the camp before Aleppo. The attempt, however, miscarried, and the murderers were seized and put to death. Saladin, incensed at this attempt on his life, and guessing well the quarter whence it came, now pressed on the siege with greater vigour.

Finding the benefit which might be derived from the daggers of the Fedavee, Kameshtegin resolved to employ them against his personal enemies. The vizir of the young prince, and two of the principal emirs, had laid a plot for his destruction. Coming to the knowledge of it, he determined to be beforehand with them, and, watching the moment when Malek-es-Saleh was about to mount his horse to go to the chase, he approached him, requesting his signature to a blank paper, under pretence of its being necessary for some affair of urgent importance. The young prince signed his name without suspicion, and Kameshtegin instantly wrote on the paper a letter to the Sheikh of the Assassins, in which Malek-es-Saleh was made to request him to send men to put those three emirs out of the way. The Ismaïlite chief readily complied with the request, as he supposed it to be, of his young friend and neighbour, and several Fedavees were despatched to execute his wishes. Two of these fell on the vizir as he was going out of the eastern gate of a mosk near his own house. They were cut to pieces on the spot. Soon after three fell on the emir Mujaheed as he was on horseback. One of them caught hold of the end of his cloak, in order to make more sure of him, but the emir gave his horse the spurs, and broke away, leaving his cloak behind. The people seized the Assassins, two of whom were recognized as being acquaintances of the emir's head groom. One of them was crucified, and along with him the groom as an accomplice : on the breast of the latter was placed this inscription, " This is the reward of the concealer of the Impious." The others were dragged to the castle, and beaten on the soles of their feet to make them confess what had induced them to attempt the commission of such a crime. In the midst of his tortures one of them cried out, " Thou didst desire of our lord Sinan the murder of thy slaves, and now thou dost punish us for performing thy wishes." Full of wrath Malek-es-Saleh wrote a letter to the sheikh Sinan filled with the bitterest reproaches. The sheikh made no other reply than that of sending him back the letter bearing his own subscription. Historians do not tell us what the final result was; and it is also in a great measure uncertain at what time this event occurred.

The Assassins did not give over their attempts upon Saladin, whose power became more formidable to them after he had deprived the family of Noor-eddeen of their honours and dominions; and he was again attacked by them in his camp before the fortress of Ezag. One of them assailed him and wounded him in the head, but the sultan (he had now assumed that title) caught him by the arm and struck him down. A second rushed on—he was cut down by the guards; a third, a fourth, shared the same fate. Terrified at their obstinate perseverance, the sultan shut himself up in his tent during several days, and ordered all strangers and suspicious persons to quit the camp.

Next year (1176) the sultan, being at peace with his other enemies, resolved to take exemplary vengeance on those who had so unprovokedly attempted his life. Assembling an army, he entered the mountains, wasted with fire and sword the territory of the Ismaïlites, and came and laid siege to Massyat. The power of the Syrian Ismaïlites would have been now extinguished but for the intercession of the Prince of Hama, the sultan's uncle, who, at the entreaty of Sinan, prevailed on his nephew to grant a peace on condition of no attempt being made at any future time on his life. Sinan gladly assented to these terms, and he honourably kept his engagement, for the great Saladin reigned fifteen years after this time, carried on continual wars, conquered Jerusalem and the Holy Land, exposed himself to danger in the field and in the camp, but no Assassin was ever again known to approach him with hostile intentions.

Chapter IX.

Sinan the Dai-al-Kebir of Syria—Offers to become a Christian —His Ambassador murdered by the Templars—Cardinal de Vitry's Account of the Assassins—Murder of the Marquis of Montferrat—Defence of King Richard.

The person who had the chief direction of the affairs of the society in Syria in the time of Saladin was one of the most remarkable characters which appear in the history of the Assassins.   His name was Rasheed-ed-deen (*Orthodox in Religion*) Sinan, the son of Suleiman of Basra.   Like so many others of the impostors who have appeared from time to time in the east, he had the audacity to give himself out for an incarnation of the Divinity.   No one ever saw him eat, drink, sleep, or even spit.   His clothing was of coarse hair-cloth.   From the rising to the setting of the sun he stood upon a lofty rock, preaching to the people, who received his words as those of a superior being.   Unfortunately for his credit, his auditors at length discovered that he had a halt in his gait, caused by a wound which he received from a stone in the great earthquake of 1157.   This did not accord with the popular idea of the perfection which should belong to the corporeal vehicle of Divinity. The credit of Sinan vanished at once, and those who had just been adoring the god now threatened to take the life of the impostor.   Sinan lost not his self-possession; he calmly entreated them to be patient, descended from his rock, caused food to be brought, invited them to eat, and by the persuasive powers of his eloquence induced them to recognise

him as their sole chief, and all unanimously swore
obedience and fidelity to him.

The neglect of chronology by the oriental historians, or their European translators and followers, is
frequently such that we are left in great uncertainty
as to the exact time of particular events, and are thus
unable to trace them to their real causes and occasions. The mention of the earthquake of 1157 would
however seem to make it probable that it was about
that time that Sinan put forward his claims to divinity;
and as, at that very period, Hassan, the son of Keäh
Mohammed, was giving himself out for the promised
imam, we may suppose that it was his example which
stimulated Sinan to his bold attempt at obtaining
independent dominion over the Syrian branch of the
Ismaïlites.

Sinan was, like Hassan, a man of considerable
learning. His works are held in high estimation by
the remains of the sect of the Ismaïlites still linger-
ing among the mountains of Syria. These works,
we are told, consist of a chaotic mixture of mutilated
passages of the Gospel and the Koran, of contradictory articles of belief, of hymns, prayers, sermons, and
regulations, which are unintelligible even to those
who receive and venerate them.

The sacred books of the Christians formed, as we
see, a part of the studies of the Sheikh of Massyat,
and, as it would appear, he thought he might derive
some advantage from his acquaintance with them.
The religio-military society of the Knights of the
Temple, whose history we shall soon have to record,
had possessions in the neighbourhood of those of the
Assassins, and their superior power had enabled them,
at what time is uncertain, to render the latter tribu-
tary. The tribute was the annual sum of 2,000
ducats, and Sinan, to whom probably all religions
were alike, and who had unbounded power over the

minds of his people, conceived the idea of releasing himself from it by professing the same religion with his neighbours.   He accordingly sent, in the year 1172, one of his most prudent and eloquent ministers on a secret embassy to Amalric King of Jerusalem, offering, in the name of himself and his people, to embrace the Christian religion, and receive the rite of baptism, provided the king would engage to make the Templars renounce the tribute of 2,000 ducats, and agree to live with them henceforward as good neighbours and friends and brethren.   Overjoyed at the prospect of making converts of such importance, the king readily assented to the desires of the Ismaïlite chief, and he at the same time assured the Templars that their house should not be a loser, as he would pay them 2,000 ducats annually out of his treasury.   The brethren of the Temple made no objection to the arrangement; and after the Ismaïlite ambassador had been detained and treated honourably for some days by the king, he set out on his return, accompanied by a guide and escort sent by the king to conduct him as far as the borders of the Ismaïlite territory.   They passed in safety through the country of Tripolis, and were now in the vicinity of the first castles of the Ismaïlites, when suddenly some Templars rushed forth from an ambush, and murdered the ambassador.   The Templars were commanded by a knight named Walter du Mesnil, a one-eyed, daring, wicked man, but who, on this occasion, it would appear, acted by the orders of his superiors, who probably did not consider the royal promise good security for the 2,000 ducats ; for, when Amalric, filled with indignation at the base and perfidious action, assembled his barons at Sidon to deliberate on what should be done, and by their advice sent two of their number to Ado de St. Amand, the Master of the Temple, to demand satisfaction for the iniqui tous deed, the master contented himself by saying that he had imposed a penance on brother Du Mesnil, and had moreover directed him to proceed to Rome without delay, to know what farther the apostolic father would order him to do, and that, on this account he must, in the name of the pope, prohibit any violence against the aforesaid brother. The king, however, was not regardless of justice and of his own dignity. Shortly afterwards, when the master and several of the Templars were at Sidon, he assembled his council again, and, with their consent, sent and dragged Du Mesnil from the house of the Templars, and threw him into prison, where he would probably have expiated his crime but for the speedy death of the king. All hopes of the conversion of the Ismaïlites were now at an end.

It is on this occasion that the Archbishop of Tyre gives an account of what he had been able to learn respecting the Assassins. As what we have previously related of them has been exclusively drawn from eastern sources, it will not be useless to insert in this place the accounts of them given by the Cardinal de Vitry, who has followed and enlarged the sketch of the archbishop*.

" In the province of Phœnicia, near the borders of the Antaradensian town which is now called Tortosa, dwells a certain people, shut in on all sides by rocks and mountains, who have ten castles, very strong and impregnable, by reason of the narrow ways and inaccessible rocks, with their suburbs and the valleys, which are most fruitful in all species of fruits and corn, and most delightful for their amenity. The number of these men, who are called Assassins, is said to exceed 40,000†. They set a captain over

---

* Gesta Dei per Francos, vol. i. pp. 994, 1062.

† William of Tyre makes their number 60,000. He declares his inability to give the origin of the na ae Assassins.

themselves, not by hereditary succession, but by the prerogative of merit, whom they call the Old Man (*Veterem* seu *Senem*), not so much on account of his advanced age as for his pre-eminence in prudence and dignity.   The first and principal *abbot* of this unhappy *religion* of theirs, and the place where they had their origin and whence they came to Syria, is in the very remote parts of the east, near the city of Bagdad and the parts of the province of Persia.   These people, who do not divide the hoof, nor make a difference between what is sacred and what is profane, believe that all obedience indifferently shown by them towards their superior is meritorious for eternal life.   Hence they are bound to their master, whom they call the Old Man, with such a bond of subjection and obedience that there is nothing so difficult or so dangerous that they would fear to undertake, or which they would not perform with a cheerful mind and ardent will, at the command of their lord.   The Old Man, their lord, causes boys of this people to be brought up in secret and delightful places, and having had them diligently trained and instructed in the different kinds of languages, sends them to various provinces with daggers, and orders them to slay the great men of the Christians, as well as of the Saracens, either because he is at enmity with them for some cause or other, or at the request of his friends, or even for the lucre of a large sum of money which has been given him, promising them, for the execution of this command, that they shall have far greater delights, and without end, in paradise, after death, than even those amidst which they had been reared.   If they chance to die in this act of obedience they are regarded as martyrs by their companions, and being placed by that people among their saints, are held in the greatest reverence.   Their parents are enriched with many gifts by the master, who is called the Old Man, and if they were slaves they are let go free ever after. Whence these wretched and misguided youths, who are sent from the convent (*conventu*) of the aforesaid brethren to different parts of the world, undertake their deadly legation with such joy and delight, and perform it with such diligence and solicitude, transforming themselves in various ways, and assuming the manners and dress of other nations, sometimes concealing themselves under the appearance of merchants, at other times under that of priests and monks, and in an infinity of other modes, that there is hardly any person in the whole world so cautious as to be able to guard against their machinations. They disdain to plot against an inferior person. The great men to whom they are hostile either redeem themselves by a large sum of money, or, going armed and attended by a body of guards, pass their life in suspicion and in dread of death. They kept the law of Mahomet and his institutions diligently and straitly beyond all other Saracens till the times of a certain master of theirs, who, being endowed with natural genius, and exercised in the study of different writings, began with all diligence to read and examine the law of the Christians and the Gospels of Christ, admiring the virtue of the miracles, and the sanctity of the doctrine. From a comparison with these he began to abominate the frivolous and irrational doctrine of Mahomet, and at length, when he knew the truth, he studied to recall his subjects by degrees from the rites of the cursed law. Wherefore he exhorted and commanded them that they should drink wine in moderation and eat the flesh of swine. At length, after many discourses and serious admonitions of their teacher, they all with one consent agreed to renounce the perfidy of Mahomet, and, by receiving the grace of baptism, to become Christians."

We may, from this account, perceive that the Crusaders had a tolerably clear idea of the nature and constitution of the society of the Assassins. The Cardinal de Vitry plainly describes them as forming a *religion*, that is, an order under an abbot; and perhaps the resemblance which Hammer traces between them and the Templars, which we shall notice when we come to speak of this last society, is not quite so fanciful as it might at first sight appear. It is curious, too, to observe that the Christians also believed that the Sheikh-al-Jebal had some mode of inspiring the Fedavee with a contempt of life and an aspiration after the joys of paradise.

The dagger had not been unsheathed against the Christian princes since, forty-two years before (1149), Raymond, the young Count of Tripolis, was murdered as he knelt at his devotions, and the altar was sprinkled with his blood. A more illustrious victim was now to bleed; and, as the question of who twas the real author of his death forms a curious historical problem, we shall here discuss it at some length.

Conrad Marquis of Montferrat, a name celebrated in the history of the third crusade, had just been named King of Jerusalem by Richard Lion-heart King of England. In the latter end of the month of April 1192 the marquis, being at Tyre, went to dine with the Bishop of Beauvais. One writer says that, the marchioness having stayed too long in the bath, and the marquis being averse to dining alone, he mounted his horse and rode to dine with the Bishop; but, finding that that prelate had already finished his meal, he was returning home to his palace. As he passed through a narrow street, and was come near the toll-house, two Assassins, having watched their opportunity, approached him. The one presented a petition, and, while he was engaged reading it, both struck him with their daggers, crying,

" Thou shalt be neither marquis nor king." One of them was cut down instantly, the other sought refuge in a neighbouring church, and, according to an Arabian historian, when the wounded marquis was brought into the same church, he rushed on him anew, and completed his crime. Others relate that the marquis was carried home to his palace, where he lived long enough to receive the holy sacrament and to give his last instructions to his wife. The two accounts, we may perceive, are by no means repugnant.

These Assassins, who were both youths, had been for some time—six months it is said—in Tyre, watching for an opportunity to perform the commission which had been given them. They had feigned a conversion from Islam, or, as some say, had assumed the habit of monks, in order to win the confidence of the marquis, and thus procure more ready access to him. One of them, we are told, had even entered his service, and the other that of Balian of Ibelin.

The question now comes, at whose instigation was the murder committed? Here we find several both oriental and occidental witnesses disposed to lay the guilt on Richard, King of England, those writers who were his own subjects indignantly repelling the accusation, and some indifferent witnesses testifying in his favour. Previous to examining these witnesses we must state that king Richard was at enmity with Philip Augustus, King of France; that though he had given the crown of Jerusalem to the Marquis of Montferrat, there was little kind feeling between them, and they had been enemies; and, finally, that the history of the English monarch exhibits no traits of such a generous chivalrous disposition as should put him beyond suspicion of being concerned in an assassination.

Of the writers who charge king Richard with the

murder it is to be observed that the only ones that
are contemporary are the Arabian historians. The
following passage is quoted from the History of
Jerusalem and Hebron, by Hammer, who regards
it as quite decisive of the guilt of the English king
—" The marquis went, on the 13th of the month
Rebi-al-Ewal, to visit the Bishop of Tyre. As he
was going out he was attacked by two Assassins, who
slew him with their daggers. When taken and
stretched on the rack, they confessed that they had
been employed by the King of England. They died
under the torture." Boha-ed-deen, the friend and
biographer of Saladin, writes to the same effect. It
is therefore evident that, at the time, it was reported
that the marquis had been murdered by persons employed by the King of England; and Vinisauf and
the other English writers assure us that the French
party and the friends of the murdered marquis endeavoured to throw the odium of the deed on king
Richard. As that mode of getting rid of an enemy
was far too familiar in the east, it was natural enough
that the Arabian writers should adopt the report
without much inquiry. This consideration alone
ought very much to invalidate their testimony. Some
German chroniclers also, following the reports which
were industriously spread to the disadvantage of the
English king at the time he was a prisoner in Austria,
did not hesitate to accuse him of the murder of the
marquis; but, as has been justly observed, these, as
well as the preceding, were either partial or at a
distance*.

In opposition to these assertions, we have the unanimous testimony of all the English writers, such as
Vinisauf (the companion and historian of king Richard's crusade), Hoveden, Brompton William of New-

* Raumer, Geschichte der Hohenstauffen, ii., p. 490. Wilken, Geschichte der Kreuzzüge, iv., 489.

bridge. The Syrian bishop, Aboo-'l-Faraj, mentions the report of the Assassin who was put to the rack having laid the guilt on king Richard, but adds that the truth came afterwards to light. Hugo Plagon, a judicious and impartial writer, so far from imputing the death of the marquis to king Richard, assigns the cause which moved the Assassin prince to order the death of the marquis, namely, the same which we shall presently see stated in the letter ascribed to the Old Man of the Mountain. Rigord, who wrote the history of Philip Augustus, does not by any means impute the murder of the marquis to king Richard, though he says that while Philip was at Pontoise letters were brought to him from beyond sea, warning him to be on his guard, as Assassins (*Arsacidæ*) had been sent, at the suggestion and command of the King of England, to kill him, " for at that time they had slain the king's kinsman, the marquis." Philip, in real, but more probably feigned alarm, immediately surrounded his person with a guard of serjeants-at-mace. The Arabic historian, Ebn-el-Athir, the friend of Saladin, says that the sultan had agreed with the Old Man of the Mountain, for a sum of 10,000 pieces of gold, to deliver him of both king Richard and the marquis, but that Sinan, not thinking it to be for his interest to relieve the sultan of the English king, had taken the money and only put the marquis out of the way. This narrative is wholly improbable, for treachery was surely no part of the character of Saladin; but it serves to prove the impartiality which is so justly ascribed to the Arabic writers in general. The testimony of Abulfeda is as follows : " And in it (the year of the Hejra 588, or A. D. 1192,) was slain the Marquis, Lord of Soor (or Tyre) ; may God, whose name be exalted, curse him ! A Batinee, or Assassin (in one copy Bati-

nees), who had entered Soor in the disguise of a
monk, slew him*."

We thus see that the evidence in favour of the King
of England greatly preponderates, not a single writer
who was on the spot laying the murder to his charge ;
on the contrary, those who had the best means of
being informed treated the imputation with contempt,
as a base calumny devised by the French party. But
there is a still more illustrious witness in his behalf, if
the testimony ascribed to him be genuine—the Old
Man of the Mountain himself. Brompton gives two
letters purporting to have been written by this personage, the one to the Duke of Austria, the other to
the princes and people of Europe in general. The
latter is also given by William of Newbridge, with
some variation. Both have been admitted by Rymer
into his Fœdera. Gibbon, who seems to have known
only the last, pronounces it to be an "absurd and
palpable forgery." Hammer, whose arguments we
shall presently consider, undertakes to demonstrate
that these epistles are forgeries. Raumer, more
prudently, only says that this last is not genuine in
its present form.

The following are translations of these documents:—

" The Old Man of the Mountain to Limpold,
Duke of Austria, greeting. Since several kings and
princes beyond sea accuse Richard, King of England,
and lord, of the death of the marquis, I swear by the
God who reigneth for ever, and by the law which we
hold, that he had no guilt in his death ; for the cause
of the death of the marquis was as follows.

" One of our brethren was coming in a ship from
Satelia (*Salteleya*) to our parts, and a tempest
chancing to drive him to Tyre the marquis had him
taken and slain, and seized a large sum of money

* Annales Muslemici, tom. iv., pp. 122, 123. Hafniae, 1792.

which he had with him. But we sent our messengers to the marquis, requiring him to restore to
us the money of our brother, and to satisfy us respecting the death of our brother, which he laid upon
Reginald, the Lord of Sidon, and we exerted ourselves through our friends till we knew of a truth that
it was he himself who had had him put to death, and
had seized his money.

"And again we sent to him another of our messengers, named Eurisus, whom he was minded to
fling into the sea; but our friends made him depart
with speed out of Tyre, and he came to us quickly
and told us these things. From that very hour we
were desirous to slay the marquis; then also we sent
two brethren to Tyre, who slew him openly, and as
it were before all the people of Tyre.

" This, then, was the cause of the death of the
marquis; and we say to you in truth that the lord
Richard, King of England, had no guilt in this death
of the marquis, and those who on account of this
have done evil to the lord King of England have done
it unjustly and without cause.

" Know for certain that we kill no man in this
world for any hire or money, unless he has first done
us evil.

" And know that we have executed these letters in
our house at our castle of Messiat, in the middle of
September. In the year from Alexander M. D. & V."

" The Old Man of the Mountain to the princes of
Europe and all the Christian people, greeting.

" We would not that the innocence of any one
should suffer by reason of what we have done, since
we never do evil to any innocent and guiltless person ; but those who have transgressed against us we
do not, with God to aid, long suffer to rejoice in the
injuries done to our simplicity.

" We therefore signify to the whole of you, testifying by him through whom we hope to be saved, that that Marquis of Montferrat was slain by no machination of the King of England, but he justly perished, by our will and command, by our satellites, for that act in which he transgressed against us, and which, when admonished, he had neglected to amend. For it is our custom first to admonish those who have acted injuriously in anything to us or our friends to give us satisfaction, which if they despise, we take care to take vengeance with severity by our ministers, who obey us with such devotion that they do not doubt but that they shall be gloriously rewarded by God if they die in executing our command.

" We have also heard that it is bruited about of that king that he has induced us, as being less upright and consistent (*minus integros et constantes*), to send some of our people to plot against the King of France, which, beyond doubt, is a false fiction, and of the vainest suspicion, when neither he, God is witness, has hitherto attempted anything against us, nor would we, in respect to our honour, permit any undeserved evil to be planned against any man. Farewell."

We will not undertake to maintain the genuineness of these two epistles, but we may be permitted to point out the futility of some of the objections made to them. Hammer pronounces the first of them to be an undoubted forgery because it commences with swearing by the law, and ends by being dated from the era of the Seleucides. Both, he says, were equally strange to the Ismaïlites, who precisely at this time had begun to trample the law under foot, and had abandoned the Hejra, the only era known in Mohammedan countries, for a new one commencing with the reign of Hassan II. He further sees, in the circumstance of a letter from the Old Man of the Mountain (*Sheikh-al-Jebal*) being dated from Massyat, a proof of the ignorance of the Crusaders respecting the true head and seat of the Ismaïlite power. These objections are regarded by Wilken as conclusive. They will, however, lose much of their force if we bear in mind that the letters are manifestly translations, and that the chief of Massyat at that time was Sinan, who some years before had offered to become a Christian, and who does not seem at all to have adopted the innovations of Hassan the Illuminator. Sinan might easily have been induced by the friends of the King of England, one of the most steady of whom was Henry of Champagne*, who succeeded Conrad of Montferrat in the kingdom, to write those letters in his justification, and it is very probable that the translations were made in Syria, where the Arabic language was of course better understood than in Europe, and sent either alone or with the originals. The translator might have rendered the title which Sinan gave himself by *Senex de Monte*, which would be better understood in the west, and he may also have given the corresponding year of the era of the Seleucides (the one in use among the Syrian Christians) for the year of the Hejra used by the Ismaïlite chief, or indeed Sinan may have employed that era himself. In this case there would remain little to object to the genuineness of the letter to the Duke of Austria. Hammer regards the expression *our simplicity (simplicitas nostra)* as being conclusive against the genuineness of the second letter. We must confess that we can see no force in the objection. Sinan might wish to represent himself as a very plain, simple, innocent sort of person. It might further be doubted

* An instance of Henry's intimacy with the Assassins has been given in p. 81.

if a European forger would venture to represent the prince of the Assassins—the formidable Old Man of the Mountain—in such a respectable light as he appears in these two epistles*.

But there is another account of the death of the Marquis of Montferrat, which is probably much better known to the generality of readers than any of the preceding ones. The far-famed author of " Waverley" has, in his romantic tale of the " Talisman," made Conrad to be wounded and vanquished in the lists by the son of the King of Scotland, the champion of king Richard, and afterwards slain by the dagger, not of the Assassins, but of his confederate in villany the Master of the Temple, to prevent his making confession of their common guilt!

Yielding to none in rational admiration of the genius of Sir W. Scott, we cannot avoid expressing a wish that he had ceased to write when he had exhausted that rich field of national feelings and manners with which he was alone familiar, and from which he drew the exquisite delineations of " Waverley" and its Scottish brethren. All his later works, no doubt, exhibit occasional scenes far beyond the power of any of his imitators; but when his muse quits her native soil, she takes leave of nature, truth, and simplicity. Even the genius of a Scott is inadequate to painting manners he never witnessed, scenery he never beheld.

The tale of the " Talisman" is a flagrant instance. Topography, chronology, historic truth, oriental manners, and individual character, are all treated with a most magnanimous neglect, indeed, even, we might say, with contempt; for, careless, from " security to please," as the author is known to have been, his vagaries must sometimes have proceeded from mere

* Sir J. Mackintosh (History of England, i. 187) seems to regard the letters as genuine.

wilfulness and caprice. It would, we apprehend, perplex our oriental travellers and geographers to point out the site of the fountain named the Diamond of the Desert, not far from the Dead Sea, and yet lying half-way between the camp of the Saracens and that of the Crusaders, which last, we are told, lay between Acre and Ascalon, that is, on the sea-coast, or to show the interminable sandy desert which stretches between the Dead Sea and the Mediterranean. As to historic truth, we may boldly say that there is hardly a single circumstance of the romance in strict accordance with history; and as to the truth of individual character, what are we to say to the grave, serious, religious Saladin, but the very year before his death, being in the flower of his age, rambling alone through the desert, like an errant knight, singing hymns to the Devil, and coming disguised as a physician to the Christian camp, to cure the malady of the English monarch, whom he never, in reality, did or would see*? We might enumerate many additional instances of the violation of every kind of unity and propriety in this single tale†.

Let not any deem it superfluous thus to point out the errors of an illustrious writer. The impressions made by his splendid pages on the youthful mind

* May it not be said that real historic characters should not be misrepresented? Sir W. Scott was at full liberty to make his Varneys and his Bois Gilberts as accomplished villains as he pleased; he might do as he pleased with his own; but what warrant had he from history for painting Conrad of Montferrat and the then Master of the Templars under such odious colours as he does?

† The author invariably writes *Montserrat* for *Montferrat*. The former is in Spain, and never was a marquisate. As it were to show that it was no error of the press, it is said, " The shield of the marquis bore, in reference to his title, a *serrated* and rocky mountain." We also find *naphtha* and *bitumen* confounded, the former being described as the solid, the latter as the liquid substance.

are permanent and ineffaceable, and, if not corrected, may lead to errors of a graver kind. The "Talisman" moreover affects a delusive show of truth and accuracy; for, in a note in one part of it, the author (ironically, no doubt) affects to correct the historians on a point of history. The natural inference, then, is that he has himself made profound researches, and adhered to truth; and we accordingly find another novelist, in what he terms a history of chivalry, declaring the "Talisman" to be a faithful picture of the manners of the age. Sir W. Scott, however, has himself informed us, in the preface to "Ivanhoe," of his secret for describing the manners of the times of Richard Cœur de Lion. With the chronicles of the time he joined that of Froissart, so rich in splendid pictures of chivalric life. Few readers of these romances perhaps are aware that this was the same in kind, though not in degree, as if, in his tales of the days of Elizabeth and James I., he had had recourse to the manner-painting pages of Henry Fielding; for the distance in point of time between the reign of Richard I. and that of Richard II., in which last Froissart wrote, is as great as that between the reigns of Elizabeth and George II.; and, in both, manners underwent a proportional change. But we are in the habit of regarding the middle ages as one single period of unvarying manners and institutions, and we are too apt to fancy that the descriptions of Froissart and his successors are equally applicable to all parts of it.

CHAPTER X.

Jellal-ed-deen—Restoration of Religion—His Harem makes the Pilgrimage to Mecca—Marries the Princess of Ghilan —Geography of the Country between Roodbar and the Caspian—Persian Romance—Zohak and Feridoon—Kei Kaoos and Roostem—Ferdoosee's Description of Mazande-ran—History of the Shah Nameh—Proof of the Antiquity of the Tales contained in it.

THE unhallowed rule of Mohammed II. lasted for the long space of thirty-five years, during which time all the practices of Islam were neglected by the Ismaïlites. The mosks were closed, the fast of Ra-mazan neglected, the solemn seasons of prayer despised. But such a state can never last; man must have religion; it is as essential to him as his food; and those pseudo-philosophers who have en-deavoured to deprive him of it have only displayed in the attempt their ignorance and folly. The purifica-tion of the popular faith is the appropriate task of the true philanthropist.

We may often observe the son to exhibit a cha-racter the diametrically opposite of that of his father, either led by nature or struck by the ill effects of his father's conduct. This common appearance was now exhibited among the Assassins. Mohammed disre-garded all the observances of the ceremonial law; his son and successor, Jellal-ed-deen (*Glory of Religion*) Hassan, distinguished himself, from his early years, by a zeal for the ordinances of Islam. The avowal of his sentiments caused considerable enmity and suspicion between him and Mohammed; the father feared the son, and the son the father. On the days of public audience, at which Jellal-ed-deen was expected to appear, the old sheikh used the precaution of wearing a shirt of mail under his clothes, and of increasing the number of his guards. His death, which occurred when his son had attained his twenty-fifth year, is ascribed by several historians, though apparently without any sufficient reason, to poison administered to him by his successor.

The succession of Jellal-ed-deen was uncontested. He immediately set about placing all things on the footing which they had been on previous to the time of *On his Memory be Peace.* The mosks were repaired and reopened; the call to prayer sounded as heretofore from the minarets; and the solemn assemblies for worship and instruction were held once more on every Friday. Imams, Koran-readers, preachers, and teachers of all kinds, were invited to Alamoot, where they were honourably entertained and richly rewarded. Jellal-ed-deen wrote to his lieutenants in Kusistan and Syria, informing them of what he had done, and inviting them to follow his example. He also wrote to the khalif, to the powerful Shah of Khaurism, and to all the princes of Persia, to assure them of the purity of his faith. His ambassadors were everywhere received with honour, and the khalif and all the princes gave to Jellal-ed-deen, in the letters which they wrote in reply, the title of prince, which had never been conceded to any of his predecessors. The imams, and the men learned in the law, loudly upheld the orthodoxy of the faith of the mountain-chief, on whom they bestowed the name of Nev (*New*) Musulman. When the people of Casveen, who had always been at enmity with the Ismaïlites, doubted of his orthodoxy, Jellal-ed-deen condescended to ask of them to send some persons of respectability to Alamoot, that he might have an opportunity of convincing them.

They came, and in their presence he committed to the flames a pile of books which he said were the writings of Hassan Sabah, and contained the secret rules and ordinances of the society. He cursed the memory of Hassan and his successors, and the envoys returned to Casveen, fully convinced of his sincerity.

In the second year of his reign Jellal-ed-deen gave a further proof of the purity of his religious faith by permitting, or, perhaps, directing, his harem, that is, his mother, his wife, and a long train of their female attendants, to undertake the pilgrimage to the holy city of Mecca, to worship at the tomb of the Prophet. The sacred banner was, according to custom, borne before the caravan of the pilgrims from Alamoot, and the Tesbeel, or distribution of water to the pilgrims, usual on such occasions*, was performed by the harem of the mountain-prince on such a scale of magnificence and liberality as far eclipsed that of the great Shah of Khaurism, whose caravan reached Bagdad at the same time on its way to Mecca. The khalif Nassir-ladin-Illah even gave precedence to the banner of the pilgrims from Alamoot, and this mark of partiality drew on him the wrath of the potent prince of Khaurism. Twice did the latter afterwards collect an

---

* "Sebil, in Arabic 'the way,' means generally the road, and the traveller is hence called *Ibn-es-sebil*, the son of the road; but it more particularly signifies the way of piety and good works, which leads to Paradise. Whatever meritorious work the Moslem undertakes, he does *Fi sebil Allah*, on the way of God, or for the love of God; and the most meritorious which he can undertake is the holy war, or the fight for his faith and his country, *on God's way*. But since pious women can have no immediate share in the contest, every thing which they can contribute to the nursing of the wounded, and the refreshment of the exhausted, is imputed to them as equally meritorious as if they had fought themselves. The distribution of water to the exhausted and wounded warriors is the highest female merit in the holy war on God's way."— *Hammer's History of the Assassins*, Wood's translation, p. 144.

I

army to make war on the successor of the Prophet.
With the first, consisting of nearly 300,000 men, he
marched against Bagdad, and had reached Hamadan
and Holuan, when a violent snow-storm obliged him
to retire. He had collected his forces a second time,
when the hordes of Chinghis Khan burst into his
dominions. His son and successor resumed his plans,
and reached Hamadan, when again a snow-storm
came to avert destruction from the City of Peace.
As the power of the Mongol conqueror was now
great and formidable, the prudent prince of Alamoot
sent in secret ambassadors to assure him of his submission, and to tender his homage.

Jellal ed-deen took a more active part in the politics of his neighbours than his predecessors had done.
He formed an alliance with the Atabeg Mozaffer-ed-
deen (*Causing the Religion to be victorious*), the governor of Azerbeijan, against the governor of Irak, who
was their common enemy. He even visited the Atabeg
at his residence, where he was received with the
utmost magnificence, and each day the Atabeg sent
1,000 dinars for the expenses of his table. The two
princes sent to the khalif for aid; their request was
granted; and they marched against, defeated, and
slew the governor of Irak, and appointed another in
his place. After an absence of eighteen months
Jellal-ed-deen returned to Alamoot, having in the
mean time, by his prudent conduct, greatly augmented
the fame of his orthodoxy. He now ventured to
aspire to a connexion with one of the ancient princely
houses of the country, and asked in marriage the
daughter of Ky Kaoos, the prince of Ghilan. The
latter having expressed his readiness to give his consent, provided that of the khalif could be obtained,
envoys were despatched to Bagdad, who speedily re
turned with the approbation of Nassir-ladin-Illah, and
the princess of Ghilan was sent to Alamoot.

The mention of Ghilan and of Ky Kaoos presents an opportunity, which we are not willing to let pass, of diversifying our narrative by an excursion into the regions of Persian geography and romance, which may cast a gleam of the sunshine of poetry over the concluding portion of our history of the dark and secret deeds of the Ismaïlites.

The mountain range named Demavend, on the south side of which Roodbar, the territory of the Ismaïlites, lies, is the northern termination of the province of Irak Ajemee, or Persian Irak. Beyond it stretches to the Caspian Sea a fertile region, partly hilly, partly plain*. This country is divided into five districts, which were in those times distinct from and independent of each other. At the foot of the mountains lay Taberistan and Dilem, the former to the east, the latter to the west. Dilem is celebrated as having been the native country of the family of Buyah, which, rising from the humblest station, exercised under the khalifs, and with the title of Ameer-al-Omra (*Prince of the Princes*), a power nearly regal over Persia during a century and a half†. North of Dilem lay Ghilan, and north of Taberistan Mazenderan, the ancient Hyrcania. In the midst of

* This part of Persia also acquires interest from the circumstance of Russia being believed to be looking forward to obtaining it, one day or other, by conquest or cession.

† Azed-ud-dowlah, one of the most celebrated of these princes, had a dyke constructed across the river Kur, in the plain of Murdasht, near the ruins of Persepolis, to confine the water, and permit of its being distributed over the country. It was called the Bund-Ameer (*Prince's Dyke*), and travellers ignorant of the Persian language have given this name to the river itself. We must not, therefore, be surprised to find in " Lalla Rookh" a lady singing,

"There's a bower of roses by Bendameer's *stream ;*"
and asking,

" Do the roses still bloom by the *calm* Bendameer ? "
Calm and still, beyond doubt, is the Bendameer.

these four provinces lay Ruyan and Rostemdar, remarkable for having been governed for a space of
800 years by one family of princes, while dynasty
after dynasty rose and fell in the neighbouring states.
In these provinces the names of the royal lines recal
to our mind the ancient history, both true and fabulous, of Irân (Persia), as we find it in the poem of
Ferdoosee, the Homer of that country. The family
of Kawpara, which governed Ruyan and Rostemdar,
affected to derive their lineage from the celebrated
blacksmith Gavah, who raised his apron as the
standard of revolt against the Assyrian tyrant Zohak;
and the family of Bavend, which ruled for nearly
seven centuries, with but two interruptions, over
Mazenderan and Taberistan, were descended from
the elder brother of Noosheerwan the Just, the most
celebrated monarch of the house of Sassan.

This region is the classic land of Persia. When,
as their romantic history relates, Jemsheed, the third
monarch of Iran after Cayamars, the first who ruled
over men, had long reigned in happiness and prosperity, his head was lifted up with pride, and God
withdrew from him his favour. His dominions were
invaded by Zohak, the prince of the Tauzees (Assy-
rians or Arabs); his subjects fell away from him, and,
after lurking for a hundred years in secret places, he
fell into the hands of the victor, who cut him asunder
with a saw. A child was born of the race of Jemsheed, named Feridoon, whom, as soon as he came to
the light (in the village of Wereghi, in Taberistan),
his mother Faranuk gave to a herdsman to rear, and
his nourishment was the milk of a female buffalo,
whose name was Poormayeh. Zohak meantime had
a dream, in which he beheld two warriors, who led
up to him a third, armed with a club which terminated in the head of a cow. The warrior struck him
on the head with his club, and took him and chained

him in the cavern of a mountain. He awoke with a loud cry, and called all the priests, and astrologers, and wise men, to interpret his dream. They feared to speak. At last they told him of the birth and nurture of Feridoon, who was destined to overcome him. Zohak fell speechless from his throne at the intelligence. On recovering, he sent persons in all directions to search for and put to death the fatal child; but the maternal anxiety of Faranuk was on the watch, and she removed the young Feridoon to the celebrated mountain Elburz, where she committed him to the care of a pious anchorite. Zohak, after a long search, discovered the place where Feridoon had been first placed by his mother, and in his rage he killed the beautiful and innocent cow Poormayeh.

Zohak is represented as a most execrable tyrant. Acting under the counsel of the Devil, he had murdered his own father to get his throne. His infernal adviser afterwards assumed the form of a young man, and became his cook. He prepared for him all manner of curious and high-seasoned dishes; for hitherto the food of mankind had been rude and plain. As a reward, he only asked permission to kiss the shoulders of the king. Zohak readily granted this apparently moderate request; but from the spots where the Devil impressed his lips grew forth two black snakes. In vain every art was employed to remove them, in vain they were cut away, they grew again like plants. The physicians were in perplexity. At length the Devil himself came in the shape of a physician, and said that the only mode of keeping them quiet was to feed them with human brains. His object, we are told, was gradually in this way to destroy the whole race of man.

The design of the Devil seemed likely to be accomplished. Each day two human beings were slain, and the serpents fed with their brains. At length

two of the tyrant's cooks discovered that the brain of
a man mixed with that of a ram satisfied the mon-
sters, and, of the two men who were given to be
killed each day, they always secretly let go one, and
those who were thus delivered became the progenitors
of the Koords who dwell in the mountains west of
Persia.   Among those unfortunate persons who were
condemned to be food for the serpents was the son
of a blacksmith named Gavah.   The afflicted father
went boldly before the tyrant, and remonstrated with
him on the injustice of his conduct.   Zohak heard
him with patience and released his son.   He also
made him bearer of a letter addressed to all the provinces of the empire, vaunting his goodness, and
calling on all to support him against the youthful
pretender to his throne.   But Gavah, instead of executing the mandate, tore the tyrant's letter, and,
raising his leathern apron on a lance by way of
standard, called on all the inhabitants of Irân to
arise and take arms in support of Feridoon, the rightful heir to the throne of Jemsheed.

Meantime Feridoon, who had attained the age of
twice eight years, came down from Elburz, and,
going to his mother, besought her to tell him from
whom he derived his birth.   Faranuk related to him
his whole history, when the young hero, in great
emotion, vowed to attack the tyrant, and avenge on
him the death of his father ; but his mother sought,
by representing the great power of Zohak; to divert
him from his purpose, and exhorted him to abandon
all such thoughts, and to enjoy in quiet the good
things of this life.   But a numerous army, led by
Gavah in search of the true heir to the throne, now
came in sight.   Feridoon, joyfully advancing to meet
them, adorned with gold and precious stones the
leathern banner, placed upon it the orb of the moon,
and, naming it Direfsh-e-Gavanee (*Gavah's Apron*),

selected it for the banner of the empire of Irân.
Each succeeding prince, we are told, at his accession, added jewels to it, and Direfsh-e-Gavanee blazed
in the front of battle like a sun. Feridoon, then
calling for smiths, drew for them in the sand the
form of a club, with a cow's head at the end of it,

From the Shah Nameh, illuminated Persian MS.

and when they had made it he named it Gawpeigor
(*Cow-face*), in honour of his nurse. Taking leave
of his mother, he marches against the tyrant; an
angel comes from heaven to aid the rightful cause;
Zohak is deserted by his troops; he falls into the
hands of Feridoon, who, by the direction of the
angel, imprisons him in a cavern of the mountain
Demavend. Feridoon, on ascending the throne of
his forefathers, governed with such mildness, firmness, and justice, that his name is to the present day
in Persia significative of the ideal of a perfect monarch*.

Mazenderan is not less celebrated in Persian romance than the region at the foot of Demavend. It
was the scene of the dangers of the light-minded Kej
Kaoos (supposed to be the Cyaxares of the Greeks),
and of the marvellous adventures called the Seven
Fables or Stages of the Hero Roostem, the Hercules
of Persia, who came to his aid. When Kej Kaoos
mounted the throne of Irân, he exulted in his wealth
and in his power. A deev (*Demon*), desirous of
luring him to his destruction, assumed the guise of a
wandering minstrel, and, coming to his court, sought
to be permitted to sing before the padisha (*Emperor*).
His request was acceded to,—his theme was the praises
of Mazenderan, and he sang to this effect:—

" Mazenderan deserves that the shah should think
on it; the rose blooms evermore in its gardens, its
hills are arrayed with tulips and jessamines, mild is
the air, the earth is bright of hue, neither cold nor
heat oppresses the lovely land, spring abides there

* Four lines, quoted by Sir J. Malcolm from the Gulistan
of Saadi, may be thus *literally* rendered in the measure of the
original:—

> The blest Feridoon an angel was not;
> Of musk or of amber he formed was not;
> By justice and mercy good ends gained he;
> Be just and merciful, thou 'lt a Feridoon be.

evermore, the nightingale sings without ceasing in
the gardens, and the deer bound joyously through
the woods. The earth is never weary of pouring
forth fruits, the air is evermore filled with fragrance,
like unto rose-water are the streams, the tulip glows
unceasingly on the meads, pure are the rivers, and
their banks are smiling: ever mayest thou behold
the falcon at the chase. All its districts are adorned
with abundance of food, beyond measure are the
treasures which are there piled up, the flowers bend
in worship before the throne, and around it stand
the men of renown richly girded with gold. Who
dwelleth not there knoweth no pleasure, as joy and
luxuriant pastime are to him unknown."

Kej Kaoos was beguiled by the tempter, and,
eager to get possession of so rich a land, he led a
large army into it. The Shah of Mazenderan was
aided by a potent demon or enchanter named the
Deev Seffeed (*White Deev*), who, by his magic arts,
cast a profound darkness over the Irânian monarch
and his host, in which they would have all been
destroyed but for the timely arrival of Roostem, who,
after surmounting all the impediments that magic
could throw in his way, slew the Deev Seffeed, and
delivered his sovereign.

Kej Kaoos, we are afterwards told by the poet,
formed the insane project of ascending to heaven,
which he attempted in the following manner. A
stage was constructed on which a throne was set for
the monarch; four javelins were placed at the corners, with pieces of goat's flesh on them, and four
hungry eagles were tied at the bottom, who, by their
efforts to reach the meat, raised the stage aloft into
the air; but when the strength of the birds was exhausted the whole fell with the royal aëronaut in the
desert, where he was found by Roostem and the
other chiefs.

From the Same.

The history of the Shah-nameh (*King-book*), in which these legends are contained, is one of the most curious in literature. The fanaticism of the Arabs, who conquered Persia, raged with indiscriminate fury cgainst the literature, as well as the religion, of that aountry; and when, in the time of Al-Mansoor and his successors Haroon-er-Rasheed and Al-Mamoon, the Arabs themselves began to devote their attention to literature and science, it was the science of Greece and the poetry of their native language that they cultivated. The Persian literature meantime languished in obscurity, and the traditional, heroic, and legendary tales of the nation were fading fast from memory, when a governor of a province, zealous, as it would appear, for the honour of the Persian nation, made a collection of them, and formed from them a continuous narrative in prose. The book thus formed was called the Bostan-nameh (*Garden-book*). It was in great repute in the northern part of Persia, where, at a distance from the court of the khalifs, the Persian manners, language, and nationality were better preserved; and when the Turkish family of the Samenee founded an empire in that part of Persia, sultan Mansoor I., of that race, gave orders to a poet named Dakeekee to turn the Bastan-nameh into Persian verse. The poet undertook the task, but he had not made more than a thousand verses when he perished by assassination. There being no one supposed capable of continuing his work, it was suspended till twenty years afterwards, when the celebrated Mahmood of Ghizni, the conqueror of India, meeting with the Bastan-nameh, gave portions of it to three of the most renowned poets of the time to versify. The palm of excellence was adjudged to Anseri, who versified the tale of Sohrab slain by his own father Roostem, one of the most pathetic and affecting narratives in any language. The sultan made him Prince of the Poets, and directed him to versify the entire work; but, diffident of his powers, Anseri shrank from the task, and having some time afterwards met a poet of Toos in Khorasan, named Isaac, the son of Sheriff-Shah, surnamed Ferdoosee

(*Paradisal**), either from his father's employment as a gardener, or from the beauty of his verses, he introduced him to the sultan, who gladly committed the task to him. Ferdoosee laboured with enthusiasm in the celebration of the ancient glories of his country; and in the space of thirty or, as some assert, of only eight years, he brought the poem to within two thousand lines of its termination, which lines were added by another poet after his death.

The Shah-nameh is, beyond comparison, the finest poem of the Mohammedan east. It consists of 60,000 rhymed couplets, and embraces the history of Persia, from the beginning of the world to the period of its conquest by the Arabs. The verses move on with spirit and rapidity, resembling more the flow of our lyrical, than that of our common heroic, lines†.

Ferdoosee wrote his poem in the early part of the eleventh century from a book which had been in existence a long time before, for he always calls it an *old book*. No proof therefore is needed that he did not invent the tales which compose the Shah-nameh, and they have every appearance of having been the ancient traditionary legends of the Persian nation. But we are able to show that these legends were popular in Persia nearly six centuries before his time; and it was chiefly with a view to establishing this

---

* Paradise, we are to recollect, is a word of Persian origin, adopted by the Greeks, from whom we have received it. A Paradise was a place planted with trees, a park, garden, or pleasure-ground, as we may term it.

† Hammer has, in his "Belles Lettres of Persia" (*Schöne Redekunst Persians*), and in the "Mines de l'Orient," translated a considerable portion of the Shah-nameh in the measure of the original. MM. Campion and Atkinson have rendered a part of it into English heroic verse. Görres has epitomised it, as far as to the death of Roostem, in German prose, under the title of " Das Heldenbuch von Iran." An epitome of the poem in English prose, by Mr. Atkinson, has also lately appeared.

curious point that we related the tale of Zohak and Feridoon.

Moses of Choren, the Armenian historian, who wrote about the year 440, thus addresses the person to whom his work is dedicated. " How should the vain and empty fables about Byrasp Astyages gain any portion of thy favour, or why shouldest thou impose on us the fatigue of elucidating the absurd, tasteless, senseless legends of the Persians about him? to wit, of his first injurious benefit of the demoniac powers which were subject to him, and how he could not deceive him who was deception and falsehood itself. Then, of the kiss on the shoulders, whence the dragons came, and how thenceforward the growth of vice destroyed mankind by the pampering of the belly, until at last a certain Rhodones bound him with chains of brass, and brought him to the mountain which is called Demavend; how Byraspes then dragged to a hill Rhodones, when he fell asleep on the way, but this last, awaking out of his sleep, brought him to a cavern of the mountain, where he chained him fast, and set an image opposite to him, so that, terrified by it, and held by the chains, he might never more escape to destroy the world."

Here we have evidently the whole story of Zohak and Feridoon current in Persia in the fifth century; and any one who has reflected on the nature of tradition must be well aware that it must have existed there for centuries before. The very names are nearly the same. Taking the first syllable from Feridoon, it becomes nearly Rodon, and Biyraspi Aidahaki (the words of the Armenian text) signify the dragon Byrasp: Zohak is evidently nearly the same with the last word. This fable could hardly have been invented in the time of the Sassanian dynasty, who had not then been more than two centuries on the throne, much less during the period of the dominion of the Parthian Arsacides, who were adverse to everything Persian. We are therefore carried back to the times of the Kejanians, the Achæmenides of the Greeks; and it is by no means impossible that the tale of Zohak and Feridoon was known even to the host which Xerxes led to the subjugation of Greece.

It is well known to those versed in oriental history that, when the founder of the house of Sassan mounted the throne of Persia in the year 226, he determined to bring back everything, as far as was possible, to its state in the time of the Kejanians, from whom he affected to be descended, and that his successors trod in his footsteps. But, as Persia had been for five centuries and a half under the dominion of the Greeks and Parthians, there was probably no authentic record of the ancient state of things remaining. Recourse was therefore had to the traditional tales of the country; and, as the legend of Zohak and Feridoon was, as we have seen, one of the most remarkable of these tales, it was at once adopted as a genuine portion of the national history, and a banner formed to represent the Apron of Gavah, which was, as the poet describes it, adorned with additional jewels by each monarch of the house of Sassan at his accession. This hypothesis will very simply explain the circumstance of this banner being unnoticed by the Greek writers, while it is an undoubted fact that it was captured by the Arabs at the battle of Kadiseäh, which broke the power of Persia, —a circumstance which has perplexed Sir John Malcolm.

We will finally observe that the historian just alluded to, as well as some others, thinks that the darkness cast by the magic art of the White Deev over Ky Kaoos and his army in Mazanderan coincides with the eclipse of the sun predicted by Thales, and which, according to Herodotus, parted the armies of the Medians and the Lydians when engaged in conflict. Little stress is however, we apprehend, to be laid on such coincidences. Tradition does not usually retain the memory of facts of this nature, though fiction is apt enough to invent them. The only circumstances which we have observed in the early part of the Shah-namch agreeing with Grecian history, are some relating to the youthful days of Kei Khoosroo, which are very like what Herodotus relates of Cyrus.

We now return to the history of the Assassins

CHAPTER X.

Death of Jellal-ed-deen—Character of Ala-ed-deen, his successor—The Sheikh Jemal-ed-deen—The Astronomer Nasir-ed-deen—The Vizir Sheref-al-Moolk—Death of Ala-ed-
deen—Succession of Rukn-ed-deen, the last Sheikh-al-Jebal.

THE reign of Jellal-ed-deen, which, unfortunately
for the society, lasted but twelve years, was unstained
by blood ; and we see no reason to doubt the judgment of the oriental historians, who consider his faith
in Islam as being sincere and pure.   It was probably
his virtue that caused his death, for his life, it was
suspected, was terminated by poison administered by
his own kindred.   His son Ala-ed-deen* (*Eminence
of Religion*), who succeeded him, was but nine years
old; but as, according to the maxims of the Ismaïlites,
the visible representative of the imam was, to a certain extent, exempted from the ordinary imperfections
of humanity, and his commands were to be regarded
as those of him whose authority he bore, the young
Ala-ed-deen was obeyed as implicitly as any of his
predecessors.   At his mandate the blood was shed
of all among his relatives who were suspected of
having participated in the murder of his father.

Ala-ed-deen proved to be a weak, inefficient ruler.
His delight was in the breeding and tending of sheep,
and he spent his days in the cotes among the herds-
men, while the affairs of the society were allowed to
run into disorder.   All the restraints imposed by his
father were removed, and every one was left to do

* This is the name which, in the form of Aladdin, is so
familiar to us from the story of the Wonderful Lamp.

what was right in his own eyes. The weakness of this prince's intellect is ascribed to his having, in the fifth year of his reign, had himself most copiously bled without the knowledge of his physician, the consequence of which was an extreme degree of debility and a deep melancholy, which never afterwards left him. From that time no one could venture to offer him advice respecting either his health or the state of the affairs of the society, without being rewarded for it by the rack or by instant death. Everything was therefore kept concealed from him, and he had neither friend nor adviser.

Yet Ala-ed-deen was not without some estimable qualities. He had a respect and esteem for learning and learned men. For the sheikh Jemal-ed-deen Ghili, who dwelt at Casveen, he testified on all occasions the utmost reverence, and sent him annually 500 dinars to defray the expenses of his household. When the people of Casveen reproached the learned sheikh with living on the bounty of the Impious, he made answer, " The imams pronounce it lawful to execute the Ismaïlites, and to confiscate their goods; how much more lawful is it for a man to make use of their property and their money when they give them voluntarily!" Ala-ed-deen, who probably heard of the reproaches directed against his friend, sent to assure the people of Casveen that it was solely on account of the sheikh that he spared them, or else he would put the earth of Casveen into bags, hang the bags about the necks of the inhabitants, and bring them to Alamoot. The following instance of his respect for the sheikh is also related. A messenger coming with a letter to him from the sheikh was so imprudent as to deliver it to him when he was drunk. Ala-ed-deen ordered him to have a hundred blows of the bastinade, at the same time crying out to him, " O foolish and thoughtless man, to give me a letter from the sheikh at the time when I was drunk! Thou shouldest have waited till I was come out of the bath, and was come to my senses."

The celebrated astronomer Nasir-ed-deen (*Victory of Religion*) had also gained the consideration of Ala-ed-deen, who was anxious to enjoy the pleasure of his society. But the philosopher, who resided at Bokhara, testified little inclination to accept of the favour intended him. Ala-ed-deen therefore sent orders to the Dai-al-Kebir of Kuhistan to convey the uncourteous sage to Alamoot. As Nasir-ed-deen was one day recreating himself in the gardens about Bokhara, he found himself suddenly surrounded by some men, who, showing him a horse, directed him to mount, telling him he had nothing to fear if he conducted himself quietly. It was in vain that he argued and remonstrated; he was far on the road to Kuhistan, which was 600 miles distant, before his friends knew he was gone. The governor made every apology for what he had been obliged to do. The philosopher was sent on to Alamoot to be the companion of Ala-ed-deen, and it was while he was there that he wrote his great work called the Morals of Nasir (*Akhlaak-Nasiree*).*

It was during the administration of Ala-ed-deen that the following event, so strongly illustrative of the modes of procedure of the Assassins, took place. The sultan Jellal-ed-deen, the last ruler of Khaurism, so well known for his heroic resistance to Chingis

---

* Malcolm's History of Persia, vol. i. In the clever work called "Traits and Stories of the Irish Peasantry," which is the best picture ever given of the language, manners, and modes of thinking of that class, there is an amusing account (and an undoubtedly true one) of the "Abduction of Mat Kavanagh," one of that curious order of men called in that country hedge-schoolmasters, which, as indicative of a passion for knowledge, may be placed in comparison with this anecdote of Ala-ed-deen.

Khan, had appointed the emir Arkhan governor of
Nishaboor, which bordered closely on the Ismaïlite
territory of Kuhistan. Arkhan being obliged to
attend the sultan, the deputy whom he left in his
stead made several destructive incursions into Kuhistan, and laid waste the Ismaïlite districts of Teem
and Kaïn. The Ismaïlites sent to demand satisfaction, but the only reply made to their complaints and
menaces by the deputy-governor was one of those
symbolical proceedings so common in the east. He
came to receive the Ismaïlite envoy with his girdle
stuck full of daggers, which he flung on the ground
before him, to signify either his disregard for the
daggers of the society, or to intimate that he could
play at that game as well as they. The Ismaïlites
were not, however, persons to be provoked with
impunity, and shortly afterwards three Fedavees were
despatched to Kunja, where Arkhan was residing at
the court of the sultan. They watched till the emir
came without the walls of the town, and then fell
upon and murdered him. They then hastened to the
house of Sheref-al-Moolk (*Nobleness of the Realm*),
the vizir, and penetrated into his divan. Fortunately
he was at that time engaged with the sultan, and
they missed him; but they wounded severely one
of his servants, and then, sallying forth, paraded the
streets, proclaiming aloud that they were Assassins.
They did not however escape the penalty of their
temerity, for the people assembled and stoned them
to death.

An envoy of the Ismaïlites, named Bedr-ed-deen
(*Full Moon of Religion*) Ahmed, was meantime on
his way to the court of the sultan. He stopped short
on hearing what had occurred, and sent to the vizir
to know whether he should go on or return. Sheref-
al-Moolk, who feared to irritate the Assassins, directed
him to continue his journey, and, when he was

arrived, showed him every mark of honour. The object of Bedr-ed-deen's mission was to obtain satisfaction for the ravages committed on the Ismaïlite territory and the cession of the fortress of Damaghan. The vizir promised the former demand without a moment's hesitation, and he made as little difficulty with regard to the second. An instrument was drawn out assigning to the Ismaïlites the fortress which they craved, on condition of their remitting annually to the royal treasury the sum of 30,000 pieces of gold.

When this affair was arranged the sultan set out for Azerbeijan, and the Ismaïlite ambassador remained the guest of the vizir. One day, after a splendid banquet, when the wine, which they had been drinking in violation of the law, had mounted into their heads, the ambassador told the vizir, by way of confidence, that there were several Ismaïlites among the pages, grooms, guards, and other persons who were immediately about the sultan. The vizir, dismayed, and at the same time curious to know who these dangerous attendants were, besought the ambassador to point them out to him, giving him his napkin as a pledge that nothing evil should happen to them. Instantly, at a sign from the envoy, five of the persons who were attendants of the chamber stepped forth, avowing themselves to be concealed Assassins. " On such a day, and at such an hour," said one of them, an Indian, to the vizir, " I might have slain thee without being seen or punished ; and, if I did not do so, it was only because I had no orders from my superiors." The vizir, timid by nature, and rendered still more so by the effects of the wine, stripped himself to his shirt, and, sitting down before the five Assassins, conjured them by their lives to spare him, protesting that he was as devotedly the slave of the sheikh Ala-ed-deen as of the sultan Jellal-ed-deen.

As soon as the sultan heard of the meanness and cowardice of his vizir, he sent a messenger to him with the keenest reproaches, and an order to burn alive the five Ismaïlites without an instant's delay. The vizir, though loth, was obliged to comply, and, in violation of his promise, the five chamberlains were cast on the flaming pyre, where they died exulting at being found worthy to suffer in the service of the great Sheikh-al-Jebal. The master of the pages was also put to death for having admitted Ismaïlites among them. The sultan then set out for Irak, leaving the vizir in Azerbeijan. While he was there an envoy arrived from Alamoot, who, on being admitted to an audience, thus spake, " Thou hast given five Ismaïlites to the flames; to redeem thy head, pay 10,000 pieces of gold for each of these unfortunate men." The vizir heaped honours on the envoy, and directed his secretary to draw out a deed in the usual forms, by which he bound himself to pay the Ismaïlites the annual sum of 10,000 pieces of gold, besides paying for them the 30,000 which went to the treasury of the sultan. Sheref-al-Moolk was then assured that he had nothing to apprehend.

The preceding very characteristic anecdote rests on good authority, for it is related by Aboo-'l-Fetah Nissavee, the vizir's secretary, in his life of sultan Jellal-ed-deen.

The astronomer Nasir-ed-deen was not the only involuntary captive of Alamoot. Ala-ed-deen sent once to Farsistan to the atabeg Mozaffer-ed-deen, to request that he would send him an able physician. Requests from Alamoot were not lightly to be disregarded, and the atabeg despatched the imam Behaed-deen, one of the most renowned physicians of the time, to the mountains of Jebal. The skill of the imam proved of great benefit to the prince, but when the physician applied for leave to return to his family he found that he was destined to pass the remainder of his days in Alamoot, unless he should outlive his patient.

The imam's release, however, was more speedy than he expected. Ala-ed-deen, who had several children, had nominated the eldest of them, Rukn-ed-deen (*Support of Religion*), while he was yet a child, to be his successor. As Rukn-ed-deen grew up the people began to hold him in equal respect with his father, and to consider his commands as equally binding on them. Ala-ed-deen took offence, and declared that he would give the succession to another of his children; but, as this directly contravened one of the Ismaïlite maxims, namely, that the first nomination was always the true one, it was little heeded. Rukn-ed-deen, in apprehension for his life, which his father threatened, retired to a strong castle to wait there the time when he should be called to the succession. Meantime the tyranny and caprice of Ala-ed-deen had given many of the principal persons about him cause to be apprehensive for their lives, and they resolved to anticipate him. There was a man at Alamoot named Hassan, a native of Mazenderan, who, though no Ismaïlite, was of a vile and profligate character. He was the object of the doating attachment of Ala-ed-deen, and consequently had free and constant access to him. Him they fixed upon as their agent, and they found no difficulty in gaining him. Ala-ed-deen, whose fondness for breeding and tending sheep had never diminished, had built for himself a wooden house close by his sheep-cotes, whither he was wont to retire, and where he indulged himself in all the excesses in which he delighted. Hassan of Mazenderan seized the moment when Ala-ed-deen was lying drunk in this house, and shot him through the neck with an arrow. Rukn-ed-deen, who is said to have been engaged in the conspiracy, assuming the part of the avenger of blood, the murderer and all his family were put to death, and their bodies committed to the flames; but this act of seeming justice did not free Rukn-ed-deen from suspicion, and the bitter reproaches of his mother were poured forth on him as a parricide.

The termination of the power of the Ismaïlites was now at hand. Rukn-ed-deen had hardly ascended the throne of his murdered father when he learned that an enemy was approaching against whom all attempts at resistance would be vain.

CHAPTER XI.

The Mongols—Hoolagoo sent against the Ismaïlites—Rukn-
ed-deen submits—Capture of Alamoot—Destruction of the
Library—Fate of Rukn-ed-deen—Massacre of the Ismaïlites
—St. Louis and the Assassins—Mission for the Conversion
of the People of Kuhistan—Conclusion.

HALF a century had now elapsed since the voice of
the Mongol seer on the banks of the Sélinga had
announced to the tribes of that race that he had seen
in a vision the Great God sitting on his throne and
giving sentence that Temujeen, one of their chiefs,
should be Chingis Khan (*Great Khan*), and the
obedient tribes had, under the leading of Temujeen,
commenced that career of conquest which extended
from the eastern extremity of Asia to the confines of
Egypt and of Germany.   At this time the chief
power over the Mongols was in the hands of Mangoo,
the grandson of Chingis, a prince advantageously
made known to Europe by the long abode of the
celebrated Venetian Marco Polo at his court.   The
Mongols had not yet invaded Persia, though they
had, under Chingis himself, overthrown and stripped
of his dominions the powerful sultan of Khaurism.
It was however evident that that country could not
long escape the fate of so many extensive and powerful states, and that a pretext would soon be found
for pouring over it the hordes of the Mongols.

We are told, though it seems scarcely credible,
that ambassadors came from the Khalif of Bagdad
to Nevian, the Mongol general who commanded on
the northern frontier of Persia, requiring safe conduct

to the court of Mangoo. The object of their mission was to implore the great khan to send his invincible troops to destroy those pests of society the bands of the Ismaïlites. The prayer of the envoys of the successor of the Prophet was supported by the Judge of Casveen, who happened to be at that time at the court of Mangoo, where he appeared in a coat of mail, to secure himself, as he professed, from the daggers of the Assassins. The khan gave orders to assemble an army; his brother Hoolagoo was appointed to command it, and, as he was setting forth, Mangoo thus addressed him :—

" With heavy cavalry and a mighty host I send thee from Tooran to Iran, the land of mighty princes. It behoves thee now strictly to observe, both in great and in small things, the laws and regulations of Chinghis Khan, and to take possession of the countries from the Oxus to the Nile. Draw closer unto thee by favour and rewards the obedient and the submissive; tread the refractory and the rebellious, with their wives and children, into the dust of contempt and misery. When thou hast done with the Assassins begin the conquest of Irak. If the Khalif of Bagdad comes forward ready to serve thee, thou shalt do him no injury; if he refuses, let him share the fate of the rest."

The army of Hoolagoo was reinforced by a thousand families of Chinese firemen to manage the battering machines and fling the flaming naphtha, known in Europe under the name of Greek fire. He set forward in the month Ramazan of the 651st year of the Hejra (A. D. 1253). His march was so slow that he did not cross the Oxus till two years afterwards. On the farther bank of this river he took the diversion of lion-hunting, but the cold came on so intense that the greater part of his horses perished, and he was obliged to wait for the ensuing spring before he could advance. All the princes of the menaced countries sent embassies to the Mongol camp announcing their submission and obedience. The head-quarters of Hoolagoo were now in Khorassan, whence he sent envoys to Rukn-ed-deen, the Ismaïlite chief, requiring his submission. By the advice of the astronomer Nasir-ed-deen, who was his counsellor and minister, Rukn-ed-deen sent to Baissoor Noobeen, one of Hoolagoo's generals, who had advanced to Hamadan, declaring his obedience and his wish to live in peace with every one. The Mongol general recommended that, as Hoolagoo himself was approaching, Rukn-ed-deen should wait on him in person. After some delay, the latter agreed to send his brother Shahinshah, who accompanied the son of Baissoor to the quarters of the Mongol prince. Meantime Baissoor, by the orders of Hoolagoo, entered the Ismaïlite territory and drew near to Alamoot. The troops of the Assassins occupied a steep hill near that place. The Mongols attacked them, but were repelled each time they attempted the ascent. Being forced to give over the attack, they contented themselves with burning the houses and ravaging the country round.

When Shahinshah reached the camp of Hoolagoo and notified the submission of his brother, orders to the following effect were transmitted to the mountain-chief :—" Since Rukn-ed-deen has sent his brother unto us, we forgive him the offences of his father and his followers. He shall himself, as, during his short reign, he has been guilty of no crime, demolish his castles and come to us." Orders were sent at the same time to Baissoor to give over ravaging the district of Roodbar. Rukn-ed-deen began casting down some of the battlements of Alamoot, and at the same time sent to beg the delay of a year before appearing in the presence of Hoolagoo. But the

orders of the Mongol were imperative; he was required to appear at once, and to commit the defence
of his territory to the Mongol officer who was the
bearer of Hoolagoo's commands. Rukn-ed-deen
hesitated. He sent again to make excuses and ask
more time; and, as a proof of his obedience, he
directed the governors of Kuhistan and Kirdkoh to
repair to the Mongol camp. The banners of Hoolagoo were now floating at the foot of Demavend, close
to the Ismaïlite territory, and once more orders came
to Maimoondees, where Rukn-ed-deen and his family
had taken refuge:—"The Ruler of the World is
now arrived at Demavend, and it is no longer time
to delay. If Rukn-ed-deen wishes to wait a few days
he may in the mean time send his son." The
affrighted chief declared his readiness to send his
son, but, at the persuasion of his women and advisers,
instead of his own, he sent the son of a slave, who
was of the same age, requesting that his brother
might be restored to him. Hoolagoo was soon informed of the imposition, but disdained to notice it
otherwise than by sending back the child, saying he
was too young, and requiring that his elder brother,
if he had one, should be sent in place of Shahinshah. He at the same time dismissed Shahinshah with these words:—"Tell thy brother to demolish Maimoondees and come to me; if he does not
come, the eternal God knows the consequences."

The Mongol troops now covered all the hills and
valleys, and Hoolagoo in person appeared before
Maimoondees. The Assassins fought bravely, but
Rukn-ed-deen had not spirit to hold out. He sent
his other brother, his son, his vizir Nasir-ed-deen,
and the principal persons of the society, bearing rich
presents to the Mongol prince. Nasir-ed-deen was
directed to magnify the strength of the Ismaïlite
fortresses in order to gain good terms for his master;

but, instead of so doing, he told Hoolagoc net to regard them, assuring him that the conjunction of the stars announced the downfal of the Ismaïlites, and that the sun of their power was hastening to its setting. It was agreed that the castle should be surrendered on condition of free egress. Rukn-ed-deeh, his ministers, and his friends, entered the Mongol camp on the first day of the month Zoo-l-Kaadeh. His wealth was divided among the Mongol troops. Hoolagoo took compassion on himself, and spoke kindly to him, and treated him as his guest. Nasir-ed-deen became the vizir of the conqueror, who afterwards built for him the observatory of Meragha.

Mongol officers were now dispatched to all the castles of the Ismaïlites in Kuhistan, Roodbar, and even in Syria, with orders from Rukn-ed-deen to the governors to surrender or demolish them. The number of these strong castles was upwards of one hundred, of which there were forty demolished in Roodbar alone. Three of the strongest castles in this province, namely, Alamoot, Lamseer, and Kirdkoh, hesitated to submit, their governors replying to the summons that they would wait till Hoolagoo should appear in person before them. In a few days the Mongol prince and his captive were at the foot of Alamoot. Rukn-ed-deen was led under the walls, and he ordered the governor to surrender. His command was disregarded, and Hoolagoo, not to waste time, removed his camp to Lamseer, leaving a corps to blockade Alamoot. The people of Lamseer came forth immediately with their homage, and a few days afterwards envoys arrived from Alamoot entreating Rukn-ed-deen to intercede for the inhabitants with the brother of Mangoo. The conqueror was moderate; he allowed them free egress, and gave them three days to collect and remove their families and property. On the third day the Mongol

troops received permission to enter and plunder the
fortress. They rushed, eager for prey, into the
hitherto invincible, now deserted, Vulture's Nest, and
rifled it of all that remained in it. As they hurried
through its subterrane recesses in search of treasure
they frequently, to their amazement, found themselves
immersed in honey, or swimming in wine; for there
were large receptacles of wine, honey, and corn, hewn
into the solid rock, the nature of which was such that,
though, as we are told, they had been filled in the
time of Hassan Sabah, the corn was perfectly sound,
and the wine had not soured. This extraordinary
circumstance was regarded by the Ismaïlites as a
miracle wrought by that founder of their society.

When Alamoot fell into the hands of the Mongols
Ata-Melek (*King's-father*) Jowainee, a celebrated
vizir and historian, craved permission of Hoolagoo to
inspect the celebrated library of that place, which had
been founded by Hassan Sabah and increased by his
successors, and to select from it such works as might
be worthy of a place in that of the khan. The permission was readily granted, and he commenced his
survey of the books. But Ata-Melek was too orthodox a Mussulman, or too lazy an examiner, to make
the best use of his opportunity; for all he did was to
take the short method of selecting the Koran and a
few other books which he deemed of value out of the
collection, and to commit the remainder, with all the
philosophical instruments, to the flames, as being
impious and heretical. All the archives of the society
were thus destroyed, and our only source of information respecting its doctrines, regulations, and history,
is derived from what Ata-Melek has related in his
own history as the result of his search among the
archives and books of the library of Alamoot, previous
to his making an *auto da fé* of them.

The fate of the last of a dynasty, however worthless

and insignificant his character may be, is always interesting from the circumstance alone of his being the last, and thus, as it were, embodying in himself the history of his predecessors. We shall therefore pause to relate the remainder of the story of the feeble Rukn-ed-deen.

When Hoolagoo, after the conclusion of his campaign against Roodbar, retired to Hamadan, where he had left his children, he took with him Rukn-ed-deen, whom he continued to treat with kindness. Here the Assassin prince became enamoured of a Mongol maiden of the very lowest class. He asked permission of Hoolagoo to espouse her, and, by the directions of that prince, the wedding was celebrated with great solemnity. He next craved to be sent to the court of Mangoo Khan. Hoolagoo, though surprised at this request, acceded to it also, and gave him a corps of Mongols as an escort. He at the same time directed him to order on his way the garrison of Kirdkoh, who still held out, to surrender, and demolish the fortress. Rukn-ed-deen, as he passed by Kirdkoh, did as directed, but sent at the same time a private message to the governor to hold out as long as possible. Arrived at Kara-Kooroom, the residence of the khan, he was not admitted to an audience, but the following message was delivered to him :—" Thus saith Mangoo : Since thou affectest to be obedient to us, wherefore has not the castle of Kirdkoh been delivered up? Go back, and demolish all the castles which remain; then mayest thou be partaker of the honour of viewing our imperial countenance." Rukn-ed-deen was obliged to return, and, soon after he had crossed the Oxus, his escort, making him dismount under pretext of an entertainment, ran him through with their swords.

Mangoo Khan was determined to exterminate the whole race of the Ismaïlites, and orders to that effect had already reached Hoolagoo, who was only waiting to execute them till Kirdkoh should have surrendered. As the garrison of that place continued obstinate, he no longer ventured to delay. Orders for indiscriminate massacre were issued, and 12,000 Ismaïlites soon fell as victims. The process was short; wherever a member of the society was met he was, without any trial, ordered to kneel down, and his head instantly rolled on the ground. Hoolagoo sent one of his vizirs to Casveen, where the family of Rukn-eddeen were residing, and the whole of them were put to death, except two (females it is said), who were reserved to glut the vengeance of the princess Boolghan Khaloon, whose father Jagatai had perished by the daggers of the Assassins

The siege of Kirdkoh was committed by Hoolagoo (who was now on his march to Bagdad to put an end to the empire of the khalifs) to the princes of Mazenderân and Ruyan. The castle held out for three years, and the siege was rendered remarkable by the following curious occurrence :—It was in the beginning of the spring when a poet named Koorbee of Ruyan came to the camp. He began to sing, in the dialect of Taberistan, a celebrated popular song of the spring, beginning with these lines :—

> When the sun from the fish to the ram doth return,
> Spring's banner waves high on the breeze of the morn.*

* " And Day, with his *banner* of radiance *unfurled,*
>   Shines in through the mountainous portal that opes
> Sublime from that valley of bliss to the world,"

says Mr. Moore in his " Lalla Rookh," undoubtedly without any knowledge of the eastern song. His original was perhaps Campbell's

>   " Andes, giant of the western star,
> His meteor *standard* to the winds *unfurled,*
> Looks from his throne of clouds o'er half the *world;*"

which was again, in all probability, suggested, like Gray's

The song awoke in the minds of princes and soldiers
the recollection of the vernal delights they had left
behind them; an invincible longing after them seized
the whole army; and, without reflecting on the consequences, they broke up the siege, and set forth to
enjoy the season of flowers in the fragrant gardens of
Mazenderân.   Hoolagoo was greatly incensed when
he heard of their conduct, and sent a body of troops
against them, but forgave them on their making due
apologies and submissions.

The Ismaïlite power in Persia was now completely
at an end; the khalifat, whose destruction had been
its great object, was also involved in its ruin, and the
power of the Mongols established over the whole of
Irân.   The Mongol troops failed in their attempts
on the Ismaïlite castles in Syria; but, at the end of
fourteen years, what they could not effect was achieved
by the great Beibars, the Circassian Mamlook sultan
of Egypt, who reduced all the strongholds of the Assassins in the Syrian mountains, and extinguished
their power in that region.

The last intercourse of the Assassins with the
western Christians which we read of was that with
St. Louis.   William of Nangis relates—but the tale
is evidently apocryphal—that in the year 1250 two of
the *Arsacidæ* were sent to France to murder that
prince, who was then only twenty-two years of age.
The *Senex de Monte* however repented, and sent
others to warn the French monarch.   These arriving
in time, the former were discovered, on which the

> " Loose his beard, and hoary hair
>   Stream'd like a *meteor* to the troubled air, '

by Milton's

> " Imperial *ensign*, which, full high advanced,
>   Shone like a *meteor* streaming to the wind."

It is thus that the particles of poetry, like those of matter,
are in eternal circulation, and forming new combinations.

king loaded them all with presents, and dismissed them with rich gifts for their master.

Rejecting this idle legend, we may safely credit the account of Joinville, that in 1250, when St. Louis was residing at Acre, after his captivity in Egypt, he was waited on by an embassy from the Old Man of the Mountain, the object of which was to procure, through his means, a remission of the tribute which he paid to the Templars and the Hospitallers. As if to obviate the answer which might naturally be made, the ambassador said that his master considered that it would be quite useless to sacrifice the lives of his people by murdering the masters of these orders, as men as good as they would be immediately appointed to succeed them. It being then morning, the king desired them to return in the evening. When they appeared again, he had with him the masters of the Temple and the Hospital, who, on the propositions being repeated, declared them to be most extravagant, and assured the ambassadors that, were it not for the sacredness of their character, and their regard for the word of the king, they would fling them into the sea. They were directed to go back, and to bring within fifteen days a satisfactory letter to the king. They departed, and, returning at the appointed time, said to the king that their chief, as the highest mark of friendship, had sent him his own shirt and his gold ring. They also brought him draught and chess-boards, adorned with amber, an elephant and a giraffe (*orafle*) of crystal. The king, not to be outdone in generosity, sent an embassy to Massyat with presents of scarlet robes, gold cups, and silver vases, for the Ismaïlite chief.

Speculative tenets will continue and be propagated long after the sect or society which holds them may have lost all temporal influence and consideration. Accordingly, seventy years after the destruction of

Alamoot, in the reign of Aboo-Zeid, the eighth successor of Hoolagoo, it was found that nearly all the
people of Kuhistan were devoted to the Ismaïlite
opinions. The monarch, who was an orthodox Soon-
nee, advised with the governor of the province, and
it was resolved to send a mission, composed of learned
and zealous divines, for the conversion of the heretics.
At the head of the mission was placed the pious and
orthodox sheikh Emad-ed-deen of Bokhara; the
other members of it were the sheikh's two sons and
four other learned ulemas (*Doctors of law*), in all
seven persons. Full of enthusiasm and zeal for the
good cause which they had in hand, the missionaries
set forth. They arrived at Kaïn, the chief place of
the province, and found with grief and indignation
none of the ordinary testimonies of Moslem devotion.
The mosks were in ruins, no morning or evening call
to prayer was to be heard, no school or hospital was
to be seen. Emad-ed-deen resolved to commence
his mission by the solemn call to prayer. Adopting
the precaution of arraying themselves in armour, he
and his companions ascended the terrace of the
castle, and all at once from its different sides shouted
forth, " Say God is great ! There is no god but God,
and Mohammed is his prophet. Up to prayer; to
good works !" The inhabitants, to whom these
sounds were unusual and offensive, ran together, determined to bestow the crown of martyrdom on the
missionaries; but these good men, whose zeal was of
a prudent complexion, did not, though armed, abide
the encounter. They took refuge in an aqueduct,
where they concealed themselves till the people had
dispersed, when they came forth once more, ascended
the terrace, and gave the call to prayer. The people
collected again, and again the missionaries sought
their retreat. By perseverance, however, and the
powerful support of the governor of the province, they

gradually accustomed the ears of the people to the forms of orthodoxy. Many years afterwards sultan Shahrokh, the son of Timoor, resolved to send a commission to ascertain the state of religion in Kohistan. At the head of it he placed Jelalee of Kaïn, the grandson of Emad-ed-deen, a man of learning and talent and a distinguished writer. Jelalee deemed himself especially selected by heaven for this purpose, as his grandsire had headed the former mission, and the Prophet had appeared to himself in a dream, and given to him a broom to sweep the land, which he interpreted to be a commission to sweep away the impurity of infidelity out of the country. He therefore entered on his office with joy, and, after a peregrination of eleven months, reported favourably of the faith of the people of Kohistan, with the exception of some dervishes and others, who were addicted to *Soofeeism.*

At the present day, nearly six centuries after the destruction of the Ismaïlite power, the sect is still in existence both in Persia and in Syria. But, like that of the Anabaptists, it has lost its terrors, and the Ismaïlite doctrine is now merely one of the speculative heresies of Islam. The Syrian Ismaïlites dwell in eighteen villages around Massyat, and pay an annual sum of 16,500 piastres to the governor of Hama, who nominates their sheikh or emir. They are divided into two sects or parties, the Sooweidanee, so named from one of their former sheikhs, and the Khisrewee, so called on account of their great reverence for Khiser, the guardian of the Well of Life. They are all externally rigid observers of the precepts of Islam, but they are said to believe in the divinity of Ali, in the uncreated light as the origin of all things, and in the sheikh Rasheed-eddeen Sinan as the last representative of God upon earth.

The Persian Ismaïlites dwell chiefly in Roodbar,

but they are to be met all over the east, and even appear as traders on the banks of the Ganges. Their imam, whose pedigree they trace up to Ismaïl, the son of Jaaffer-es-Sadik, resides, under the protection of the Shah of Persia, at the village of Khekh, in the district of Koom. As, according to their doctrine, he is an incarnate ray of the Divinity, they hold him in the utmost veneration, and make pilgrimages from the most distant places to obtain his blessing.

We have thus traced the origin, the growth, and the decline of this formidable society, only to be paralleled by that of the Jesuits in extent of power and unity of plan and purpose. Unlike this last, however, its object was purely evil, and its career was one of blood: it has therefore left no deeds to which its apologists might appeal in its defence. Its history, notwithstanding, will always form a curious and instructive chapter in that of the human race.

THE TEMPLARS.

CHAPTER I.

Introduction—The Crusades—Wrong Ideas respecting their
Origin—True Causes of them—Pilgrimage—Pilgrimage of
Frotmond—Of the Count of Anjou—Striking Difference
between the Christianity of the East and that of the West
—Causes of their different Characters—Feudalism—The
Extent and Force of this Principle.

AMONG the many extraordinary phenomena which
the middle ages present, none is more deserving of
attention, or more characteristic of the times and the
state of society and opinion, than the institution of
the religio-military orders of the Hospitallers, the
Templars, and the Teutonic Knights. Of these
orders, all of which owed their origin to the Crusades,
and commenced in the 12th century, the last, after
the final loss of the Holy Land, transferring the
scene of their activity to the north of Germany, and
directing their arms against the heathens who still
occupied the south coast of the Baltic, became the
founders, in a great measure, of the Prussian power;
while the first, planting their standard on the Isle of
Rhodes, long gallantly withstood the forces of the
Ottoman Turks, and, when at length obliged to resign
that island, took their station on the rock of Malta,
where they bravely repelled the troops of the greatest
of the Ottoman sultans, and maintained at least a
nominal independence till the close of the 18th cen-

L

tury. A less glorious fate attended the Knights of the Temple. They became the victims of the unprincipled rapacity of a merciless prince; their property was seized and confiscated; their noblest members perished in the flames; their memory was traduced and maligned; the foulest crimes were laid to their charge; and a secret doctrine, subversive of social tranquillity and national independence, was asserted to have animated their councils. Though many able defenders of these injured knights have arisen, the charges against them have been reiterated even in the present day; and a distinguished Orientalist (Von Hammer) has recently even attempted to bring forward additional and novel proofs of their secret guilt.* To add one more to the number of their defenders, to trace the origin, develope the internal constitution of their society, narrate their actions, examine the history of their condemnation and suppression, and show how absurd and frivolous were the charges against them, are the objects of the present writer, who, though he is persuaded, and hopes to prove, that they held no secret doctrine, yet places them among the secret societies of the middle ages, because it is by many confidently maintained that they were such.

As the society of the Templars was indebted for its origin to the Crusades, we will, before entering on our narrative, endeavour to correct some erroneous notions respecting the causes and nature of these celebrated expeditions.

The opinion of the Crusades having been an ema-

* The principal works on the subject of the Templars are Raynouard Monumens historiques relatifs à la Condamnation des Templiers; Dupuy Histoire de la Condamnation des Templiers; Münter Statutenbuch des Ordens der Tempelherren, and Wilike Geschichte des Tempelherrenordens. There is scarcely anything on the subject in English.

nation of the spirit of chivalry is one of the most erroneous that can be conceived, yet it is one most widely spread. Romancers, and those who write history as if it were romance, exert all their power to keep up the illusion, and the very sound of the word Crusade conjures up in most minds the ideas of waving plumes, gaudy surcoats, emblazoned shields, with lady's love, knightly honour, and courteous feats of arms. A vast deal of this perversion of truth is no doubt to be ascribed to the illustrious writer of the splendid epic whose subject is the first Crusade. Tasso, who, living at the time when the last faint gleam of expiring chivalry was fitfully glowing through the moral and political gloom which was overspreading the former abodes of freedom and industry in Italy, may be excused if, young and unversed in the philosophy of history, he mistook the character of European society six centuries before his time, or deemed himself at liberty to minister to the taste of a court which loved the fancied image of former times, and stimulate it to a generous emulation by representing the heroes of the first Crusade as animated with the spirit and the virtues of the ideal chivalry. But the same excuse is not to be made for those who, writing at the present day, confound chivalry and the Crusades, give an epitome of the history of the latter under the title of that of the former, and venture to assert that the valiant Tancred was the *beau ideal* of chivalry, and that the " Talisman" contains a faithful picture of the spirit and character of the Crusades.*

* On the subject of chivalry see Ste. Palaye Mémoires sur la Chevalerie, Sir W. Scott's Essay on the same subject, and Mills's and James's histories of chivalry. We do not recollect that any of these writers has fairly proved that the chivalry which they describe ever existed as an institution, and we must demur to the principle which they all assume of romances like Perceforest being good authority for the manners of the age in which they were composed.

We venture to assert that the Crusades did *not*
originate in chivalry, and that the first Crusade, the
most important of them, and that which gave the
tone and character to all the succeeding ones, does
not present a single vestige of what is usually understood by the term chivalry, not a trace of what the
imagination rather than the knowledge of Burke
described as embodying " the generous loyalty to
rank and sex, the proud submission, the dignified
obedience, and that subordination of the heart which
kept alive, even in servitude itself, the spirit of an
exalted freedom—that sensibility of principle, that
chastity of honour, which felt a stain like a wound,
which inspired courage whilst it mitigated ferocity,
which ennobled whatever it touched, and under which
vice itself lost half its evil by losing all its grossness."
Little surely does he know of the 11th century and
its spirit who can suppose any part of the foregoing
description to apply to those who marched in arms to
Asia to free the sepulchre of Christ; slightly must
he have perused the *Gesta Tancredi* of Radulphus
Cadomens, who can conceive that gallant warrior, as
he undoubtedly was, to have been the mirror of
chivalry.

Chivalry and the Crusades commenced in the
same century, and drew their origin from the same
source. One was not the cause of the other, but
both were effects of the same cause, and that cause
was *feudalism*. This inculcated " the proud submission, the dignified obedience," &c., &c., which
were gradually idealised into chivalry; it impressed
on the mind of the vassal those principles of re
gard to the rights and property of his lord which
seemed to justify and sanction the Holy War. Previously, however, to explaining the manner in
which this motive acted, we must stop to notice
another concurring cause of the Crusades, with-

out which it would perhaps never have begun to operate.

Man has at all periods been led by a strong impulse of his nature to visit those spots which have been distinguished as the scenes of great and celebrated actions, or the abode of distinguished personages. The operation of this natural feeling is still stronger when it is combined with religion, and there arises a conviction that the object of his worship is gratified by this act of attention, and his favour thereby secured to the votary. Hence we find *pilgrimage*, or the practice of taking distant journeys to celebrated temples, and other places of devotion, to have prevailed in all ages of the world. In the most remote periods of the mythic history of Greece, where historic truth is not to be sought, and only manners and modes of thinking are to be discerned, we constantly meet the *theoria*, or pilgrimage to Delphi, mentioned in the history of the heroes, whence we may with certainty collect that it formed at all times a portion of the manners of the Greeks. India, at the present day, witnesses annually the pilgrimage of myriads to the temple of Juggernaut, and Jerusalem has been for thousands of years the resort of pious Israelites.

The country which had witnessed the life and death of their Lord naturally acquired importance in the eyes of the early Christians, many of whom, moreover, were Jews by birth, and had always viewed Jerusalem with feelings of veneration. All, too, confounded—as has unfortunately been too much the case in later times—the old and the new law, and saw not that the former was but " beggarly elements" in comparison with the latter, and deemed that the political and economical precepts designed for a single nation, inhabiting one small region, were obligatory on the church of Christ, which was intended to comprise the whole human race. Many of the practices of Judaism were therefore observed by the Christians, and to this principle we are perhaps in a great measure to ascribe the rapid progress of the practice, and the belief in the efficacy, of pilgrimage to the Holy City.

The abuses of pilgrimage were early discerned, and some of the more pious Fathers of the Church preached and wrote against the practice. But piety and eloquence were vain, and could little avail to stem the torrent when men believed that the waters of Jordan had efficacy to wash every sin, though unattended by sincere repentance. The Church, as she advanced in corruption, improved in worldly wisdom, and, taking pilgrimage under her protection, made it a part of her penal discipline. The sinner was now ordered a journey to the Holy Land as a means of freeing his soul from the guilt of his perhaps manifold enormities. Each year saw the number of the pilgrims augment, while the growing veneration for relics, of which those which came from the Holy Land were esteemed the most efficacious, stimulated pilgrimage by adding the incentive of profit, as a small stock of money laid out in the purchase of the generally counterfeit relics always on sale at Jerusalem would produce perhaps a thousand per cent. on the return of the pilgrim to his native country. A pilgrim was also held in respect and veneration wherever he came, as an especial favourite of the Divinity, having been admitted by him to the high privilege of visiting the sacred places, a portion of whose sanctity it would be supposed might still adhere to him.

The 11th century was the great season of pilgrimage. A strange misconception of the meaning of a portion of Scripture had led men to fancy that the year 1000 was to be that of the advent of Christ, to judge the world. As the valley of Jehoshaphat was believed to be the spot on which this awful event would take place, the same feeling which leads people at the present day to lay a flattering unction to their souls by supposing that death-bed repentance will prove equivalent in the sight of God to a life passed in obedience to his will and in the exercise of virtue, impelled numbers to journey to the Holy Land, in the belief that this officiousness, as it were, of hitherto negligent servants would be well taken by their Lord, and procure them an indulgent hearing before his judgment-seat. Pilgrimage, therefore, increased greatly; the failure of their expectations, the appointed time having passed away without the Son of Man coming in the clouds of Heaven, gave it no check, but, on the contrary, rather an additional impulse; and during this century the caravans of pilgrims attained to such magnitude and strength as to be deserving of the appellation of *The armies of the Lord*—precursive of the first and greatest Crusade.

In truth the belief in the merit and even the obligation of a pilgrimage to Jerusalem, in the sight of God, was now as firmly impressed on the mind of every Christian, be his rank what it might, as that of the necessity and advantage of one to the Kaaba of Mecca is in the apprehension of the followers of Mohammed; and in the degraded state of the human intellect at that period a pilgrimage was deemed adequate to the removal of all sin. As a proof of this we shall narrate the pilgrimages of two distinguished personages of those times. The first occurred in the 9th, the second in the 11th century.

In the reign of Lothaire, son of Louis the Debonnaire, a nobleman of Brittany, named Frotmond, who had murdered his uncle and his youngest brother, began to feel remorse for his crimes. Arrayed in the habit of a penitent, he presented himself before the monarch and an assembly of his prelates, and made confession

of his guilty deeds. The king and bishops had him
straitly bound in chains of iron, and then commanded
him, in expiation of his guilt, to set forth for the East,
and visit all the holy places, clad in hair-cloth, and
his forehead marked with ashes. Accompanied by
his servants and the partners of his crime, the Breton
lord directed his course to Palestine, which he reached
in safety. Having, in obedience to the mandates of
his sovereign and of the church, visited all the holy
places, he crossed the Arabian desert, which had been
the scene of the wanderings of Israel, and entered
Egypt. He thence traversed a part of Africa, and
went as far as Carthage, whence he sailed for Rome.
Here the Pope, on being consulted, advised him to
make a second pilgrimage, in order to complete his
penance, and obtain the perfect remission of his sins.
Frotmond · accordingly set forth once more, and
having performed the requisite duties at the Holy
City, proceeded to the shore of the Red Sea, and
there took up his abode for three years on Mount
Sinai, after which time he made a journey to Armenia,
and visited the mountain on which the ark of Noah
had rested. His crimes being now, according to the
ideas of those times, expiated, he returned to his
native country, where he was received as a saint, and
taking up his abode in the convent of Redon, passed
there the remainder of his days, and died deeply re-
gretted by his brethren.*

Fulk de Nerra, Count of Anjou, had spilt much
innocent blood ; he had had his first wife burnt alive,
and forced his second wife to seek refuge from his
barbarity in the Holy Land. The public odium pursued him, and conscience asserting her rights presented to his disturbed imagination the forms of those
who had perished by him issuing from their tombs,
and reproaching him with his crimes. Anxious to

* Michaud, Histoire des Croisades, I., p. 59.

escape from his invisible tormentors, the count put
on him the habit of a pilgrim, and set forth for
Palestine. The tempests which he encountered in
the Syrian seas seemed to his guilty soul the instruments of divine vengeance, and augmented the fer-
vour of his repentance. Having reached Jerusalem
in safety, he set heartily about the work of penance.
He traversed the streets of the Holy City with a
cord about his neck, and beaten with rods by his servants, while he repeated these words, *Lord, have
mercy on a faithless and perjured Christian, on a
sinner wandering far from his home.* During his
abode in Jerusalem he gave abundant alms, relieving
the wants of the pilgrims, and leaving numerous
monuments of his piety and munificence.

Deep as was the penitence of the Count of Anjou,
it did not stand in the way of the exercise of a little
pious fraud. By an ingenious device he deceived
the impious malignity of the profane Saracens, who
would have made him defile the holy sepulchre; and
the chroniclers tell us that as he lay prostrate before
the sacred tomb he contrived to detach from it a
precious stone, which he carried back with him to
the West. On his return to his duchy he built, at the
castle of Loches, a church after the model of that of
the Resurrection at Jerusalem, and here he every day
implored with tears the divine forgiveness. His
mind, however, could not yet rest; he was still
haunted by the same horrid images; and he once
more visited the Holy Land, and edified the faithful by
the austerity of his penance. Returning home by
the way of Italy, he delivered the supreme pontiff
from a formidable enemy who was ravaging his territory, and the grateful pope conferred on him in return
the full absolution of all his sins. Fulk brought with
him to Anjou a great quantity of relics, with which he
adorned the churches of Loches and Angers; and his

chief occupation thenceforward was the building of towns and monasteries, whence he acquired the name of *The Great Builder*. His people, who blessed heaven for his conversion, honoured and loved him ; the guilt of his sins had been removed by the means which were then deemed of sovereign efficacy; yet still the monitor placed by God in the human breast, and which in a noble mind no power can reduce to perfect silence, did not rest ; and the Holy Land beheld, for the third time, the Count of Anjou watering the sepulchre of Christ with his tears, and groaning afresh over his transgressions. He quitted Jerusalem for the last time, recommending his soul to the prayers of the pious brethren whose office it was to receive the pilgrims, and turned his face homewards. But Anjou he was never more to behold; death surprised him at Metz. His body was transferred to Loches, and buried in his church of the Holy Sepulchre.

These instances may suffice to show what the opinion of the efficacy and merit of pilgrimage to the Holy Land was at the time of which we write. We here find convincing proof that in the minds of princes and prelates, the highest and most enlightened order of society, it was confidently believed to avail to remove the guilt of crimes of the deepest die. And let not any one say that the clergy took advantage of the ignorance of the people, and made it the instrument of extending their own power and influence; for such an assertion would evince ignorance both of human nature in general and of the temper and conduct of the Romish hierarchy at that, and we might almost say at all periods of its existence. However profligate the lives of many of the clergy may have been, they never called in question the truth of the dogmas of their religion. Even the great and daring Gregory VII., in the midst of what appear to us his arrogant and almost impious assumptions, never for moment doubted of the course which he was pursuing being the right one, and agreeable to heaven. The clergy, as well as the laity, were firmly persuaded of the efficacy of pilgrimage, and in both the persuasion was naturally stronger in proportion to the ignorance of the believer. We accordingly find that vast numbers of all ranks, and both sexes, clergy as well as laity, annually repaired to the tomb of Christ.

It remains to be explained what the principle was which gave origin to the idea of the right and justice of recovering the Holy Land, which was now in the hands of the fanatic Turks, instead of those of the tolerant Saracens. This cause was, as we have above asserted, the feudal spirit, that is, the spirit of the age, and not that emanation of it termed chivalry.

Religion, whatever its original nature and character, will always take a tinge from the manners and temper of those who adopt it. Nothing can be more illustrative of the truth of this observation than the history of the Christian religion. Any one who opens the Gospel, and reads it without preconception or prejudice, cannot fail at once to recognise the rational and fervent piety, the active benevolence, the pure morality, the noble freedom from the trammels of the world, joined with the zealous discharge of all the social duties, which every page of it inculcates. Yet we find this religion in the East degenerating into abject grovelling superstition and metaphysical quibbling, pursued with all the rancour of the *odium theologicum*, while in the West it assumed a fiery fanatic character, and deemed the sword an instrument of conversion superior to reason and argument. This difference, apparently so strange, arose from the difference of the social state and political institutions of the people of the East and of the West at the time when they embraced Christianity.

The free spirit had long since fled from Greece

when the first Christian missionaries preached the
faith among its people. But the temper of the Greek
was still lively, and his reasoning powers acute.
Moreover, he had still the same leaning towards a
sensible and material religion which has at all times
distinguished him, and the increasing despotism of
the empire depressed and enfeebled more and more
every day the martial spirit which he had displayed
in the days of his freedom.   No field remained for
his mental activity but that of philosophy and religion.
The former, which had long been his delight, he
had contrived to subtilize into an almost unintelligible mysticism ; and in this form it speedily spread
its infection through his new faith, which was besides
further metamorphosed and changed in character by
an infusion from the dualistic system of Persia.
Meantime the ascetic spirit which had come from
the East joined with the timidity engendered by the
pressure of despotism to make him mistake the spirit
of the Gospel, and convert Christianity into a crouch-
ing cowardly superstition.   When the emperor Nice-
phorus Phocas sought to infuse a martial and fanatic
spirit into his subjects, and to rouse them to vigorous
exertion against the Saracens, his bishops replied to
his exhortations by citing a canon of St. Basil, which
directed that he who had slain an enemy in battle
should abstain during three years from participation
in the holy sacraments.   The priest of a little town
in Cilicia was engaged one day in saying mass when
a band of Saracens burst in, and began to plunder
the town.   Without waiting to take off his sacerdotal
vestments, he seized the hammer, which in the
churches of the East frequently serves the purpose of
a bell, and, flying among the infidels, plied his weapon
to such effect that he forced them to a precipitate
flight, and saved the town.   What was the reward
of the gallant priest ?   He was censured by his dio-

cesan, interdicted the exercise of his ghostly functions, and so ill-treated in other respects, that he
flung off his robes and joined the Saracens, whose
more martial and energetic creed accorded better
with his manly sentiments. When the pilgrims of
the first Crusade began to arrive in such terrific numbers at Constantinople, the Greek emperor and his
subjects could hardly persuade themselves of the
possibility of religion being the actuating cause of
such a portentous movement—so little did religion
and deeds of arms accord in their minds !

But with the nations of the West the case was
different. In these the ruling portion, that which
gave tone to the whole, were of the Gothic and Germanic races, whose hardy bands had dashed to pieces
the worn-out fabric of the Western empire. Wor-
shippers in their native forests of Thor and Odin,
and the other deities of Valhalla, who admitted none
but the valiant dead to share in the celestial pork and
mead which each day crowned the board in their lucid
abode, their manners, their sentiments, their whole
being was martial, and they infused this spirit into
the religion which they adopted from their Roman
subjects. In making this change in its tone they
derived aid from the Jewish portion of the sacred
volume, which has been in all ages abused, by men
ignorant of its character and original use, to purposes
of fanaticism and persecution ; and the religion of
Christian Europe, from the fifth century downwards,
became of a martial and conquering character. By
the sword Charlemagne converted the pagan Saxons ;
his successors employed the sword against the heathen
Vends ; and by fire and sword Olof Triggva-son spread
Christianity throughout the North. In former times
this mode of conversion had been in a great degree
foreign to the Western church ; and persuasion had

M

been chiefly employed in the dissemination of the faith among the heathen nations.

The religion of the West we thus see was martial; but this spirit alone would not have sufficed to produce the Crusade which was to interest and appear as a duty to all orders of men. Here the feudal principle came into operation, and gave the requisite impulse.

In the 11th century the feudal system was completely developed in France and Germany, and the modes of thinking, speaking, and acting derived from it pervaded all the relations of life. From the top to the bottom of society the mutual obligations of lords and vassals were recognised and acted upon, and each vassal deemed it a most sacred duty to defend by arms the honour and property of his superior lord. There was also a kind of supreme temporal chief of the Christian world acknowledged in the person of the Emperor of Germany, who was viewed as the successor of Charlemagne, and the representative of the Roman emperors. The feudal ideas extended even to the hierarchy, which now put forth such exorbitant claims to supremacy over the temporal power. The head of the church was an acknowledged vicegerent of Him who was styled in scripture Lord of all the kingdoms of the earth. Jesus Christ was, therefore, the apex of the pyramid of feudal society; he was the great suzerain and lord paramount of all princes and peoples, and all were equally under obligation to defend his rights and honour. Such were evidently the sentiments of the age.

It is hardly necessary to remind the reader that the religion of the period which we treat of was of a gross and material character, and that the passions and infirmities of human nature were freely bestowed on the glorified Son of God. He was deemed to take a peculiar interest in the spot of land where he had sojourned when on earth, and more especially in the tomb in which his body had been deposited, and with grief and indignation to see them in the hands of those who contemptuously derided his divinity, and treated with insult and cruelty those of his faithful vassals who underwent the toils and dangers of a distant journey to offer their homage at his tomb. Nothing could, therefore, be more grateful to his feelings than to behold the sacred soil of Palestine free from heathen pollution, and occupied and defended by his faithful vassals, and no true son of the church could hesitate a moment to believe that it was his bounden duty to arm himself in the cause of his lord, and help to reinstate him in his heritage. Here, then, without having recourse to the romantic principle of chivalry, we have an adequate solution of the phenomenon of the first Crusade. Here we have a motive calculated to operate on the minds of all orders, equally effectual with men of piety, virtue, and wealth, like Godfrey of Bouillon and Stephen of Chartres, who looked for no temporal advantages, as with the meanest and most superstitious of the vassals and serfs who might be supposed to have only sought a refuge from misery and oppression by assuming the cross. We would not by any means be supposed to deny that many other causes and motives were in operation at the same time; but this we deem the grand one. This was the motive which gave dignity to and hallowed all others, and which affected the mind of every Crusader, be his rank or station in society what it might.

Pilgrimage then was esteemed a duty, and a powerful mean of removing guilt and appeasing the wrath of the Almighty; the spirit of the age was martial, and its religion, tinged by the ancient system of the North of Europe, was of the same character; the feudal principle was in its vigour, and extended even

M 2

to the relations of man with the deity; the rude and
barbarous Turks had usurped the heritage, the very
crown-lands, as we may say, of Jesus Christ, and insulted his servants, whose duty it plainly was to
punish them, and free the tomb of their lord;—the
natural result of such a state of circumstances and
opinion was the first Crusade.

CHAPTER II.

First Hospital at Jerusalem—Church of Santa Maria de Latina—Hospital of St. John—The Hospitallers—Origin of the Templars—Their original Poverty—They acquire Consideration—St. Bernard—His Character of the Templars —The Order approved of and confirmed by the Council of Troyes—Proofs of the Esteem in which they were held.

In consequence of the resort of pilgrims and traders from the West to Jerusalem it had been found necessary to build there, with the consent of the Saracens, *hospitia*, or places of entertainment for them during their abode in the holy city. For they could not, consistently with the religious animosity which prevailed between them and the Moslems, seek the hospitality of these last, and the Christians of the Greek church who dwelt in the Holy City, besides that they had no very friendly feeling towards their Catholic brethren, were loth to admit them into their houses, on account of the imprudent language and indecorous acts in which they were too frequently in the habit of indulging, and which were so likely to compromise their hosts with their Saracen lords. Accordingly the monk Bernard, who visited Jerusalem in the year 870, found there, in the valley of Jehoshaphat, near the church of the Holy Virgin, a hospital consisting of twelve mansions, for western pilgrims, which was in the possession of some gardens, vineyards, and corn-fields. It had also a good collection of books, the gift of Charlemagne. There was a market held in front of it, which was much resorted to, and every

dealer paid two pieces of gold to the overseer for permission to have a stand there.

In the 11th century, when the ardour of pilgrimage
was inflamed anew, there was a hospital within the
walls of Jerusalem for the use of the Latin pilgrims,
which had been erected by Italian traders, chiefly of
Amalfi.   Near this hospital, and within a stone's
cast of the church of the Holy Sepulchre, they erected,
with the permission of the Egyptian khalif, a church
dedicated to the Holy Virgin, which was usually called
Sta. Maria de Latina.   In this hospital abode an
abbot and a good number of monks, who were of the
Latin church, and followed the rule of St. Benedict.
They devoted themselves to the reception and entertainment of pilgrims, and gave alms to those who
were poor, or had been rifled by robbers, to enable
them to pay the tax required by the Moslems for
permission to visit the holy places.   When the number of the pilgrims became so great that the hospital
was incapable of receiving them all, the monks raised
another *hospitium* close by their church, with a chapel
dedicated to a canonized patriarch of Alexandria,
named St. John Eleëmon, or the Compassionate.
This new hospital had no income of its own ; the
monks and the pilgrims whom they received derived
their support from the bounty of the abbot of the
convent of the Holy Virgin, or from the alms of
pious Christians.

At the time when the army of the crusaders appeared before the walls of Jerusalem the Hospital of
St. John was presided over by Gerard, a native of
Provence, a man of great uprightness and of exemplary piety. His benevolence was of a truly Christian
character, and far transcended that of his age in
general ; for during the period of the siege he relieved all who applied to him for succour, and not
merely did the schismatic Greek share his bounty,

even the unbelieving Moslem was not repelled when
he implored his aid. When the city was taken,
numbers of the wounded pilgrims were received, and
their wounds tended in the hospital of St. John, and
the pious Duke Godfrey, on visiting them some days
afterwards, heard nothing but the praises of the good
Gerard and his monks.

Emboldened by the universal favour which they
enjoyed, Gerard and his companions expressed their
wish to separate themselves from the monastery of
Sta. Maria de Latina, and pursue their works of
charity alone and independently. Their desire met
no opposition: they drew up a rule for themselves,
to which they made a vow of obedience in presence
of the patriarch, and assumed as their dress a black
mantle with a white cross on the breast. The humility of these Hospitallers was extreme. They styled
the poor and the sick their lords and themselves their
servants; to them they were liberal and compassionate, to themselves rigid and austere. The finest
flour went to compose the food which they gave to
the sick and poor; what remained after they were
satisfied, mingled with clay, was the repast of the
monks.

As long as the brotherhood were poor they continued in obedience to the abbot of Sta. Maria de
Latina, and also paid tithes to the patriarch. But a
tide of wealth soon began to flow in upon them.
Duke Godfrey, enamoured of their virtue, bestowed
on them his lordship of Montboire, in Brabant, with
all its appurtenances; and his brother and successor,
Baldwin, gave them a share of all the booty taken
from the infidels. These examples were followed by
other Christian princes; so that within the space of
a very few years the Hospital of St. John was in
possession of numerous manors both in the East and
in Europe, which were placed under the manage-

ment of members of their society. The Hospitallers now coveted a total remission of all the burdens to which they were subject, and they found no difficulty in obtaining all that they desired. Pope Paschal II., in the year 1113, confirmed their rule, gave them permission, on the death of Gerard, to elect their own head, without the interference of any temporal or spiritual power whatever, freed them from the obligation of paying tithes to the patriarch, and confirmed all the donations made or to be made to them. The brotherhood of the Hospital was now greatly advanced in consideration, and reckoned among its members many gallant knights, who laid aside their arms, and devoted themselves to the humble office of ministering to the sick and needy.

The worthy Gerard died in the same year with King Baldwin I. (1118), and Raymond Dupuy, a knight of Dauphiné, who had become a brother of the order, was unanimously elected to succeed him in his office. Raymond, who was a man of great vigour and capacity, drew up a series of rules for the direction of the society, adapted to its present state of consequence and extent. From these rules it appears that the order of St. John admitted both the clergy and the laity among its members, and that both were alike bound to yield the most implicit obedience to the commands of their superior. Whether Raymond had any ulterior views is uncertain, but in the regulations which he made we cannot discern any traces of the spirit which afterwards animated the order of St. John.

Just, however, as Raymond had completed his regulations there sprang up a new society, with different maxims, whose example that of St. John found itself afterwards obliged to adopt and follow. The Holy Land was at that time in a very disturbed and unquiet state; the Egyptian power pressed it on the

south, the Turkish on the north and east; the Arab
tribes indulged in their usual predatory habits, and
infested it with hostile incursions; the Mussulman inhabitants were still numerous; the Syrian Christians
were ill affected towards the Latins, from whom they
frequently experienced the grossest ill-treatment;
the Latins were few and scattered. Hence the pilgrim was exposed to numerous dangers; peril beset
him on his way from the port at which he landed to
the Holy City, and new perils awaited him when he
visited the banks of the Jordan, or went to pluck his
branch of consecrated palm in the gardens of Jericho.
Many a pilgrim had lost his life on these occasions.

Viewing these evils, nine valiant and pious knights
resolved to form themselves into an association which
should unite the characters of the monk and the
knight, by devoting themselves to a life of chastity
and piety at the tomb of the Saviour, and by employing their swords in the protection of the pilgrims on
their visits to the holy places. They selected as their
patroness the *sweet* Mother of God (*La doce Mère
de Dieu*), and their resolution, according so perfectly
with the spirit of the Crusades, which combined piety
and valour, gained at once the warm approbation of
the king and the patriarch. In the presence of the
latter they took the three ordinary vows of chastity,
poverty, and obedience, and a fourth of fighting in-
cessantly in the cause of pilgrims and the Holy Land
against the heathen. They bound themselves to live
according to the rule of the canons of St. Augustine,
and elected as their first master Hugh de Payens.
The king, Baldwin II., assigned them a portion of
his palace for their abode, and he and his barons
contributed to their support. As the palace stood
close by the church and convent of the Temple, the
abbot and canons gave them a street leading from it
to the palace, for keeping their magazines and equip-

M 5

ments in, and hence they styled themselves the Soldiery of the Temple (*Militia Templi*), and Templars. They attracted such immediate consideration, owing in great part, no doubt, to the novelty of their plan, that the very year after their establishment (1120), Fulk, Count of Anjou, who was come on pilgrimage to Jerusalem, joined their society as a married brother, and on his return home annually remitted them thirty pounds of silver in furtherance of their pious objects, and the example of the Count of Anjou was followed by several other princes and nobles of the West.

The English historian, Brompton, who wrote in the 12th century, asserts that the founders of the order of the Temple had originally been members of that of St. John. We know not what degree of credit this may be entitled to *, but it is certain that there had been as yet nothing of a military character in this last, and that its assumption of such a character was an imitation of the society of the Temple; for, urged by the praise which they saw lavished on the Templars for their meritorious conduct, the Hospitallers resolved to add the task of protecting to that of tending and relieving pilgrims, and such of their members as were knights resumed their arms, joyful to employ them once more in the cause of God. The amplitude of their revenues enabled them to take a number of knights and footmen into their pay—a practice in which they had probably been preceded by the Templars, who thus employed the money which was remitted to them from Europe. But during the lifetime of Raymond Dupuy the order of the Hospital did not become completely a military one; he always

* The other writers of that century agree in the account given above. Brompton's authority has been preferred by some modern writers, who probably wished to pay their court to the order of Malta.

bore the simple title of director (*procurator*) of the
Hospital, and it was not till some time afterwards that
the head of the society was, like that of the Templars,
styled master, and led its troops to battle. At all
times the tendence of the poor and the sick formed a
part of the duties of the brethren of the Hospital, and
this was always a marked distinction between them
and the rival order of the Temple, whose only task
was that of fighting against the infidels.

During the first nine years which elapsed after the
institution of their order the knights of the Temple
lived in poverty, religiously devoting all the money
which was sent to them from Europe to the advantage
of the Holy Land, and the service of pilgrims. They
had no peculiar habit, their raiment was such as the

charity of the faithful bestowed upon them; and though knights, and engaged in constant warfare against the infidels, their poverty and moderation were such that Hugh des Payens and his companion, Godfrey, of St. Omer, had but one war-horse between them—a circumstance which they afterwards, in their brilliant period, commemorated by their seal, which represented two knights mounted on the one horse, a device chosen with a view to inculcating humility on the brethren, now beginning to wax haughty and insolent.

A chief cause of the extraordinary success of the first Crusaders had been the want of union among their enemies. The Saracens and Turks mutually hated each other, and would not combine for a common object, and the Turks were, moreover, at enmity among themselves, and one prince frequently allied himself with the Christians against another. But they were now beginning to perceive the necessity of union, and were becoming every day more formidable to their Christian neighbours. King Baldwin II., who had been a prisoner in their hands, made every effort when he had obtained his freedom to strengthen his kingdom, and, among other means for this purpose, he resolved to gain for the Templars, whose valour, humility, and single-mindedness were the theme of general applause, additional consideration, by obtaining from the Holy Father the confirmation of their order. With this view he despatched, in the year 1127, two of their members, named Andreas and Gundemar, to Rome, with this request to the Pope, to whom they were also to make a strong representation of the perilous state of the Holy Land. The king, moreover, furnished them with a letter of recommendation to St. Bernard, Abbot of Clairvaux, whose influence was then all-powerful in the Christian world, and who was nephew of the envoy Andreas.

Shortly afterwards Hugh de Payens himself arrived in Europe with five others of the brethren.

Nothing could be more advantageous to the new order than the favour and countenance of the illustrious Abbot of Clairvaux, who had been for some time past an admirer of its objects and deeds. Three years before this time he had written a letter to the Count of Champagne, who had entered the order of the Templars, praising the act as one of eminent merit in the sight of God. He now, on occasion of the visit of the Master *, wrote, at his request, an eloquent work, exhorting the brethren of the new order to persevere in their toilsome but highly laudable task of fighting against the tyranny of the heathens, and commending their piety to the attention of all the faithful, setting in strong opposition to the luxury of the knights of his time the modesty and simplicity of these holy warriors. He extolled the unlimited obedience of the Templars to their Master, both at home and in the field. " They go and come," says he, "at a sign from their Master ; they wear the clothing which he gives them, and ask neither food nor clothing from any one else ; they live cheerfully and temperately together, without wives and children, and, that nothing may be wanting for evangelical perfection, without property, in one house, endeavouring to preserve the unity of the spirit in the bond of peace, so that one heart and one soul would appear to dwell in them all. They never sit idle, or go about gaping after news. When they are resting from warfare against the infidels, a thing which rarely occurs, not to eat the bread of idleness, they employ themselves in repairing their clothes and arms, or do something which the command of the Master or the common need enjoins. There is with

* Wilken I. 28, gives 1135 as the year in which this piece was written.

them no respect of persons; the best, not the noblest, are the most highly regarded; they endeavour to anticipate one another in respect and to lighten each other's burdens.   No unseemly word or light mocking, no murmur or immoderate laughter, is let to pass unreproved, if any one should allow himself to indulge in such.   They avoid games of chess and tables; they are adverse to the chase, and equally so to hawking, in which others so much delight.   They hate all jugglers and mountebanks, all wanton songs and plays, as vanities and follies of this world.   They cut their hair in obedience to these words of the apostle, ' it is not seemly in a man to have long hair;' no one ever sees them dressed out; they are seldom ever washed; they are mostly to be seen with disordered hair, and covered with dust, brown from their corslets and the heat of the sun.   When they go forth to war they arm themselves within with faith, without with iron, but never adorn themselves with gold, wishing to excite fear in the enemy, and not the desire of booty.   They delight in horses which are strong and swift, not in such as are handsomely marked and richly caparisoned, wishing to inspire terror rather than admiration.   They go not impetuously and headlong into battle, but with care and foresight, peacefully, as the true children of Israel.   But as soon as the fight has begun, then they rush without delay on the foes, esteeming them but as sheep; and know no fear, even though they should be few, relying on the aid of the Lord of Sabaoth.   Hence one of them has often put a thousand, and two of them ten thousand, to flight. Thus they are, in union strange, at the same time gentler than lambs and grimmer than lions, so that one may doubt whether to call them monks or knights. But both names suit them, for theirs is the mildness of the monk and the valour of the knight.   What remains to be said but that this is the Lord's doing, and it is wonderful in our eyes? Such are they whom God has chosen out of the bravest in Israel, that, watchful and true, they may guard the holy sepulchre, armed with swords, and well skilled in war."

Though in these expressions of St. Bernard there may be perceived some marks of rhetorical exaggeration, they prove incontestibly the high character and sincere virtue of the founders of the society of the Templars, and that it was organized and regulated with none but worthy objects in view. They also offer, if such were required, an additional proof that the crusade was no emanation of chivalry; for those to whom St. Bernard throughout sets the Templars in opposition were the chivalry of the age.

This epistle of the Abbot of Clairvaux had been circulated, and every other just and honest mean employed to conciliate the public favour for the Templars, when, on the 31st January, 1128, the Master, Hugh de Payens, appeared before the council of Troyes, consisting of the Archbishops of Rheims and Sens, ten bishops, and a number of abbots, among whom was St. Bernard himself, and presided over by the Cardinal of Albano, the papal legate. The Master having given an account of the principles and exploits of the Templars, the assembled fathers approved of the new order, and gave them a new rule, containing their own previous regulations, with several additions drawn from that of the Benedictines, and chiefly relating to spiritual matters. The validity of this rule was made to depend on the approbation of it by the Holy Father and by the Patriarch of Jerusalem, neither of whom hesitated to confirm it. By the direction of the Pope Honorius, the synod appointed a white mantle to be the distinguishing dress of the brethren of the Temple, that of those of the Hospital being black. This mantle was plain, without any cross, and such it remained till the pontifi-

cate of Pope Eugenius III., who, in 1146, appointed
the Templars to wear a *red* cross on the breast, as a
symbol of the martyrdom to which they stood constantly exposed : the cross worn on their black mantles, by the knights of St. John, was, as we have seen*,
white. The order now assumed, or were assigned, a
peculiar banner, formed of cloth, striped black and
white, called in old French, *Bauseant*†, which word
became the battle-cry of the knights of the Temple,
and often struck terror into the hearts of the infidels.
It bore on it the ruddy cross of the order, and the
pious and humble inscription, *Non nobis, Domine,
non nobis, sed nomini tuo, da gloriam*, (Not to us,
O Lord, not to us, but to thy name give the glory !)

Several knights now assumed the habit of the
order, and in a progress which Hugh de Payens,
accompanied by some of the brethren, made through
France and England, he acquired for it universal
favour. He did not neglect the charge, committed to
him by the king of Jerusalem, of invoking aid for
the Holy Land, now so hard bested, and his exhortations were not without effect.   Fulk, Count of

---

* *See* p. 187. Sir W. Scott describes his Templar in Ivanhoe,
as wearing a white mantle with a *black* cross of eight points.
The original cross of the Hospitallers, we may observe, had
not eight points. That of the order of Malta was of this form.

† *Bauseant*, or *Bausant*, was, in old French, a piebald horse,
or a horse marked white and black. Ducange, Roquefort. The
word is still preserved with its original meaning in the Scotch
dialect, in the form *Bawsent :*
        " His honest, sonsie, baws'nt face
        Aye gat him friends in ilka place,"
says Burns, describing the "ploughman's collie," in his tale
of the " Twa Dogs ;" and in the Glossary, Dr. Currie explains
Baws'nt as meaning " having a white stripe down the face."
As, however, some notion of handsomeness or attractiveness of
appearance seems to be involved in the epithet, *Bauseant*, or
Beauséant, may possibly be merely an older form of the present
French word, *Bienséant.*

Anjou, now rejoined his Master and brethren; but as he had gotten an invitation to repair to Jerusalem, and espouse the only daughter of the King, he set out before them to the East.

Hugh de Payens would admit no knight into the order who did not terminate all his feuds and enmities, and amend his life. Thus, when a knight, named Hugh d'Amboise, who had oppressed the people of Marmoutier, and had refused obedience to the judicial sentence of the Count of Anjou, was desirous to enter the order, he refused to admit him to take the vows till he had given perfect satisfaction to those whom he had injured.

Honour and respect awaited the Templars wherever they appeared, and persons of all ranks were eager to do what might be grateful to them. When the Templar who came with the seal of Godfrey of St. Omer, as his credential to the governor of that place, to demand his goods which Godfrey had given the order, he met with a most favourable reception, not only from the governor, but from the bishop; and on their applying, as was necessary in this case, to the Count of Flanders and Alsatia, that prince was so far from throwing any impediments in the way, that, in a very short space of time, the buildings which had belonged to Godfrey were converted into a church and a temple-house. Many Flemish gentlemen followed the example of Godfrey, and bestowed a part of their property on the Templars. King Henry I. of England, who met and conversed with Hugh de Payens in Normandy, was so pleased with his account of the new order, that he presented him with many rich gifts, and gave him strong recommendations to the principal of the English barons. The Emperor Lothaire bestowed in 1130 on the order a large part of his patrimony of Supplinburg. The old Count Raymond Berenger, of Barcelona and Provence, weary of the world and of the toils of government, became a Templar, and took up his abode in the temple-house at Barcelona; and, as he could not go personally to combat the infidels in the Holy Land, he continually sent rich gifts to the brethren at Jerusalem, and he complied rigorously wlth all the other duties of the order.   In 1133 Alfonso, king of Arragon and Navarre, a valiant and warlike monarch, who had been victor in nine and twenty battles against the Moors, finding himself old and without children, made a will, by which he appointed the knights of the Temple and of the Hospital, together with the canons of the Holy Sepulchre, to be his joint-heirs, deeming, perhaps, that the most gallant defenders of the Holy Land would best prosecute his favourite object of breaking the power of the infidels.   The aged monarch fell the following year in the battle of Fraga, against the Moors; and, negligent of his disposition of the realm, the nobles of Arragon and Navarre met and chose sovereigns out of his family. The orders were not strong enough to assert their rights; and this instance, therefore, only serves to show the high degree of consideration to which they had so early attained.

Seal of the Templars.

CHAPTER III.

Return of the Templars to the East—Exoneration and Refutation of the Charge of a Connection with the Ismaïlites—Actions of the Templars—Crusade of Louis VII.—Siege of Ascalon—Sale of Nassir-ed-deen—Corruption of the Hospitallers—The bull, *Omne Datum Optimum*—Refusal of the Templars to march against Egypt—Murder of the Ismaïlite Envoy.

In the year 1129 Hugh de Payens, accompanied by 300 knights of the noblest families in Europe, who had become members of the order, and followed by a large train of pilgrims, returned to the Holy Land. Shortly after his arrival, the unlucky expedition to Damascus above narrated*, was undertaken, and the Templars formed a portion of the troops which marched, as they fancied, to take possession of that city. As has been observed, this is the first occasion on which we find the Christians in alliance and connection with the Ismaïlites; and as Hammer, the historian of the last, makes the grave charge against Hugh de Payens, of having modelled his new society on the plan of that deadly association, and of having been the chief planner and instigator of the treacherous attempt on Damascus, we will suspend the course of our narration, to discuss the probability of that opinion, though in so doing we must anticipate a little respecting the organisation of the Order of the Temple.

Hammer argues an identity between the two

* *See* p. 88.

orders, as he styles them, of the Ismaïlites and the
Templars, from the similarity of their dress, their internal organisation, and their secret doctrine ; and
as the two societies existed in the same country, and
that of the Ismaïlites was first instituted, he infers
that this was the original, and that of the Templars
the copy.

First, with respect to the outward habiliment, the
dress of the order. Nothing, as appears to us, can
be weaker than to lay any stress on so casual a circumstance as similarity of forms or colours, more
especially when a true and distinct cause for the
assumption of them on either side can be assigned.
The colour of the khalifs of the house of Ommiyah
was *white;* hence the house of Abbas, in their contest
with them, adopted *black,* as their distinguishing hue ;
and hence, when the Abbasides were in possession
of the supreme power, all those who, under pretence
of supporting the rights of the family of Ali, or on any
other pretext, raised the standard of revolt against
them, naturally selected *white,* as the sign of their
opposition. Hassan Sabah, therefore, only retained the
use of the colour which he found already established.
When he formed the institution of the Fedavee, or
the *Devoted to Death,* what more suitable mark of
distinction could he assign them than a *red* girdle or
cap, which indicated their readiness to spill their own
blood or that of others ? With respect to the Templars, the society of the Hospitallers was already
existing when Hugh de Payens and his companions
resolved to form themselves into a new association.
The mantle worn by the members of the Hospital
was *black :* what colour then was so natural for them
to adopt as its opposite, *white ?* and when, nearly
thirty years after their institution, the pope appointed
them or gave them permission to wear a cross on
their mantle, like the rival order, no colour could

present itself so well suited to those who daily and hourly exposed themselves to martyrdom, as that of blood, in which there was so much of what was symbolical.

With respect to internal organisation, it will, we apprehend, be always found that this is, for the most part, the growth of time and the product of circumstances, and is always nearly the same where these last are similar. The dominion of the Assassins extended over large tracks of country; hence arose the necessity of appointing lieutenants. In like manner, when the Templars got large possessions in the West and the East, they could not avoid, after the example of the Hospitallers, appointing persons to manage the affairs of the society in different countries. Hence, then, as the Ismaïlites had their Sheikh-al-Jebal, with his Dais-al-Kebir of Kuhistan and Syria, so the Templars had their Master and their Priors of different provinces. The resemblance is so far exact, but, as we see, easily accounted for. That which Hammer goes on to draw between the component parts of each society is altogether fanciful. To the Refeek, Fedavee and Lazik of the Ismaïlites, he sets as counterparts the knights, esquires, and serving-brethren of the Templars. It is needless to point out the arbitrariness of this comparison. The chaplains of the Templars, we may see, are omitted, and it was, perhaps, they who bore the greatest resemblance to the Refeeks, while neither knights nor esquires had the smallest similarity to the Fedavee.

As to a secret doctrine, we shall hereafter discuss the question whether the Templars had one or not. Here we shall only observe, that the proof of it, and of the ultimate object of the Templars being the same with that of the Ismaïlites, namely, the acquisition of independent power, adduced by Hammer, is by no means satisfactory. He says that it was the object of both societies to make themselves masters of the surrounding country, by the possession of fortresses and castles, and thus become formidable rivals to princes; and he sees, in the preceptories or houses of the Templars, the copies of the hill-forts of the Ismaïlites. That such was the design of this last society is quite apparent from the preceding part of our work; but what resemblance is there between such formidable places of defence as Alamoot and Lamseer, and the simple structures in which a few knights and their attendants dwelt in the different parts of Europe, and which were hardly, if at all, stronger than the ordinary baronial residences? and what resistance could the Temple of London or that of Paris offer to the royal strength, if put forth? Hammer has here again fallen into his usual error of arguing too hastily from accidental resemblances. The preceptories of the Templars were, as we shall show, the necessary consequence of the acquisition of property by the order, and had nothing hostile to society in their nature.

When we reflect on the character of the first crusaders, and particularly on that of the first Templars, and call to mind their piety, ignorance, and simplicity, nothing can appear more absurd than to ascribe to them secret philosophical doctrines of impiety, imbibed from those whose language they did not even understand, and whose religion and manners they held in abhorrence, and to suppose that the first poor knights of the Temple could have had visions of the future power of their order, and have looked forward to its dominion over the Christian world. " But this is a common mistake with ingenious men, who are for ever ascribing to the founders of empires, religions, and societies, that attribute of divinity which sees from the beginning the ultimate end, and forms all its plans and projects with a view to it. It is thus that some would fain persuade us that Mahommed, in his solitary cave at Mecca, saw clearly and distinctly the future triumphs of Islam, and its banners floating at the Pyrenees and the Oxus ; that Cromwell, when an obscure individual, already in fancy grasped the sceptre of England ; and that Loyola beheld the members of his order governing the consciences of kings, and ruling an empire in Paraguay. All such results are in fact the slow and gradual growth of time ; one step leads to another, till the individual or the society looks back with amazement to the feeble commencement."

The Templars and the Ismaïlites are mentioned together by history in only one more relation, that is, on occasion of the tribute paid to the former by the Syrian branch of the latter, and the murder of the Ismaïlite ambassador above related*. As this act was very probably committed by order of the Master of the Temple, who, it might be, doubted the ability or the future inclination of the king to pay the 3000 byzants a year, it testifies but little for any very friendly feeling between the Templars and the Ismaïlites. Yet Hammer opines that the 3000 byzants were paid, not as the tribute of the weaker to the stronger, but by way of pension for the secret services which the Templars were in the habit of rendering their cause; such, for example, as refusing on one occasion to join in the expedition against the khalif of Egypt, the great head of the society of the Assassins.

To narrate the various exploits of the knights of the Temple would be to write the history of the Crusades ; for, from the time that the order acquired strength and consistency, no action with the Infidels ever was fought in which the chivalry of the Temple

* Page 116.

did not bear a distinguished part. Their war-cry was
ever heard in the thickest of the fray, and rarely was
Bauseant seen to waver or give back in the conflict.
The knights of St. John fought with emulative valour; the example of the rival orders stimulated all
parts of the Christian army ; and to this influence
may be, in great measure, ascribed many of the most
wonderful triumphs of the Cross during the twelfth
century.

In the year 1147, when Pope Eugenius III. came
to Paris to arrange the proposed crusade with Louis
VII., both the pope and the king honoured with their
presence a general chapter of the order of the Temple, which was holden at that place. It was probably
on this occasion that the supreme pontiff conferred
on the order the important privilege of having mass
said once a year in places lying under interdict. The
newly-elected Master of the Temple, Eberhard de
Bar, and 130 knights, accompanied the king on his
march for the Holy Land ; and their valour and their
skill greatly contributed towards the preservation of
the crusading army in their unfortunate march through
Lesser Asia. The siege of Damascus, which was
undertaken after the arrival of the French and German kings in the Holy Land, miscarried, as is well
known, through treachery. The traitors were doubtless the *Pullani*, as the Latins of Syria were called,
who were at this time capable of every thing that is
bad. Some writers most unjustly charge the Templars with this guilt; but those who are the best
informed on the subject make no accusation against
them. The charge, however, while it shows the
power and consideration of the Templars at that
time, may be considered to prove also that they had
degenerated somewhat from their original virtue;
for otherwise it could never have been made.

The Christian army laid siege in 1153 to the town

of Ascalon, which the Saracens still held, and would have taken it, but for the cupidity of the Templars. A large heap of wood had been piled by the besiegers against a part of the wall, and set fire to. The wind blew strong towards the town during an entire night, carrying the smoke and heat into the town, so that the garrison was forced to retire from that quarter. The Christians fed the flames with pitch, oil, and other inflammable substances, and the wall next the pile, cracked by the heat, fell down, leaving a considerable breach. The army was preparing to enter at this opening when Bernard de Tremelai, the Master of the Temple, taking his station at it with his knights, refused all ingress. It was the law of war in those days, among the crusaders, that whatever house or spoil any one took when a town was stormed, became his property. The Templars, therefore, were eager to have the first choice; and having kept off all others, Tremelai, with forty of his knights, boldly entered a strongly-garrisoned town. But they paid the penalty of their rashness and cupidity; for the garrison surrounded and slew them all, and then closed up the breach.

One of the most disgraceful acts which stain the annals of the Templars occurred in the year 1155, when Bertrand de Blancford, whom William of Tyre calls a " pious and God-fearing man," was Master of the order. In a contest for the supreme power in Egypt, which the viziers, bearing the proud title of *Sultan*, exercised under the phantom-khalifs, Sultan Abbas, who had put to death the khalif his master, found himself obliged to fly from before the vengeance of the incensed people. With his harem, and his own and a great part of the royal treasures, he took his way through the Desert. A body of Christians, chiefly Templars, lay in wait for the fugitives near Ascalon; the resistance offered by the

N

Moslems was slight and ineffectual ; Abbas himself was either slain or fled, and his son Nassir-ed-deen and the treasures became the prize of the victors. The far larger part of the booty of course fell to the Templars; but this did not satisfy their avarice; and though Nassir-ed-deen had professed his desire to become a Christian, and had begun, by way of preparation for that change, to learn the Latin language they sold him to his father's enemies for 60,000 pieces of gold, and stood by to see him bound hand and foot, and placed in a sort of cage or iron-latticed sedan, on a camel, to be conducted to Egypt where a death by protracted torture awaited him.

The Hospitallers were at this time become as corrupt as the Templars; and in this same year, when the patriarch demanded from them the tithes which they were bound to pay him, they treated the demand with scorn; raised, to show their superior wealth, stately and lofty buildings, before the humble church of the Holy Sepulchre ; and whenever the patriarch entered it to exhort the people, or pronounce the absolution of sins, they rang, by order of their Master, the bells of the Hospital so loud, that, with the utmost efforts, he could not succeed in making himself heard. One day, when the congregation was assembled in the church, the Hospitallers rushed into it in arms, and shot arrows among them as if they were robbers or infidels. These arrows were collected and hung up on Mount Calvary, where Christ had been crucified, to the scandal of these recreant knights. On applying to the Pope Adrian IV. for redress, the Syrian clergy found him and his cardinals so prepossessed in favour of their enemies,—bribed by them, as was said,—that they had no chance of relief. The insolence of the Hospitallers became in consequence greater than ever.

In fact, as an extremely judicious writer* observes, valiantly as the knights of the spiritual orders fought against the heathens, and great as was their undoubted merit in the defence of the helpless pilgrims, it cannot be denied that these knights were, if not the original promoters, at least active participators in all the mischiefs which prevailed in the Holy Land, and that they were often led to a shameful dereliction of their duties, by avarice and thirst after booty.

The year 1162 is conspicuous in the annals of the Templars, as the date of the bull *Omne Datum Optimum*, the Magna Charta of the order, and the great key-stone of their power. On the death of Adrian IV. two rival popes were elected,—Alexander III. by the Sicilian,—Victor III. by the Imperial party. The Templars at first acknowledged the latter; but at a synod, held at Nazareth, in 1161, they took the side of his rival. Alexander, who came off victor, was not ungrateful; and on the 7th January, of the following year, the aforesaid bull was issued. By this document, which would almost appear to be the dictation of the order, the Templars were released from all spiritual obedience except to the Holy See; they were allowed to have peculiar burial-grounds at their houses, and to have chaplains of their own; they were freed from the obligation to pay tithes, and could, with the consent of the bishop, receive them. It was also prohibited to any one who had once entered the order, to leave it, unless it were to enter into a stricter one. These great privileges necessarily awakened the envy and enmity of the clergy against the Templars and the Hospitallers, which last were equally favoured by the pontiffs; but these artful prelates, who were now aiming at universal power, knew well the advantage which they might derive from attaching firmly to them

* Wilken Geschichte der Kreuzzüge, Vol. iii. pt. ii. p. 39.

these associations, which united the valour of the
knight to the obedience of the monk, whose members
were of the noblest families in Europe, and whose
possessions were extensive and spread over all parts
of the Christian world.

In 1167 occurred one of the few instances of cowardice, or rather, we might say, treachery, which the
annals of the Templars present.   Almeric, king of
Jerusalem, had committed to the Templars the charge
of guarding one of those strong fortified caverns
which were on the other side of the Jordan.   Here
they were besieged by the Turks. and, though the
king was hastening to their relief, they capitulated.
Almeric, incensed at their conduct, though he was a
great friend of the order, and particularly of the
Master, Philip of Naploos, instantly had twelve of the
cowardly or treacherous knights hanged, and he experienced no opposition whatever on the part of the
order.   Philip, we may observe, was the first Master
of the Temple who was a born Syrian ; but he appears
to have been a man of fair and honourable character.
He was lord of the fortresses of Krak and Montreal
in the Stony Arabia, which he had obtained with his
wife.   It was not till after her death that he became
a Templar.   After holding the dignity of Master for
three years he resigned it.   The cause of his resignation is unknown ; but he was highly honoured and
respected during the remainder of his life, and was
employed on various important occasions.

It was during the mastership of Philip of Naploos,
that King Almeric, at the instigation of the Master of
the Hospital, and in violation of a solemn treaty,
undertook an unprosperous expedition into Egypt.
The Templars loudly protested against this act of
perfidy, and refused to take any share in the war,
either, as William, the honest Archbishop of Tyre,
observes, " because it was against their conscience, or

because the Master of the rival order was the author and projector of it." The prelate seems to regard the more honourable as the true cause. Perhaps we should express ourselves correctly if we said that in this, as in many other cases, duty and prejudice happily combined, and the path which was the most agreeable was also the most honourable.

In the mastership of Ado of St. Amando, the successor of Philip of Naploos, occurred the treacherous murder of the Ismaïlite envoy above narrated *—an act which brought the Templars into great disrepute with pious Christians, as it was quite manifest that they preferred money to winning souls to Christ.

* Page 116.

CHAPTER IV.

Heroism of the Templars and Hospitallers—Battle of Hittin
—Crusade of Richard of England and Philip of France—
Corruption of the Order—Pope Innocent III. writes a Letter of Censure—Frederic II.—Great Slaughter of the Templars—Henry III. of England and the Templars—Power of
the Templars in Moravia—Slaughter of them by the Hospitallers—Fall of Acre.

THE fall of the Christian power in the East was
now fast approaching, and it was not a little hastened
by the enmity of the rival orders. The truth of the
old sentence, that the Deity deprives of sense those
whom he will destroy, was manifested on this as on
so many other similar occasions ; and while the great
and able Saladin was consolidating his power and
preparing for the accompl shment of the object which,
as a true Moslem, lay nearest his heart, the recovery
of the Holy City, discord, enmity, and animosity,
prevailed among those who should have been actuated
by one soul and by one spirit.

Yet the two orders of religious chivalry had not
derogated from their original valour, and the last
days of Jerusalem were illumined by some noble
feats of prowess. On the 1st of May, 1187, when
Malek-el-Afdal, the son of Saladin, was returning
from an expedition into the Holy Land, which he had
undertaken with the consent of the Count of Tripolis,
regent of the kingdom, the Masters of the Temple
and of the Hospital, having collected about 140
knights and 500 footmen, met the Mo lems, who were

7,000 in number, at the celebrated brook Kishon.
They immediately charged them with the utmost im-
petuosity ; the Turks, according to custom, turned
and fled ; the Christian knights pursued, leaving their
infantry unprotected.   Suddenly a large body of the
Turks emerged from a valley, and fell on and slaugh-
tered the footmen.   Their cries brought back the
knights to their aid, but, impeded by the narrowness
of the ground, they could neither lay their lances in
rest nor run their horses against the enemy, and all
fell beneath the weapons of the Turks, with the exception of the Master of the Temple and three of
his knights, who were saved by the fleetness of their
horses.   The Master of the Hospital was among the
slain.   In this unfortunate fight, James De Mailly,
the marshal of the Templars, and a Hospitaller,
named Henry, especially distinguished themselves.
After all their brave companions had been slain
around them, they still maintained the conflict; the
Turks, filled with admiration of their valour, repeatedly offered them quarter, but in vain ; and they fell
at last, overwhelmed with darts flung from a distance,
no one venturing to approach them.   The historian,
Vinisauf, tells us that De Mailly was mounted on a
white horse, which, joined with his relucent arms and
white mantle, made him appear to the infidels to be
St. George, and they exulted greatly in having slain
the tutelar saint of the Christians.   He adds, what
is not an unlikely circumstance, that the Turks covered
his body with dust, which they afterwards powdered
on their heads, thinking thereby to acquire some portion of his valour.

At the fatal battle of Hittin, where 30,000 Christians lost their lives, where the king and all his
princes became captives, and where the Latin power
in the East was broken for ever, the Master of the
Temple, Gerard of Ridefort, and several of his

knights and those of the Hospital, were among the captives. Saladin, who bore a particular hatred to the spiritual knights, would spare them on no condition but that of their renouncing their faith. To a man they gallantly refused; and, with the exception of the Master, the heads of all were struck off. Many who belonged not to the orders, smit with desire for the glory of martyrdom, cast the mantles of Templars around them, and went cheerfully to death as such. One Templar, named Nicolaus, evinced such joy and impatience for this glorious fate, that, according to the ideas of those times, heaven was believed to testify its approbation by a visible sign, and during three nights a celestial light illumined the unburied corpse of the Christian martyr.

It was indeed rare for a Templar to renounce his faith: prejudice, or honour, we may style it, or a better principle, always kept him steady in it, whatever the irregularities of his life might be. We recollect but one instance of a brother of the Temple abjuring his faith, and he was unhappily an English knight, named Robert of St. Albans. From some unassigned cause, he flung away the dress of his order, broke his vows, went over to Saladin, and became a Musselman. The sultan gave him one of his female relatives in marriage, and the recreant knight appeared before Jerusalemn at the head of an army of the infidels. He had promised to Saladin to reduce the Holy City; but her hour was not yet come; and after wasting all the country from Montroyal to Jericho with fire and sword, he was forced to retreat before the chivalry of Jerusalem, who came forth with the holy cross, and gave him a signal defeat. This event occurred in the year 1184; and the apostacy of this Templar caused extreme dismay among the Christians, and excited great ill-will against the order in general.

It had hitherto been the maxim of the order, not to redeem any of their members out of captivity with any higher ransom than a girdle, or a knife, or some other insignificant matter, acting in this on the same principle with the old Romans, who never redeemed prisoners. The Master, Ado de St. Amando, had died in captivity; but to redeem Gerard de Ridefort, no less a ransom was given than the city of Ascalon.—Gerard died of a wound received in battle the following year.

During the memorable crusade of Philip of France and Richard of England to the Holy Land, which their rivalry and animosity rendered utterly ineffectual, we find the Hospitallers on the side of the king of England, and of course the Templars the warm partizans of the king of France. Yet, when Richard was on his return to Europe, he sent for the Master of the Temple, and said to him, that he knew by many he was not loved, and that he ran great risk of his life on his way to his kingdom; he therefore besought him that he would permit him to assume the dress of the order, and send two of the brethren with him. The Master readily granted the request of so potent a monarch, and the king went on board in the habit of a Templar. It was probably on account of the known enmity of the order to him, that King Richard adopted this expedient, thinking that no one would ever suspect him of being with the Templars. His brother John, we may here observe, was, on the contrary, a great favourer of the order, to whom he gave Lundy Island, at the mouth of the Bristol Channel. Throughout his reign, this odious prince attached himself to the Templars as the faithful servants of his lord the pope, reckoning on their aid against his gallant barons, who would not leave the liberties of the nation at the feet of a faithless tyrant. It was now very much the custom for monarchs to deposit their treasures in the Temple houses; and in the year 1213 we find King John demanding 20,000 marks which he had committed to the Templars to keep. We meet with no instance of breach of trust on the part of the knights.

The Templars shared in the common dishonesty of the church with respect to false miracles, and they felt no scruple at augmenting their wealth by deceptions calculated to impose on the ignorance and zeal of the laity. In the year 1204 it was given out that an image of the Virgin, in a convent not far from Damascus, had become clothed with flesh, and that there issued from its breasts a kind of juice or liquor of wondrous efficacy in removing the sins of pious pilgrims. As the place was distant, and the road beset with danger, the knights of the Temple took upon themselves the task of fetching the mirific fluid to the part of the coast still held by the Latins, and accommodating pilgrims with it, and the coffers of the order were largely replenished by this pious traffic.

Though, like all other proprietors in the Holy Land, the order of the Temple had been losers in consequence of the conquest of it by Saladin, their possessions in the West were so extensive that they hardly felt the loss. At this very time we find the number of their possessions of various kinds in Europe stated at 7050, principally situated in France and in England. Their arrogance and luxury naturally kept pace with their wealth; and, though writers of the twelfth century, and even the Troubadours— the satirists of the age—always speak of the knights of the Temple with honour, there was a secret dislike of them gaining ground, especially with the clergy, in consequence of the great privileges granted to them by the bull *Omne Datum Optimum*, and the insolent manner in which these privileges were exercised.

Accordingly we find, in the year 1208, the grea.

Innocent III. the most ambitious of popes, and one who was a steady friend to the order, under the necessity of passing the first public censure of them, and endeavouring to set, by authority, a limit to their excesses. In his epistle to the Master on this occasion, the holy father says that they abused the privilege of having mass celebrated in places which were under interdict, by causing their churches to be thrown open, and mass to be said every day, with loud ringing of bells, bearing the cross of Christ on their breast, but not caring to follow his doctrines, who forbids to give offence to any of the little ones who believe on him. He goes on to state that, following the doctrines of demons, they affixed the cross of their order on the breast of (i. e. *affiliated*) every kind of scoundrel, asserting that whoever, by paying two or three pence a year, became one of their fraternity, could not, even though interdicted, be deprived of Christian burial; and that hence, known adulterers, usurers, and others who were lying under sentence of interdict, were honourably interred in their cemeteries; " and thus they themselves, being captive to the devil, cease not to make captive the souls of the faithful, seeking to make alive those whom they know to be dead." The pontiff laments, that instead of, like religious men, using the world for the sake of God, they employed their religious character as a means of indulging in the pleasures of the world. Though, on account of these and such abuses, they deserved to be deprived of the privileges which had been conferred on them, the holy father will not proceed to extremity, relying on the exertions of the Master to effect a reformation.

In this epistle we have all the charges, which, as will hereafter appear, could be at any time brought with justice against the order, whose corruption pro-

ceeded in the ordinary course of human nature, and
no otherwise,—privileges and exemptions producing
insolence and assumption, and wealth generating
luxury and relaxation of morals.　It was the lavish
generosity of popes, princes, and nobles, that caused
the ruin of the Templars.

The Templars bore a distinguished part in the expedition to Egypt and siege of Damietta, in 1219, as
the chief commander on that occasion was the papal
legate, whose conduct, under show of obedience,
they chiefly directed.　But when, in 1228, the Emperor Frederic II., then under the sentence of the
church, undertook the crusade which he had vowed,
he found nothing but opposition and treachery from
these staunch adherents of the pope.　Considering
the spirit of the age, their opposition is, perhaps, not
so much to be blamed ; but no principle will excuse
the act of their writing to inform the Egyptian sultan
of the plans of the emperor.　The generous Moslem,
instead of taking advantage of this treachery, sent
the letter to Frederic, to the confusion of its authors.
Frederic checked his indignation at the time, but on
his return to Europe he took his satisfaction on those
who were most guilty, and he seized the property of
the order in Sicily and his Italian dominions.　Though
he was excommunicated again for so doing, Frederic
persisted in his enmity both to them and the Hospitallers ; and though, perhaps, the least given to superstition and illiberality of any man of his age, he
did not disdain to make friendly intercourse with
the Moslems a serious charge against them.　" The
haughty religion of the Templars," writes he, " reared
on the pleasures of the native barons of the land,
waxes wanton..... We know, on good authority, that
sultans and their trains are received with pompous
alacrity within the gates of the Temple, and that the

Templars suffer them to celebrate secular plays, and to perform their superstitious rites with invocation of Mahommet."

The hostility between the Templars and the Hospitallers still continued, though the Christian power was now nearly restricted to the walls of Acre. The Templars were in alliance with the prince of Damascus: the Hospitallers were the friends of the sultan of Egypt. The Templars extended their enmity against the emperor to the Teutonic knights, whom they deprived of their possessions in Syria. The appearance of a new enemy, however, brought concord for a time among them. The Turks of Khaurizm, on the east of the Caspian, were now in flight before the hordes of the Mongols, and 20,000 of their horsemen burst into the Holy Land. They took and plundered Jerusalem, which was unfortified and open, and then united themselves with the troops of Egypt. The Christians applied to the prince of Damascus for aid, who forthwith sent the required troops, and their combined forces went in quest of the foes. In the battle the Templars and the militia occupied the centre; the Hospitallers were posted on the left wing, the light horse on the right. The battle lasted two days, and ended in the total defeat of the Christians, a result which is ascribed, though probably with injustice, to the treachery of the Damascenes. The Master of the Temple and the whole chapter, with the knights, in all 300, were slain; only four knights and fourteen esquires escaped.

The improvident and needy Henry III. of England, in general such a dutiful son of the holy father, who, for a share of the spoil, usually aided him in the pious work of robbing his subjects, summoned courage in 1252 to speak of seizing some of the property of the church and the military orders. " You prelates and religious," said he, " especially you

o

Templars and Hospitallers, have so many liberties
and charters, that your enormous possessions make
you rave with pride and haughtiness.   What was
imprudently given, must be therefore prudently revoked ; and what was inconsiderately bestowed must
be considerately recalled.... I will break this and
other charters which my predecessors and myself have
rashly granted." But the prior of the Templars immediately replied, "What sayest thou, O king ? Far
be it that thy mouth should utter so disagreeable and
silly a word.   So long as thou dost exercise justice
thou wilt reign ; but if thou infringe it, thou wilt
cease to be a king !" These bold words appear to have
checked the feeble king, who next year besought the
two orders to become his security for a large sum of
money which he owed.   They refused his request,
and Henry thenceforth did them all the injury in his
power.

There occurred an event in Moravia in 1252, which
may serve to show the power of the order in Europe.
A nobleman, named Vratislaf, who had been obliged
to fly from that country, became a Templar in France.
He made over all his property, among which was
the castle of Eichhorn in Moravia, to the order.
But his elder brother, Burian, took possession of his
property, as having fallen to himself as head of
the family.   King Winzel, on being applied to, decided in favour of the order.   Burian, however, still
kept possession.   The next year the Templars collected some thousands of men, and marched, under
the command of their Great Prior, to take the castle.
Burian, assembling 6000 men, 900 of whom he
placed in the castle, advanced to give them battle.
The engagement was bloody ; 1700 men, among
them the Great Prior of the Templars, lay slain, when
night terminated the conflict.   A truce was made for
three days, at the end of which Burian and his men

were driven into the castle, which they defended bravely, till king Attocar sent to threaten them with his wrath if they did not give it up. Burian surrendered it, and Vratislaf, returning to Moravia, became Prior of Eichhorn, in which thirty Templars took up their abode.

Though the Templars were so extremely numerous in Europe, they were little disposed to go out to the East to encounter toil and danger, in the performance of their duties. They preferred living in ease and luxury on their rich possessions in the West; and the members of the chapter alone, with a few knights, and other persons attached to the order, abode in Syria. It would even seem that the heads of the society were meditating a final retreat from the East, where they probably saw that nothing of permanent advantage was to be achieved. The Hospitallers, on the other hand, whatever may have been the cause, appear to have been more zealous in their calling, and to have had a greater number of their members in Syria; and it is, probably, to this cause, that we are to assign the total defeat which they were enabled to give their rivals in 1259: for the animosity between the orders had come to such a height, that, in this year, they came to open war. A bloody battle was fought, in which the Templars were defeated, when, such was the bitterness of their enmity, that the victors made no prisoners, but cut to pieces every Templar who fell into their hands, and scarce a Templar remained to carry the intelligence to Europe.

From this period till the capture of Acre and final destruction of the Latin power in the East in 1291, after a continuance of nearly two centuries, the annals of the Templars are bare of events. The rivalry between them and the other orders still continued; and in the opinion of some historians, it was their jealousy that hastened the fall of that last remnant of the Christian dominion in the East. Not more than ten knights of the Temple escaped in the storm of the town, and these, with the remnants of the other orders, and the garrison, sought a retreat in Cyprus.

We have now traced the history of the order from its institution to within a few years of the period of its suppression. Of this most important event we shall delay the consideration for some time, and shall occupy the intervening space with an account of the internal organisation of the society, its officers, its wealth, and various possessions. This will, we trust, prove no slight contribution to our knowledge of one of the most curious portions of the history of the world—that of the middle ages—and gratify the reader by the display of manners and institutions which have long since passed away*.

* The organisation and the rules of the Hospitallers were similar to those of the Templars; but as that order existed down to modern times, the rules, &c., given by Vertot, contain a great number of modern additions.

CHAPTER V.

Classes of the Templars—The Knights—Their Qualifications
—Mode of Reception—Dress and Arms of the Knight—
Mode of Burial—The Chaplains—Mode of Reception—
Dress—Duties and Privileges—The Serving-Brethren—
Mode of Reception—Their Duties—The Affiliated—Causes
and Advantages of Affiliation—The Donates and Oblates.

THE founders of the order of the Templars were,
as we have seen, knights; and they were the first
who conceived the novel idea, and happy one, as we
may call it in accordance with the sentiments of
those times, of uniting in the same person the two
characters held in highest estimation—the knight
and the monk. The latter added sanctity to the former, the former gave dignity and consideration to
the latter, in the eyes of a martial generation. Hence,
the Templar naturally regarded himself as the first
of men; and the proudest nobles of the Christian
world esteemed it an honour to belong to the order.
The knights were, therefore, the strength, the flower,
the ornament of the society.

The order of the Templars, when it was fully developed, consisted not of *degrees*, but of distinct and
separate *classes*. These were the knights, the chaplains, and the serving-brethren; to which may be
added the affiliated, the donates, and the oblates, or
persons attached to the order without taking the
vows.

I. THE KNIGHTS.—Whoever presented himself to
be received as a knight of the order must solemnly

aver that he was sprung from a knightly family, and
that his father was or might have been a knight. He
was further to prove, that he was born in lawful wedlock, for, like the church in general, the Templars
excluded bastards from their society. In this rule
there was prudence, though, possibly, it was merely
established in accordance with the ideas of the time;
for, had a king of France or an emperor of Germany
been able to get his natural child into the order, and
should he then have been chosen Master of it, as he
probably would, it might have lost its independence,
and become the mere tool of the monarch. The candidate was, moreover, to declare that he was free from
all previous obligations; that he was neither married
nor betrothed; had not made any vows, or received
any consecration in another order; and that he was
not involved in debt. He had finally to declare himself to be of a sound and healthy constitution, and free
from disease. When the order was grown great and
powerful, and candidates for admission were numerous
and of the highest families, it became the custom to
require the payment of a large fee on admission.

It was necessary that the candidate for admission
among the knights of the Temple should already be a
a knight; for as knighthood was a secular honour, the
order would have regarded it as derogating from its
dignity if any of its members were to receive it. The
Hospitallers and Teutonic knights thought differently,
and with them the aspirant was knighted on his admission. If the candidate Templar, therefore, had not
been knighted, he was obliged to receive knighthood,
in the usual manner, from a secular knight, or a
bishop, previous to taking his vows.

A noviciate forms an essential and reasonable part
of the course of admission into the spiritual orders in
general; for it is but right that a person should become, in some measure, acquainted with the rules and

duties of a society before he enters it. But, though the original rule of the Templars enjoined a noviciate, it was totally neglected in practice; a matter which was afterwards made one of the charges against the order. Perhaps there was in their case little necessity for this preparatory process; the Templars were so much in the world, and those who joined them had been in general so frequently among them, and were consequently so well acquainted with their mode of life, that they hardly required any such preliminary discipline to familiarize them with their duties. The neglect of the practice at the same time gave the Templars an advantage over the rival orders who enjoined it; for a young nobleman would, in all likelihood, feel most disposed to join the society into which he could be admitted at once; and perhaps no small part of the corruption of the Templars, in which they undoubtedly surpassed their rivals, may be ascribed to the facility which was thus afforded to unworthy persons entering among them.

With respect to the age at which persons were admitted, it is plain, from the previously required reception of knighthood, that it must have been that of adolescence or manhood. All that is said by the statutes is, that no child could be received; and that the parents or relatives of a child destined to be a member of the order, should keep and breed him till *he could manfully and with armed hand extirpate the enemies of Christ out of the land.* This formed a marked distinction between the Templars and the mere religious orders, who, even at the present day, we believe, admit children, taking the charge of their rearing and education; whereas, children could only be destined to the order of the Temple, and could not be presented for admission, till able to bear arms, that is, usually in the twenty-first year of their age.

The reception of a knight took place in one of the chapels of the order, in presence of the assembled chapter. It was secret, not even the relatives of the candidate being allowed to be present. The ceremony commenced by the Master * or prior, who presided, saying, " Beloved brethren, ye see that the majority are agreed to receive this man as a brother. If there be any among you who knows any thing of him, on account of which he cannot lawfully become a brother, let him say it; for it is better that this should be signified beforehand than after he is brought before us."

The aspirant, if no objection was made, was then led into a chamber near the chapter-room; and two or three reputable knights of the oldest in the house were sent to lay before him what it was needful for him to know. They commenced by saying, " Brother, are you desirous of being associated to the order?" If he replied in the affirmative, they stated to him the whole rigour of the order. Should he reply that he was willing to endure everything for God's sake, and to be all his life long the servant and slave of the order, they asked him if he had a wife or was betrothed? if he had made profession or vows in any other order? if he owed to any man in the world more than he could pay? if he was of sound body, and had no secret infirmity, and if he was the servant of any one? Should his answers be in the negative, the brethren went back to the chapter and informed the Master or his representative of the result of the examination. The latter then asked once more, if any one knew any thing to the contrary. If all were silent, he said " Are you willing that he should be brought in in God's name?" The knights then

* When we use the word " Master," we would always be understood to mean the Master or his representative.

said, " Let him be brought in in God's name."
Those who had been already with him then went out
again, and asked him if he persisted in his resolution.
If he said that he did, they instructed him in what
he was to do when suing for admission.   They then
led him back to the chapter, where, casting himself
on his knees, with folded hands, before the receptor,
he said, " Sir, I am come, before God, and before
you and the brethren, and pray and beseech you, for
the sake of God and our dear Lady, to admit me into
your society, and the good deeds of the order, as one
who will be, all his life long, the servant and slave of
the order."   The receptor then replied, " Beloved
brother, you are desirous of a great matter, for you
see nothing but the outward shell of our order.   It
it is only the outward shell when you see that we have
fine horses and rich caparisons, that we eat and drink
well, and are splendidly clothed.   From this you conclude that you will be well off with us.   But you
know not the rigorous maxims which are in our interior.   For it is a hard matter for you, who are your
own master, to become the servant of another.   You
will hardly be able to perform, in future, what you
wish yourself.   For when you may wish to be on this
side of the sea, you will be sent to the other side;
when you will wish to be in Acre, you will be sent to
the district of Antioch, to Tripolis, or to Armenia ; or
you will be sent to Apulia, to Sicily, or to Lombardy,
or to Burgundy, France, England, or any other
country where we have houses and possessions.   When
you will wish to sleep you will be ordered to watch ;
when you will wish to watch, then you will be ordereo
to go to bed ; when you will wish to eat, then you
will be ordered to do something else.   And as both
we and you might suffer great inconvenience from
whta you have, mayhap, concealed from us, look here

on the holy Evangelists and the word of God, and answer the truth to the questions which we shall put to you ;. for if you lie you will be perjured, and may be expelled the order, from which God keep you!"

He was now asked over again, by the receptor, the same questions as before; and, moreover, if he had made any simoniacal contract with a Templar or any other for admission. If his answers proved satisfactory, the receptor proceeded, " Beloved brother, take good care that you have spoken the truth to us; for should you have spoken false in any one point, you might be put out of the order, from which God keep you! Now, beloved brother, attend strictly to what we shall say unto you. Do you promise to God, and our dear Lady Mary, to be, all your life long, obedient to the Master of the Temple, and to the prior who shall be set over you?"

" Yea, Sir, with the help of God!"

" Do you promise to God, and our dear Lady Mary, to live chaste of your body all your life long?"

" Yea, Sir, with the help of God!"

" Do you promise to God, and our dear Lady Mary, to observe, all your life long, the laudable manners and customs of our order, both those which are already in use, and those which the Master and knights may add?"

" Yea, Sir, with the help of God!"

" Do you promise to God, and our dear Lady Mary, that you will, with the strength and powers which God has bestowed on you, help, as long as you live, to conquer the Holy Land of Jerusalem; and that you will, with all your strength, aid to keep and guard that which the Christians possess?"

" Yea, Sir, with the help of God!"

" Do you promise to God, and our dear Lady Mary, never to hold this order for stronger or weaker, for better or worse, than with permission of the Master, or of the chapter which has the authority *?"

" Yea, Sir, with the help of God !"

" Do you finally promise to God, and our dear Lady Mary, never to be present when a Christian is unjustly and unlawfully despoiled of his heritage, and that you will never, by counsel or by act, take part therein ?"

" Yea, Sir, with the help of God !"

" In the name, then, of God, and our dear Lady Mary, and in the name of St. Peter of Rome, and of our father the pope, and in the name of all the brethren of the Temple, we receive to all the good works of the order which have been performed from the beginning, and shall be performed to the end, you, your father, your mother, and all of your family whom you will let have share therein. In like manner do you receive us to all the good works which you have performed and shall perform. We assure you of bread and water, and the poor clothing of the order, and labour and toil enow."

The Master then took the distinguishing habit of the order, namely, the white mantle with the red cross, and putting it about the neck of the candidate, clasped it firmly. The chaplain then repeated the 132d psalm, *Ecce quam bonum*, and the prayer of the Holy Ghost, *Deus qui corda fidelium*, and each brother repeated a *Pater noster*. The Master and the chaplain then kissed him on the mouth; and he sat down before the Master, who delivered to him a discourse, of which the following is the substance.

He was not to strike or wound any Christian ; not to swear ; not to receive any service or attendance from a woman without the permission of his superiors; not on any account to kiss a woman, even if

---

* That is, never to quit the order.

she was his mother or his sister; to hold no child at
the baptismal font, or be a god-father; to abuse no
man or call him foul names; but to be always courteous
and polite. He was to sleep in a linen shirt, drawers,
and hose, and girded with a small girdle. He was
to attend divine service punctually, and at table he
was to commence and conclude with prayer; during
the meal he was to preserve silence. When the Master died, he was, be he where he might, to repeat 200
Pater nosters for the repose of his soul.

Each knight was supplied with clothes, arms, and
equipments, out of the funds of the order. His dress
was a long white tunic, nearly resembling that of
priests in shape, with a red cross on the back and
front of it; his girdle was under this, over his linen
shirt. Over all he wore his white mantle with its red
cross of four arms (the under one being the longest,
so that it resembled that on which the Saviour suffered)
on the left breast. His head was covered by a cap or
a hood attached to his mantle. His arms were shield,
sword, lance, and mace; and, owing to the heat of
the East, and the necessity of activity in combats
with the Turks and Saracens, his arms and equipments in general were lighter than those used by the
secular knights. He was allowed three horses and
an esquire, who was either a serving-brother of the
order or some layman who was hired for the purpose.
At times this office was performed by youths of noble
birth, whom their parents and relatives gladly placed
in the service of distinguished knights of the Temple, that they might have an opportunity of acquiring
the knightly virtues; and these often became afterwards members of the order.

When a knight had become, from age or wounds,
incapable of service, he took up his abode in one of
the temple-houses, where he lived in ease, and was
treated with the utmost respect and consideration.

Costume of Knight Templar.

These emeriti knights are frequently mentioned under the name of *Prodomes* (*Good men*); they were present at all deliberations of importance; and their experience and knowledge of the rules of the order were highly prized and attended to.

When the Templar died, he was placed in a coffin in his habit, and with his legs crossed, and thus buried. Masses were said for his soul; his arms and clothes were partly given back to the marshal or draper of the order—partly distributed among the poor.

II. THE CHAPLAINS.—The order of the Templars, being purely military in its commencement, consisted then solely of laymen. That of the Hospital, on the contrary, on account of its office of attending the sick, had, necessarily, priests in it from its origin. This advantage of the latter society excited the jealousy of the Templars, and they were urgent with the popes to be allowed a similar privilege. But the pontiffs were loth to give offence to the oriental prelates, already displeased at the exemption from their control granted in this case to the Hospitallers; and it was not till the year 1162, that is, four years after the founding of the order, when their great favourer, Alexander III., occupied the papal throne, that the Templars attained their object.

The bull, *Omne Datum Optimum*, issued on this occasion, gave permission to the Templars to receive into their houses spiritual persons, in all countries, who were not bound by previous vows. If they were clergy of the vicinity, they were to ask them of the bishop; and if he refused his consent, they were empowered, by the bull, to receive them without it. The clergy of the Temple were to perform a noviciate of a year—a practice which, as in the case of the knights, was dispensed with in the days of the power and corruption of the order. The reception of the clergy was the same as that of the knights, with the omission

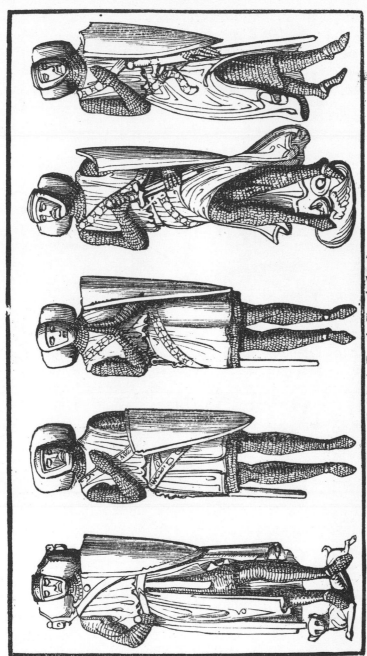

Knights in Temple Church, London.

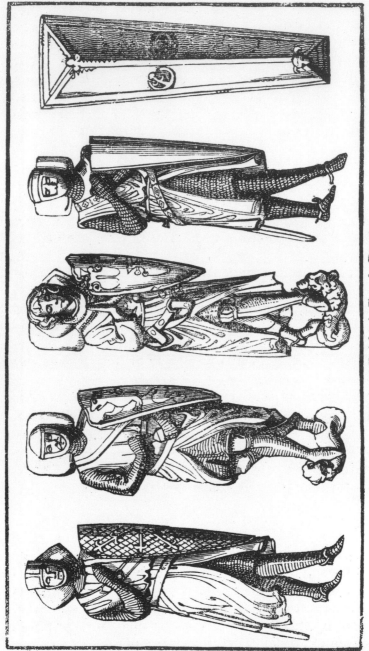

Effigies of Knights in Temple Church.

of such questions as did not apply to them. They were only required to take the three vows of poverty, chastity, and obedience. The ritual of their reception was in Latin, and was almost precisely the same with that of the Benedictines. Like that of the knights, their reception was secret. When the psalms had been sung the Master put on the recipient the dress of the order and the girdle, and, if he was a priest, the cap called *baret*.

The habit of the chaplains of the order was a white close-fitting tunic, with a red cross on the left breast. Though, according to the statutes, they were to have the best clothes in the order, they were not permitted to assume the white mantle as long as they were mere priests. But should one of them, as was not unfrequently the case, arrive at the episcopal dignity, he was, if desirous of it, cheerfully granted that privilege. It was a further distinction between the knights and the chaplains, that the former wore their beards, while the latter were close-shaven. The chaplains were also to wear gloves, *out of respect to the body of the Lord.*

All who had received the *first tonsure* were eligible to the office of chaplain to the order. When those who were only sub-deacons and deacons were to be raised to the rank of priests, the Master or his deputy sent them with letters dimissory to a bishop of the vicinity, who was bound to confer the required order.

The clergy were, like all other members of the order, bound to obey the Master and the chapter. The Master and the chief officers of the order had always chaplains in their train to celebrate mass and other religious offices, as also to act as secretaries, the knights being in general as illiterate as their secular brethren. It was by this last office that the chaplains acquired their chief influence in the society; mind and superior knowledge vindicating, as they always do, their natural rights. For though it was specially provided that the clergy should take no share in the government of the society without being invited thereto by their superiors, the opinion of the secretary was naturally taken in general, and if he was a man of sense and talent, it was most commonly followed*.

The duties of the clergy of the order were nearly the same as those of monks in general. They performed all religious offices, and officiated at all the ceremonies of the order, such as the admission of members, the installation of a Master, &c. Their privileges were very unimportant; they had merely the best clothes, sat next the Master in the chapter and in the refectory, and were first served at table; when they committed any offence, they were also more lightly punished than others. They could, however, if it so pleased the heads of the order, arrive at high rank in it; and we find that they were not unfrequently among the preceptors. The attorney-general of the order at Rome, who was always a person of considerable importance, was most probably a priest of the order; at least we know that Peter de Bononia, the last of them, was such.

It is worthy of notice, that even in the most flourishing period of the order it never had a sufficient number of chaplains, and was always obliged to have recourse to the ministry of secular priests. The causes of this were probably the circumstance of the order having attained its full form and consistency long before the clergy formed a part of it, and they consequently had not an opportunity of arranging it so as

* This influence of the clergy excited the spleen of the knights. Gerard de Caux, in his examination hereafter to be noticed, said, " The aged men of the order were unanimous in maintaining that the order had gained nothing in *internal goodness* by the admission of learned members."

to give themselves their due share of power and importance. It must have been galling to the pride of those who were used to rule, obeying only their spiritual superiors, to find themselves subject to the command of mere laymen, as they esteemed the knights of the order. Further, though they shared in the good things of the order and enjoyed the advantage of the consideration in which it stood, yet they had no dignities to look forward to; whereas an entrance into a Benedictine order held out to the ambitious a prospect of rich priories, abbacies, and bishoprics, and, at the least, a voice in the chapter. It may well be supposed that the pride of the knights of the Temple refused to admit into their society such persons as those who afterwards joined the mendicant orders—peasants and others who preferred a life of ease and idleness to the labours of the plough and the workshop. The number consequently of those who presented themselves for admission was small. But the knights felt no disadvantage thereby; enow of secular priests were to be had, who were willing to have the master of the Temple as their ordinary, and to share in the good things of the order, and as neither party was bound to the other, they could easily part if they disagreed.

III. THE SERVING-BRETHREN. The order, consisting at first of only knights and men of noble birth, had no serving-brethren in it. The knights probably found esquires for a limited time among those who fought under their banner and received their pay. The Hospitallers seem to have set the example of introducing into the order the class of serving-brethren, which is not to be found with the Templars till some time after the council of Troyes. The advantage of this alteration was very apparent. Hitherto only knights and nobles were interested in the fate of the society to which their relatives belonged; the regards of burghers and traders would now be obtained by the formation of this class, to admission into which their sons and brothers were eligible. They felt themselves honoured by their relatives coming into contact with knights, and were therefore liberal in the admission-fee and in other contributions to the *quêtes* of the order.

We should be wrong in supposing the serving-brethren to have been all persons of mean birth. The high consideration in which the order stood induced many men of wealth, talent, and valour, but who were not of noble birth, to join it. We thus find among the serving-brethren William of Arteblay, almoner to the king of France; Radulf de Gisi, collector of the taxes in Champagne; John de Folkay, an eminent lawyer. Bartholomew Bartholet gave property to the amount of 1,000 *livres Tournois* to be admitted; William of Liege gave 200 *livres Tournois* a year. The serving-brother, indeed, could never arrive at the dignity of knight (for which he was disqualified by birth), and consequently never exercise any of the higher offices of the order, but in other respects he enjoyed the same advantages and privileges as the knights and priests.

The reception of the serving-brethren was the same as that of the two higher classes, the necessary difference being made in the questions which were asked. As the order would receive no slave into their body, the candidate was required to aver that he was a free-born man: he was moreover obliged to declare that he was not a knight. This last condition may cause surprise, but it was probably justified by experience, as it is not unlikely that evil may have been felt or apprehended from men of noble birth, out of humility, or by way of atoning for the sins of their youth, or from some other of the causes which might operate on the minds of superstitious men, or even from poverty, if, as is likely, the admission-fee was lower for a serving-brother than for a knight, concealing their birth, and entering the order as serving-brethren. As the more disagreeable duties of the order probably fell to their share, the general duties and obligations were laid before them in stronger and more explicit terms than were thought necessary in the case of knights and priests.

In the times of the poverty of the order, the clothing of the serving-brethren was the cast-off garments of the knights. But this custom did not long continue, and as some abuses arose from all the members of the order being clad in white, the serving-brethren were appointed to wear black or brown kirtles, with the red cross upon them, to indicate that they belonged to the order. In battle, their arms were nearly the same as those of the knights, but of a lighter kind, as they had frequently to jump down from their horses, and fight on foot. A serving-brother was allowed but one horse by the order, but the Master was empowered to lend him another if he thought it expedient, which horse was to be afterwards returned.

The serving-brethren were originally all of one kind; they fought in the field; they performed the menial offices in the houses of the order; but, in after-times, we find them divided into two classes— the brethren-in-arms (*Frères servons des armes*), and the handicraft-brethren (*Frères servons des mestiers*). These last, who were the least esteemed of the two, dwelt in the houses and on the lands of the order, exercising their various trades, or looking after the property of the society. We read in the statutes of the smiths and bakers of the order, and we hear of *preceptors* (as was the phrase) of the mares, cows, swine, &c. of the order. These handicraft-brethren practised the usual religious duties of the order, and were even allowed to be present at chapters. The farrier, who was also armourer, enjoyed a much higher degree of consideration than the other handicraft-brethren, for this profession was highly prized by the martial generation of the middle ages*.

The other class were more highly regarded. The knights associated with them on a footing of equality. They ate in the same refectory with the knights and priests, although at separate tables, and with always one dish less than the higher classes. They were, however, strictly subordinate to the knights; the master and all the great officers of the order had each several serving-brethren to attend him, and each knight had some of the serving-brethren among his esquires. The statutes provided carefully against their being tyrannized over or otherwise ill-treated by the knights.

The statutes make a distinction between the serving-brethren who were armed with iron and those who were not. The former were the proper light-horse of the order; they were chiefly intended to support the knights in the action, and were usually placed in the second rank. The place of the unarmed was with the baggage; and as they were exposed to little danger, they wore only linen corslets. The others were enjoined to fight, without flinching, as long as a Christian banner flew on the field: it was matter of praise to these last if they managed to come safe out of the fight. When the troops of the Temple were on their march, the esquires rode before the knights with their baggage. When the knights were going to action, one esquire rode before each with his lance, another behind with his war-horse.

There were various offices in the society, hereafter to be noticed, which were appropriated to the serving-brethren, or to which they were eligible.

* Sir W. Scott is perfectly correct in making the smith so important a character in his St. Valentine's Eve.

The knights, the chaplains, and the serving-brethren, were the proper members of the order, and it is to them alone that the name Templars applies. But both the Templars and the Hospitallers devised a mode of attaching secular persons to their interest, and of deriving advantages from their connexion with them, in which they were afterwards imitated by the mendicant orders of the Franciscans and Dominicans; the Jesuits also, who were always so keen at discerning what might be for the advantage of their society, adopted it; and it is, we believe, still practised in Catholic countries. This system is styled *affiliation*.

The affiliated were persons of various ranks in society, and of both sexes, who, without giving up their secular mode of life, or wearing any peculiar habit, joined the order, with a view to the advantages, both spiritual and temporal, which they expected to derive from it. These advantages will appear to have been very considerable when we recollect that all who joined the order were admitted to a share in the merits of its good works, which were what those times esteemed of the highest order. Nothing could have more contributed to the extent of affiliation than the exemption which the Templars enjoyed from the effects of interdict. At a time when it was in the power of every bishop to lay entire towns under this formidable sentence it must have been highly consolatory to pious or superstitious minds to belong to a society who disregarded this spiritual thunder, and who could afford them an opportunity of at least occasionally hearing mass and receiving the sacraments, and secured them, if they should die while the interdict continued, the advantage of Christian burial. In those days also, when club-law prevailed so universally, and a man's safety depended not so much on his innocence or the justice of his cause as on the

strength of his party, it was a matter of no small
consequence to belong to so powerful a body as the
Templars, and it must have been highly gratifying
to both the secular and spiritual pride of a lawyer or
a, burgher to be a member of the same body with the
high-born soldier-monks of the Temple.

These important advantages were not conceded by
the Templars without equivalent considerations. This
ambitious and covetous order required that he who
sought the honour of affiliation with them should,
besides taking the three vows, pledge himself to lead
a reputable life, to further the interests of the order
to the best of his power, and leave it the entire of his
property at his death. If he was married, and died
before his wife, he might leave her a competent pro-
vision for life ; but from the day of his admission
into the order he was to abstain from her bed, though
he might continue to reside in the same house with
her ; for were he to have children, he might provide
for them to the disadvantage of the order, or on his
death they might give trouble to it by claiming his
property. For a similar reason the affiliated were
forbidden to be sponsors, lest they might covertly or
openly give some of their property to their god-
children. They were not even permitted to give
offerings to the clergy. If they dared to violate these
injunctions, a severe punishment—in general, confinement for life—awaited them.

All orders of men were ambitious of a union with
this honourable and powerful society. We find among
the affiliated both sovereign princes and dignified
prelates : even the great Pope Innocent III., in one
of his bulls, declares himself to stand in this relation
to the order. Many of the knights who dwelt with
the Templars, and fought under their banner, were
also affiliated, and the history of the order more than
once makes mention of the *sisters*—that is, women

who were affiliated to it, for there were no nuns of the Temple similar to those of the order of Malta in later times.

In less intimate connexion with the order than the affiliated stood those who were styled *Donates* and *Oblates*. These were persons who, as their titles denote, were given or presented to the order. They were either children whom their parents or relations destined to the service of the order when they should have attained a sufficient age, or they were full-grown persons who pledged themselves to serve the order as long as they lived without reward, purely out of reverence to it, and with a view to enjoying its protection, and sharing in its good works. Persons of all ranks, princes and priests, as well as others, were to be found among the oblates of the Temple.

Chapter VI.

Provinces of the Order — Eastern Provinces — Jerusalem — Houses of this Province—Tripolis— Antioch — Cyprus— Western Provinces—Portugal—Castile and Leon—Aragon —France and Auvergne — Normandy — Aquitaine — Provence—England—Germany—Upper and Central Italy— Apulia and Sicily.

WE have thus seen what a number of persons of all ranks were more or less intimately connected with the order of the Temple, and how powerful its influence must have been throughout the Christian world. To enable the reader to form some conception of its wealth and power, we shall, previous to explaining its system of internal regulation, give a view of its possessions in various countries.

The extensive possessions of the order of the Temple, in Asia and in Europe, were divided into provinces, each containing numerous preceptories or temple-houses, and each under its appointed governor. These provinces may be classified under the heads of Eastern and Western.

The eastern provinces of the order were,—

I. JERUSALEM. — This province was always regarded as the ruling one; the chief seat and capital of the order. The Master and chapter resided here as long as the Holy City was in the hands of the Christians. This being the province which was first established, its regulations and organization served as a model for all others. Its provincial Master, or, as he was styled, the Preceptor of the Land and Kingdom of Jerusalem, took precedence of all others of the same rank.

The bailiwicks, or commanderies, in this province, were,—

1. The Temple of Jerusalem, the cradle of the order, and the original residence of the Master and the chapter.

2. Chateau Pélerin, or the Pilgrim's Castle, renowned in the history of the crusades. This castle was built by the Templars in 1217, in order that it might be their chief seat after the loss of Jerusalem. It was situated on the east side of Mount Carmel, which runs out into the sea between Caipha and Cæsarea. The Templars had long had a tower at a pass of this mountain, called *Destruction*, or the Tower of the Pass, for the defence of pilgrims against the robbers who lurked in the gorges of the mountains. They were aided in building the castle, which was also designed to be a defence to Acre, by Walter D'Avesnes and by the German knights and pilgrims who were at that time in the Holy Land, and hence, perhaps, they called it Chateau Pélerin. The Cardinal de Vitry, who was at that time bishop of Acre, thus describes it. It was built on the promontory, three sides of which were washed by the sea. As they were sinking the foundation, they came to two walls of ancient masonry, and to some springs of remarkably pure water; they also found a quantity of ancient coins with unknown inscriptions, given, as the bishop piously deems, by God to his beloved sons and warriors, to alleviate the toil and expense which they were at. The place had probably been fortified in former times by the Jews or the Romans. The builders raised two huge towers of large masses of rock on the landward side, each 100 feet high, and 74 broad; these were united by a lofty wall, broad enough at its summit for

an armed knight to stand at his ease upon it. It had a parapet and battlements, with steps leading up to them. In the space within this wall were a chapel, a palace, and several houses, with fish-ponds, salt-works, woods, meads, gardens, and vineyards. Lying at a distance of six miles from Mount Tabor, it commanded the interjacent plain and the sea-coast to Acre. There the Master and the chapter took up their final abode, after having dwelt from 1118 to 1187 at Jerusalem, from 1187 to 1191 at Antioch, and from this last year till 1217 at Acre. " The chief use," says D'Vitry, " of this edifice is, that the whole chapter of the Templars, withdrawn from the sinful city of Acre, which is full of all impurity, will reside under the protection of this castle till the walls of Jerusalem are rebuilt." A prophecy never to be fulfilled! On the fall of Acre, in 1291, Chateau Pélerin was abandoned by the knights, and its walls were levelled by the infidels.

3. The castle of Safat, at the foot of Mount Tabor. This strong castle was taken by Saladin. It was demolished in 1220, by Coradin, but afterwards rebuilt by the Templars, who then held it till 1266, when they lost it finally.

4. The temple at Acre, a remarkably strong building, the last place taken in the capture of that town.

5. The hill-fort, Dok, between Bethel and Jericho.

6. Faba, the ancient Aphek, not far from Tyre, in the territory of the ancient tribe of Ashur.

7. Some small castles near Acre, mentioned in the history of the war with Saladin, such as *La Cave*, *Marle, Citerne-rouge, Castel-blanc, La Sommellerie du Temple*.

8. The house at Gaza.

9. The castle of Jacob's-ford, at the Jordan, built in 1178 by King Baldwin IV., to check the incur-

sions of the roving Arabs. When Saladin took this castle, he treated the Templars whom he found in it with great cruelty.

10. The house at Jaffa.

11. The castle of Assur, near this town.

12. *Gerinum parvum.*

13. The castle of Beaufort, near Sidon, purchased by the order, in 1260, from Julian, the lord of that town.

We may observe that most of these abodes of the Templars were strong castles and fortresses. It was only by means of such that possession could be retained of a country like Palestine, subject to the constant inroads of the Turks and Saracens. The Templars possessed, besides these strongholds, large farms and tracts of land, of which, though their names are unknown, frequent mention is made in the history of the order.

II. TRIPOLIS.—The principal houses of the order in this province were at Tripolis itself; Tortosa, the ancient Antaradus; Castel-blanc, in the same neighbourhood; Laodicea, Tyre, Sidon, and Berytus.

III. ANTIOCH.—Of this province but little is known. There was a house at Aleppo; and the jurisdiction of the prior probably extended into Armenia*, where the order had estates to the value of 20,000 byzants.

IV. CYPRUS.—As long as the Templars maintained their footing on the continent, Cyprus, it would appear, formed no distinct province, but belonged either to that of Tripolis or of Antioch. At the time when Richard, King of England, made the conquest of this island, he sold the sovereignty of it for 25,000 marks of silver to the Templars, who had already extensive possessions in it. The following year, with the consent of the order, who were, of course, reimbursed, he

* The Armenia of the crusades was a part of Cilicia.

transferred the dominion to Guy de Lusignan, King of Jerusalem. On the capture of Acre the chief seat of the order was fixed at Limesal, also called Limissa and Nemosia, in this island, which town, having an excellent harbour, they strongly fortified. They had also a house at Nicosia, and one at the ancient Paphos, named Gastira, and, at the same place, the impregnable castle of Colossa.

Some idea of the value of the possessions of the Templars in Cyprus may be formed from the circumstance, that when, in 1316, after the suppression of the order, the Pope directed the Bishop of Limissa to transfer their property there to the Hospitallers, there were found, in the house in that town, 26,000 byzants of coined money, and silver plate to the value of 1,500 marks. As the last Master, when setting out for France ten years before, had carried with him the treasure of the order, this property must have been accumulated during that time out of the surplus revenue of the possessions of the order in the island

The Western provinces of the order were—

I. Portugal.—So early as the year 1130 (a strong proof of the rapid increase of the order) Galdin Paez, the first provincial master of the Temple in Portugal, built the castles of Tomar, Monsento, and Idanna. The Templars had also settlements at Castromarin, Almural, and Langrovia. Tomar was the residence of the great-prior.

II. Castile and Leon.—In this province the possessions of the order were so extensive as to form twenty-four bailiwicks in Castile alone. It is needless to enumerate their names *.

III. Aragon.—In this province, which abounded in castles, several belonged to the Templars; and the bailiwick of Majorca, where they were also settled,

* They will be found in Campomanes. p. 80, and Münter p. 424.

was under the jurisdiction of the great-prior of Aragon.

It is to be observed that most of the castles possessed by the order in Spain and Portugal were on the borders of the Moorish territory. Some of these had been given to the Templars as the inveterate foes of the infidels ; others had been conquered by them from the Moors.

France, where the possessions of the order were so considerable, was divided into four provinces, namely—

IV. FRANCE AND AUVERGNE, including Flanders and the Netherlands.

V. NORMANDY.

VI. AQUITAINE, or POITOU.

VII. PROVENCE.

The residences of the great-priors of these four provinces were, for France, the capacious and stately Temple at Paris, which was, as we are informed by Matthew Paris, large and roomy enough to contain an army; for Normandy, as is supposed, *La ville D'eu en la Montagne;* for Poitou, the Temple at Poitiers; for Provence, that at Montpellier.

VIII. ENGLAND.—The province of England included Scotland and Ireland. Though each of these two last kingdoms had its own great-prior, they were subordinate to the great-prior of England, who resided at the Temple of London.

The principal bailiwicks of England were—1. London ; 2. Kent ; 3 Warwick ; 4. Waesdone ; 5. Lincoln ; 6. Lindsey ; 7. Bolingbroke ; 8. Widine ; 9. Agerstone ; 10. York. In these were seventeen preceptories ; and the number of churches, houses, farms, mills, &c., possessed by the order was very considerable *.

* The possessions of the Templars in England will be found in the works of Dugdale and Tanner.

Interior of Round Tower, in Temple Church, London.

Saxon Doorway, Temple Church, London.

Details of Saxon Capitals.

Round Temple Church, Cambridge.

The chief seat of the order in Scotland appears to have been Blancradox. Its possessions were not extensive in that poor and turbulent country; and in Ireland the Templars seem to have been few, and confined to the Pale. We hear of but three of their houses in that country—namely, Glaukhorp, in the diocese of Dublin; Wilbride, in that of Ferns; and Siewerk, in that of Kildare.

IX. GERMANY.—It is difficult to ascertain how the order was regulated in Germany, where its possessions were very extensive. We hear of three great-priors: those of Upper Germany, of Brandenburg, and of Bohemia and Moravia; one of whom, but it cannot be determined which, had probably authority over the others. Though the Templars got lands in Germany as early as the year 1130, their acquisitions were not large in that country till the thirteenth century. Poland was included in the province of Germany. Great-prior in Alemania and Slavia was a usual title of the great-prior of Germany. Though the possessions of the Templars in Hungary were very considerable, there are no grounds for supposing that it formed a separate province: it was probably subject to the great-prior of Germany.

X. UPPER AND CENTRAL ITALY.—There was no town of any importance in this part of the Italian peninsula in which the Templars had not a house. The principal was that on the Aventine Hill at Rome, in which the great-prior resided. Its church still remains, and is called *Il Priorato*, or the Priory.

XI. APULIA AND SICILY.—The possessions of the Templars in Sicily were very considerable. They had houses and lands at Syracuse, Palermo, Trapani, Butera, Lentini, &c.; all of which were dependent on the principal house, which was in Messina. The great-prior resided either at Messina or at Benevento in Apulia. Possibly the seat was removed to this last place, after the Emperor Frederic II. had seized so much of the property of the order in Sicily.

In Denmark, Norway, and Sweden, the order had no possessions whatever. Though the people of these countries took some share in the crusades, and were, therefore, not deficient in religious zeal, their poor and little-known lands offered no strong inducements to the avarice or ambition of the knights of the Temple, and they never sought a settlement in them.

We thus see that, with the exception of the northern kingdoms, there was no part of Europe in which the order of the Temple was not established. Everywhere they had churches, chapels, tithes, farms, villages, mills, rights of pasturage, of fishing, of venery, and of wood. They had also, in many places, the right of holding annual fairs, which were managed, and the tolls received, either by some of the brethren of the nearest houses or by their *donates* and servants. The number of their preceptories is, by the most moderate computation, rated at 9,000; and the annual income of the order at about six millions sterling—an enormous sum for those times! Masters of such a revenue, descended from the noblest houses of Christendom, uniting in their persons the most esteemed secular and religious characters, regarded as the chosen champions of Christ, and the flower of Christian knights, it was not possible for the Templars, in such lax times as the twelfth and thirteenth centuries, to escape falling into the vices of extravagant luxury and overweening pride. Nor are we to wonder at their becoming objects of jealousy and aversion to both the clergy and the laity, and exciting the fears and the cupidity of an avaricious and faithless prince.

Chapter VII.

Officers of the Order—The Master—Mode of Election—His Rights and Privileges—Restraints on him—The Seneschal —The Marshal—The Treasurer—The Draper—The Turcopilar—Great-Priors — Commanders—Visitors —Sub-Marshal—Standard-bearer.

An order consisting of so many members, and whose wealth and possessions were of such extent, must necessarily have had numerous officers and various ranks and dignities. The elucidation of this branch of their constitution is now to engage our attention.

At the head of the order stood the Master, or, as he was sometimes called, the Great-Master * of the Temple. This personage was always a knight, and had generally held one of the higher dignities of the order. Though, like the Doge of Venice, his power was greatly controlled by the chapter, he enjoyed very great consideration, and was always regarded as the representative of the order. In the councils, the Masters of the Temple and the Hospital took precedence of all ambassadors, and sat next the prelates. All monarchs conceded princely rank and place to the Master of the Temple.

A situation which offered so much state and consi-

* *Magister, Maistre,* is the almost invariable expression in the historians, the statutes of the order, and most documents. *Magnus Magister* was, however, early employed. Terricus, the Master of the order, thus styles himself when writing to Henry II. of England. The term Grand-Master is apt to convey erroneous ideas of pomp and magnificence to the minds of many readers.

deration must, of necessity, have been an object of ambition ; but the scanty records remaining of the society do not enable us to point out any specific cases of intrigue employed for the attainment of it. That of the last Master, hereafter to be mentioned, is somewhat problematic.

The election of a Master of the Temple was as follows :—

When the Master was dead, an event which always occurred in the East, as he was bound to reside there, if it took place in the kingdom of Jerusalem, and the marshal of the order was on the spot, he took upon him the exercise of the vacant dignity till, with the aid of the chapter and of all the bailiffs on this side of the sea (*i.e.* in the East), he had appointed a great-prior to represent the Master. But this election did not take place till after the funeral. Should the death of the Master have occurred in the province of Tripolis, or that of Antioch, the prior of the province took the direction of the order till the great-prior was appointed.

Owing to the constant state of war which prevailed in the East, and to other causes, a considerable space of time occasionally intervened between the death of one Master and the appointment of his successor. During the *interregnum* the society was directed by the great-prior who bore the seal of the Master.

When the day appointed for the election was arrived, the great officers of the order and all the bailiffs who were invited to be present assembled in the place selected for holding the election—generally the chapel of the order. The great-prior, taking several of the knights aside, consulted with them ; and they then made two or three or more of the knights who were most highly-esteemed retire. The great-prior took the voices of those present on the merits of the absent knights; and he who had most in his favour was declared the electing-prior. The knights were then called in, and the choice of the assembly notified to them. A knight, possessing the same virtues of piety, love of peace, and impartiality with himself, was then assigned for an assistant to the electing-prior: and the whole assemblage withdrew, leaving the two alone in the chapel, where they passed the entire night in prayer.

Early next morning, after performing their usual devotions and hearing the mass of the Holy Ghost, the chapter re-assembled. The great-prior then exhorted the two electing brethren to perform their duty truly and honestly. These, then retiring, chose two other brethren; these four chose two more, and so on, till the number amounted to twelve, in honour of the apostles. The twelve then chose a brother-chaplain to represent the person of Jesus Christ, and maintain peace and concord. It was necessary that these thirteen should be of different provinces—eight of them knights, four serving-brethren, and one priest. The thirteen electors then returned to the chapter, and the electing-prior besought all present to pray for them, as a great task had been laid on them. All then fell on their knees and prayed; and the great-prior solemnly reminded the electors of their duty, and conjured them to perform it truly and uprightly. Having again implored the prayers of the assembly, the electing-prior and his companions retired to the place appointed for their deliberations. If the electors, or the majority of them, declared for any knight on this or the other side of the sea, he was appointed; if they were divided into parties, the electing-prior came with one of the knights, and, informing the assembly of the circumstance, asked their prayers. All fell on their knees, and the two electors returned to their companions; if they now agreed, the person whom they chose was declared Master.

Should the object of their choice be, as was not unfrequently the case, actually present in the chapter, the thirteen came in; and the electing-prior speaking in their name, said, " Beloved sirs, give praise and thanks to our Lord Jesus Christ, and to our dear Lady, and to all the saints, that we are agreed, and have, according to your command, chosen, in the name of God, a Master of the Temple. Are ye content with what we have done?" All then replied, " In the name of God!" " Do ye promise to yield him obedience as long as he lives?" " Yea, with the help of God!" The electing-prior then turned to the great-prior, and said, " Prior, if God and we have chosen thee for the Master, wilt thou promise to obey the chapter as long as thou live, and to maintain the good morals and good usages of the order?" and he answered, " Yea, with the aid of God!" The same question was then put to some of the most distinguished knights; and if the person elected was present, the electing-prior went up to him, and said, " In the name of the Father, the Son, and the Holy Ghost, we have chosen you brother, N. N., for Master, and do choose you!" He then said, " Beloved sirs and brethren, give thanks unto God: behold our Master." The chaplains then chanted aloud the *Te Deum laudamus*, the brethren arose, and, with the utmost reverence and joy, taking the new Master in their arms, carried him into the chapel, and placed him before the altar, where he continued kneeling while the brethren prayed, the chaplains repeating *Kyrie Eleïson*, *Pater noster*, and other devotional forms.

The election of the Master of the Temple required

no papal confirmation : the choice of the chapter was conclusive. Two knights were assigned to him as his companions.

The allowances and train of the Master were suitable to the rank which he was to support in the world, and to the dignity of the order which he represented. He was allowed four horses, and an esquire of noble birth. He had a chaplain and two secretaries ; one for managing his Latin correspondence, whom he might, after a time, admit to become a knight of the order ; the other, who was called his Saracenic secretary, and who was probably an eastern Christian, for carrying on his Arabic correspondence with the Infidels. He had, moreover, a farrier, a cook, and a Turcopole *, two footmen, and a Turcoman †, to serve as guide. On a march, the Turcoman rode on a horse behind an esquire : during the time of war he was led by a cord, to prevent his escape. On any ordinary journey, the Master might take two beasts of burden with him ; but in war-time, or in case of his going beyond the Jordan, or the Dog's Pass ‡, he might extend the number to four, which the statutes thriftily direct to be put into the stable when he arrives at the house where he is going to stop, and to be employed in the service of the house. The Master was finally commander-in-chief

* The Turcopoles were the offspring of a Turkish father, by a Christian mother ; or also those who had been reared among the Turks, and had learned their mode of fighting. The Christians employed them as light cavalry ; and the Templars had always a number of them in their pay.

† The Turcomans were, as their name denotes, born Turks. The Christians used them as guides on their expeditions.

‡ *Le pas de chien.* Münter (p. 66) declares his ignorance of where it lay. It was evidently the dangerous pass at the Nahr-el-Kelb, (*Dog's River*), near the sea, on the way to Antioch.

of the order in the field; and then, like the Spartan
kings, he could act in some degree unfettered by the
chapter.   When he died, he was buried with great
solemnity and pomp, by the light of torches and wax
tapers—an honour bestowed by the order on no other
of its members.   All the knights were required to
attend the funeral; and the prelates were invited to
give their presence at it.   Each brother who was
present was to repeat 200 *Pater nosters* within seven
days, for the repose of the soul of the deceased; and
100 poor persons were fed at home in the evening,
with the same design.

On the other hand, the Master was bound to obey
the chapter; and he could do nothing without con-
sulting some of the brethren.   He could not nominate
to any of the higher dignities of the order; but he
might, with the advice and consent of some of the
most reputable knights, appoint to the inferior priories
and preceptories.   He could not sell, or in any other
way dispose of, any of the lands of the order, without
the consent of the chapter; neither could he make
peace or truce without their approbation.   Their consent was also required to enable him to make any
alteration in the laws of the society, to receive any
person into it, or to send a brother beyond sea.   He
could take no money out of the treasury without the
consent of the prior of Jerusalem, who was the
treasurer of the society.   In fact, the Master of the
Temple was so curbed and restrained in every way,
and his office made so much an honorary one, that
his dignity may best be compared with that of a
Spartan king or a Venetian doge.   It is rather curious
that the Master of the Temple should be thus limited
in authority, when the abbot of the Benedictines,
whose rules the Templars in a great measure adopted,
enjoyed monarchical power.

Next in rank to the Master stood the seneschal, who, as his name denotes*, was the Master's representative and lieutenant. He had a right to be present at all chapters of the order; and to be acquainted with all transactions of consequence. He was allowed the same number of horses as the Master; but, instead of a mule, he was to have a palfrey: he had two esquires, and was assigned a knight as his companion; a deacon acted as his chaplain and Latin secretary; he had also a Saracenic secretary and a Turcopole, with two footmen. Like the Master, he bore the seal of the order.

The marshal was the general of the order; he had charge of the banner, and led the brethren to battle. All the arms, equipments, and stables of the order were under his superintendence. It was he who nominated the sub-marshal and the standard-bearer. Like all the other great officers, he was appointed by the Master and the chapter. As we have seen, when the Master died in the kingdom of Jerusalem, the marshal occupied his place till a great-prior was chosen. The marshal was allowed four horses, two esquires, a serving-brother, and a Turcopole.

The office of treasurer of the order was always united with the dignity of preceptor of the kingdom of Jerusalem. This officer had the charge of all the receipts and expenditure of the order, of which he was bound to give an account, when required, to the Master and the chapter. The wardrobe of the order was also under him; and the draper was assigned as his companion, without whose knowledge he could not dispose of any of the clothes. As the ships, though few in number, which the Templars possessed, were under him, he may be regarded as,

---

* Seneschal is one *qui alterius vicem gerit.* Charpentier Supplem. ad Dufresne Gloss. iii. p. 759.

also, in some sort, the admiral of the order; and on this account the preceptor of Acre was subordinate to him. The treasurer had the same allowance of horses, &c. as the seneschal.

The draper had charge of the clothing of the order: he was to see that each brother was decently and properly dressed. His allowance was four horses, two esquires, and a pack-servant.

The Turcopilar was the commander of the light horse. All the armed serving-brethren and the Turcopoles were under his command. He was himself subordinate to the marshal. When he was going into action, some of the knights were sent with him. These were under his orders; but if their number amounted to ten, and they had with them a banner and a knight-preceptor, the Turcopilar became subordinate to this officer; which proves that the office of Turcopilar was not one of the higher dignitaries of the order. The Turcopilar was allowed four horses.

Besides these offices of the order in the East, there were the great-priors, great-preceptors, or provincial-masters (for the terms are synonimous) of the three provinces of Jerusalem, Tripolis, and Antioch; and the preceptors, who were subordinate to them.

The great-prior of the kingdom of Jerusalem was also treasurer. His office has been already noticed. The great-priors of Tripolis and Antioch had the superintendence over the brethren and the possessions of the order in these provinces. They had the same allowances of attendants and horses as the seneschal. The prior of Antioch, when on a journey to Armenia, which bordered on his province, and in which the order had possessions, was allowed to take with him a chaplain and a portable chapel, as the Armenians were monophysite heretics, with whom

the orthodox brethren of the Temple could not join
in worship.

The prior of the town of Jerusalem had peculiar
duties to perform. It was his office, with ten knights
who stood under his command, to escort the pilgrims
on their way to and from the Jordan—one of the
principal objects of the institution of the order. On
this occasion he had with him the banner of the order
and a round tent, into which he might take any persons whom he should find sick when he encamped ;
he was also to take with him provisions, and beasts
of burden on which to place such of the pilgrims as
might be fatigued on the return.

When the true cross was brought forth on any expedition, it was the duty of the prior of Jerusalem
to keep by it, with his ten knights, night and day,
and to guard it ; he was to encamp close to it ; and
two brethren were to watch it every night.

All the secular knights who associated themselves
to the order in Jerusalem were under his orders, and
fought beneath his banner. All the brethren of the
order who were in Jerusalem were, in the absence of
the marshal, under his command. One half of the
booty captured beyond the Jordan fell to him, the
other half to the prior of the kingdom.

As we have seen above, the West was, like the
East, divided into provinces of the order. Each of
these provinces was presided over by a lieutenant of
the master, named the provincial-master, great-prior,
or great-preceptor, with his chapter and officers corresponding to those of the kingdom of Jerusalem.
He was appointed, as it would appear, by the Master
and chapter ; and when entering on his office, he
bound himself by oath to defend the Catholic religion, not only with his lips, but with arms and all
his strength ; to follow the rules drawn up by St. Bernard ; to obey the Master ; to come over the sea to his

aid whenever it was necessary ; to defend him against
all unbelieving kings and princes; not to fly before
these unbelieving foes; not to alienate the goods of
the order; to be loyal to the prince of the country;
to be chaste; and to aid all spiritual persons, especially the Cistercians, by words and by deeds.

Under the provincial-masters stood the priors,
bailiffs, or masters, who governed large districts of
the provinces, and had under their inspection several
of the houses of the order and their preceptors.
They dwelt in large temple-houses, with a good
number of knights ; they had the power of holding
chapters, and of receiving members into the order.

The preceptors were subordinate to the priors;
they presided over one or more houses. They were
generally knights, but they were sometimes priests.
They were of two kinds—house-preceptors and
knight-preceptors ; the former, as their name denotes,
merely presided over the houses, and might be priests
or serving-brethren; the latter, who were probably
only to be found in the East or in Spain, led each
ten knights in the battle.

Another office to be found among the Templars
was that of visitors. These were knights, who, as
the representatives of the Master, visited the different
provinces of the order, especially in the West, to reform abuses, make new regulations, and terminate
such disputes and law-suits as were usually reserved
for the decision of the Master and the chapter. All
the provincial officers, even the great-priors. were subject to the visitors, as the representatives of the Master. The powers of the visitors ceased as soon as
the business ended for which they were sent, or when
they were recalled.

Besides the foregoing offices, which were almost
exclusively confined to the knights, there were some
inferior ones appropriated to the serving-brethren.

Preceptory, Swingfield, Dover

These offices were five in number—namely, those of
sub-marshal, standard-bearer, farrier, cook, and preceptor of the coast of Acre.   Each of these was
allowed two horses.

The sub-marshal had the charge of all the inferior
sort of accoutrements (*le petit harnois*) of the order,
in which the horse-furniture seems to have been included.   All the handicraftsmen of the order were
under him, and were obliged to account to him for
their work. He supplied them with the needful tools
and materials; could send them where he pleased
on the service of the house; and on holidays give
them permission to go from one house to another to
amuse themselves.   The sub-marshal and the standard-bearer were each the representative of the other
in his absence.

The standard-bearer had the command over all
the esquires of the house ; that is, those who were engaged for a limited time in the service of the order,
whom he was bound to make acquainted with the
rules to which they were subject, and the punishments
to which they were liable in case of disobedience ;
he was also to pay them their wages. Whenever
the esquires took the horses out to graze, he was
bound to precede them with a standard of the order.
He always presided at the table of the serving-
brethren and esquires. When the order was marching
to battle, it was his task to ride before the standard,
which was borne after him by an esquire, or carried
on a wain*; he was to lead whithersoever the marshal directed him. When the battle commenced,
those esquires who led the horses of the knights
were to combat behind their masters ; the others
were to take the mules on which their masters rode,
and remain with the standard-bearer, who was to

* The *Carroccio* of the Italian republics.

have a banner rolled about his lance, which, when
he saw the marshal engaged in action, he was to
unfurl, and draw up the esquires in as handsome
order as possible behind the combatants, in order to
support them.

The serving-brethren were eligible to the office of
house-preceptor; but there was this distinction made
between them and knights who held that office, that,
the serving-brethren being allowed but one horse,
their esquire was a serving-brother. As Acre was
the sea-port at which all the shipments of the order
to and from Europe took place, the preceptory there
was necessarily an office which entailed a good deal
of toil and business on the person who held that
situation, and required a knowledge of commerce
and of the affairs of the world. It was therefore
not considered suitable to a knight, and was always
given to a serving-brother. The serving-brethren
were also set over the various farms and estates of the
order. These were named the brother-stewards,—in
Latin, *grangiarii* and *preceptores grangiarum*,—
and were probably selected from the craftsmen of
the order. They were allowed two horses and an
esquire.

CHAPTER VIII.

Chapters—Mode of holding them—Templars' Mode of Living —Amusements—Conduct in War.

SUCH as we have described them were the members, the possessions, and the various offices of the powerful society of the Temple. In order to complete our view, it only remains to trace its internal government and most important regulations. We shall therefore commence with an account of the chapters, from which all the acts and rules of the society emanated.

It is frequently declared in the statutes, that the Master was in the place of God; and that all his commands were to be obeyed as those of God. But these expressions, which were borrowed from the rule of the Benedictines, are, as we have already seen, not to be understood too literally; for the constitution of the order of the Templars was aristocratic, and not monarchic; and the Master was anything but absolute. In every matter he was to be guided by the opinion of the majority of the chapter.

The general chapter, or high legislative assembly of the order, consisted of all the great officers, of the great-priors of the provinces, and the most distinguished of the knights who could attend. Every brother, even the lowest of the serving-brethren, was at liberty to be present as a spectator; but only the proper members of the chapter had the privilege of speaking. The place of holding the chapter was undetermined, and was left to the choice of the Master. All laws and regulations were made or confirmed in

the general chapter : there brethren were received—
the great officers appointed—visitors chosen to be
sent to the different provinces.   It is remarkable,
that a papal legate never seems to have been present
at a chapter of the Templars; though the legates frequently assisted at those of the other orders.   This
is, most probably, to be ascribed to the secrecy in
which the Templars were pleased to envelope their
councils and proceedings; and as they rarely held
general chapters, a suitable pretext could not well be
wanting for freeing themselves from the presence of
the legate when they desired it.   Those who impute
to the Templars the holding of a secret doctrine
naturally regard this as the cause of their not admitting to their chapters those who were not initiated
in it.

A general chapter was not often assembled—a circumstance easily to be accounted for.   Though the
order was wealthy, it might not be well able to bear,
without inconvenience, the expense of deputies from
all the provinces journeying to the kingdom of Jerusalem, where the chapters were in general held ; and
further, it was obviously the interest of the Master
and the great officers to avoid assembling a body
which would at once assume the powers which they
were in the habit of exercising.

In the intervals between the meetings of general
chapters, the powers of the order were exercised by
the chapter of the Temple at Jerusalem.   This was
composed of the Master, the dignitaries of the order,
such of the provincial masters as happened to be
present, the two assistants of the Master, and such
knights as he chose to invite to it.   This last provi-
sion was the great source of the Master's power ;
and, when he was a man of talent and address, he
could, by managing to get his friends and those
whom he could depend on into the different offices,

and by summoning to the chapter such knights as were attached or looked up to him, contrive to carry any matters that he desired.   The laws, however, by way of check upon him, made it imperative that the high officers of the order should have seats in the chapter; and as these were not appointed by the Master, and were independent of him, it was supposed that they would not be his creatures.   This chapter could decide on all matters relating to the order, some important affairs, such as war and peace, excepted; make laws and regulations, which were binding on the whole society; and send visitors to the different provinces.   All public documents, such as papal bulls, were addressed to it and the Master; all decisions in matters of importance came from it; and all the brethren who were received in the West were sent to it to be distributed where they might be wanting.   The declaration made by a French knight on his examination, that the receptions in the chapter of Jerusalem were rare, as the members could be seldom brought to agree respecting a candidate, gives a hint that it was not in general a scene of the greatest harmony and unity.   It is, indeed, but natural to suppose, that, as it was the chief seat of the power of the order, it was also the great theatre of intrigue and cabal.

Each province of the order had its general chapter, and also a smaller one, presided over by the great-prior, and composed of the principal officers and such knights of character and estimation as the prior chose to call to it.   In like manner every preceptory and every large house of the order had its chapter, at which all the brethren were required to attend.   The commander was president, and each question was decided by the majority of voices.   The chief transactions in it consisted in the reception of new brethren, and the making up of quarrels and disputes, which must have frequently fallen out among men like the Templars, who were almost all soldiers. It was holden early on a Sunday morning; and the strictest secrecy, as to what took place, was enjoined on all present, for *secrecy was the soul of the order.*

The ordinary chapters were held in the following manner. Each brother, as he entered, made the sign of the cross, and, unless he was bald, took off his cap. The president then rose and said, " Stand up, beloved brethren, and pray to God to send his holy grace among us to-day." Each member repeated a *pater noster,* and, if there was a chaplain present, he said a prayer. Search was then made to see that there was no one present but those who belonged to the order. The president then delivered a discourse, exhorting the brethren to amendment of life. During this discourse no one was on any account to leave the room. When it was ended, any one who had transgressions to acknowledge went up to the president and made confession. He then retired out of sight and hearing, and the sentiments of the assembly were taken, which were afterwards signified to him. The brethren were also to remind each other of their transgressions, and exhort to confession and penitence. If any one accused a brother falsely, he was severely punished for it: while the inquiry was going on the accused was obliged to retire from the chapter. The discipline was usually administered in presence of the assembled chapter, with a scourge, or with a girdle. Those who were sick were not punished till they were recovered.

When these matters were over, the president explained a portion of the statutes, and exhorted all present to live suitably thereto. He then said, " Beloved brethren, we may now close our chapter, for, praise be to God, all is well; and may God and our dear Lady grant that it may so continue, and goodness be every day increased. Beloved brethren, ye must know how it is with pardon in our chapter, and who has not part therein ; know, then, that those have no part either in the pardon of our chapter, or in the other good works of the chapter ; who live as they should not; who depart from the righteousness of the order; who do not acknowledge their offences and do penance in the mode prescribed by the order; who treat the alms of the order as their own property, or in any other way contrary to law, and squander them in an unrighteous, scandalous, and foolish manner. But those who honestly acknowledge their faults, and conceal nothing out of shame or fear of the punishment of the order, and are right sorry for their transgressions, have a large share in the forgiveness of our chapter, and in the good works which take place in our order. And to such, in virtue of my authority, I dispense forgiveness in the name of God and of our dear Lady, in the names of the apostles Peter and Paul, of our father the pope, and of you all who have given me authority ; and pray to God that, according to his mercy, he will, for the merits of his mother, and of himself, and all the saints, forgive you your sins, as he forgave the famous Mary Magdalene." He then implored the forgiveness of those to whom he might have given any offence or done any injury ; and prayed for peace, for the church, for the holy kingdom of Jerusalem, for the order and all its houses and people, for the brethren and sisters of the order, and for its living and dead benefactors; finally, for all the dead who waited for the mercy of God, especially those who lay buried in the Temple burial-grounds, and for the souls of the fathers and mothers of the Templars. The chaplain, if present, repeated a confession of sin, in which all followed him, and then pronounced an absolution. If there was no chaplain present, each brother repeated a *pater* and an *ave*, and so the chapter ended.

The statutes of the order are full of the most minute directions respecting the equipment, clothing, and mode of living of the various members of the order. They were obliged to attend divine service punctually each day at all the different hours at which it was celebrated, and regularly to observe all the fasts of the church; they were also to have at their houses both public and private devotions. Their meals were also strictly regulated. They assembled by sound of bell: if there was a priest in the house he said grace for them, if not, each brother repeated a *pater* before he began to eat. During the meal a clergyman read out something edifying for them, and when it was over no one was to speak till grace was said. There was no difference made in the quality of the food; all, both high and low, fared alike, and they ate two off one plate. They had flesh-meat but three times a week, unless when festival days occurred. On days when they had no flesh-meat they had but two dishes. When the order were in the field a server regulated the supply and distribution of provisions. Before giving out the provisions he was to direct the serving-brethren to notify it to the superiors of the order, that they might come and select the best for themselves; he distributed the remainder without any other distinction than that of giving the best to the sick. The plate given to every two of the brethren was so large that what remained when they were done was sufficient to satisfy two of the poor. Two brethren were allowed as much food as three Turcopoles, and two of these as much as three of the servants. The brethren were not allowed to seek for any food elsewhere than from the server, vegetables, game, and venison excepted. But as by

the rules of the order the chase was prohibited
to them, they could not procure these themselves.

Amusements could not be rigorously prohibited to
men who were semi-secular, and had to mingle so
much in the world as the Templars. They were
therefore allowed to tilt, but only with headless
lances; whether only among themselves, or also at
public tournaments, is uncertain*. They were permitted to run races with their horses, but for no
higher wager than a headless cross-bow bolt, or
some other trifle. Chess and draughts were prohibited games; nor were they allowed to play at
any other game whatever for a stake. Hawking
was absolutely forbidden to the Templar, probably
on account of the high price of hawks, and of
this being the favourite amusement of the secular
knights. The reason assigned by the statutes is:—
" Because it is not seemly in the members of an
order to play sinfully, but willingly to hearken to the
commands of God, to pray often, and daily in their
prayers before God to bewail their sins with weeping
and tears." A Templar might not even accompany
one who was going out a-hawking. Moreover, as
shouting and bawling were unseemly in a member
of an order, he might not go a-hunting in a wood
with bow and crossbow, nor accompany any one thus
engaged, except to protect him against the heathen.
In fine, every species of chase was forbidden to the
Templar, except that of the lion ' who goes about
seeking whom he may devour, whose hand is against
every one, and every one's hand against him' †."

The battle was the Templar's scene of glory, and

---

* Sir W. Scott would probably find some difficulty in justi-
fying his making his Templar accept the combat à *outrance* at
the " gentle and free passage of Ashby de la Zouche."

† It is not clear whether this is to be understood literally
or metaphorically.

consequently every thing relating to the conduct of the order in war was strictly regulated. On the march the Templars, as the guardians of the holy cross, formed the vanguard of the Christian army; in the array they were in the right wing. The Hospitallers usually formed the rear-guard, and in the field were posted on the left. The Templars mounted and set forward at the voice of their marshal, the standard-bearer preceding them with the standard of the order. They moved in a walk or a small trot. The march usually took place by night, on account of the heat of eastern climes, and every precaution was adopted to prevent confusion or inconvenience. When the standard halted for emcampment, the marshal selected a place for his own tent and the chapel, which was to contain the true cross; the tents of the server, and of the great-prior of the province, had also their places marked out. It was then cried out, " Brethren, pitch your tents in the name of God!" on which each Templar forthwith raised his tent in his rank. All the tents were around the chapel, outside of its cords. The herald pitched by the standard. No brother was allowed, on any account, to go out of hearing of the war-cry, or to visit the quarters of any others than the Hospitallers, in case these last should be encamped beside them. The place for encamping was selected by the prior of the province in which the war was, who was therefore in some sort quartermaster-general; the marshal assigned the different quarters, and over each he set a knight-preceptor to govern and regulate it.

When the battle commenced, the marshal usually took the standard out of the hands of the sub-marshal and unfurled it in the name of God. He then nominated from five to ten of the brethren to

surround and guard it; one of these he made a
knight-preceptor, who was to keep close by him with
a banner furled on a spear, that, in case of that which
the marshal carried being torn, or having fallen, or
met with any other mishap, he might display it. If
the marshal was wounded or surrounded, this knight
was to raise the banner in his stead. No one was to
lower a banner, or thrust with it, on any account,
for fear of causing confusion. The brethren were to
fight on all sides, and in every way in which they
could annoy the foe, but still to keep near enough to
be able to defend the banner of the order, if needful.
But if a Templar saw a Christian in imminent danger,
he was at liberty to follow the dictates of his conscience, and hasten to his relief. He was to return
to his place as speedily as possible; but if the Turks
had gotten between him and the banner, he was to
join the nearest Christian squadron, giving the pre-
ference to the Hospitallers, if they were at hand.
Should the Christians meet with defeat, the Templar,
under penalty of expulsion from the order, was not to
quit the field so long as the banner of the order flew;
and, should there be no red-cross flag to be seen, he
was to join that of the Hospitallers, or any other.
Should every Christian banner have disappeared, he
was to retreat as well as he could.

Such were the military principles of the order of
the Temple—principles which,

> instead of rage,
> Deliberate valour breathed, firm and unmoved
> With dread of death to flight or foul retreat;

and never, unquestionably, was more unflinching
valour displayed than by the Templars. Where all
were brave and daring as the fabled heroes of romance, the Templar was still regarded as prominent,
and the Cardinal of Vitry could thus speak of them in

the early part of the thirteenth century, when they may be regarded as somewhat declined from their original elevation :—

" They seek to expel the enemies of the cross of Christ from the lands of the Christians, by fighting manfully, and by moving to battle at the signal and command of him who is at the head of their forces, *not impetuously or disorderedly, but prudently and with all caution*—the first in advance, the last in retreat; nor is it permitted to them to turn their backs in flight, or to retreat without orders. They are become so formidable to the adversaries of the faith of Christ, that one chases a thousand, and two ten thousand; not asking, when there is a call to arms, how many they are, but where they are: lions in war, gentle lambs at home; rugged warriors on an expedition, like monks and eremites in the church." The language of the worthy cardinal is no doubt declamatory, and rhetorical, and some deduction must consequently be made from it; but still enough will remain to prove that the chivalry of the Temple must still have retained no small portion of the virtues for which they had been originally renowned.

CHAPTER IX.

Molay elected Master—Last attempt of the Christians in
Syria—Conduct of the Three Military Orders—Philip the
Fair and Pope Boniface VIII.—Seizure of the Pope—
Election of Clement V.—The Papal See removed to France
—Causes of Philip's enmity to the Templars—Arrival of
Molay in France—His interviews with the Pope—Charges
made against the Templars—Seizure of the Knights—Pro-
ceedings in England—Nature of the Charges against the
Order.

WE have, in what precedes, traced the order of the
Templars from its institution to the period when the
Latin dominion was overthrown for ever on the coast
of Syria, and have described, at some length, its internal organisation, and exhibited its power and extent
of possessions. It remains for us to tell how this
mighty order was suddenly annihilated, to examine
the charges made against it*, and, as we have promised, to establish the falsehood and futility of them—
a task far from ungrateful, though not unattended
with pain ; for it is of advantage to strengthen our love
of justice and hatred of tyranny and oppression, by
vindicating the memory even of those who perished
their victims centuries agone. It is also of use to
furnish one instance more to the world of the operation of the principle which will be found so generally

* The proceedings against the Templars have been published .from the original documents by Mowdenhaler, in Germany ; but the work has been bought up by the freemasons,
who fancy themselves descended from the Templars, so that
we have been unable to procure a copy of it. Wilike has,
however, extracted largely from it.

to prevail, that, let falsehood and sophistry exert their utmost to conceal the truth, means will always remain of refuting them, and of displaying vice, however high seated, in its true colours.

In the year 1297, when the order had established its head-quarters in the isle of Cyprus, James de Molay, a native of Besançon, in the Franche Comté, was elected Master. The character of Molay appears to have been at all times noble and estimable; but if we are to credit the statement of a knight named Hugh de Travaux, he attained his dignity by an artifice not unlike that said. to have been employed by Sixtus V. for arriving at the papacy. The chapter, according to De Travaux, could not agree, one part being for Molay, the other, and the stronger, for Hugh de Peyraud. Molay, seeing that he had little chance of success, assured some of the principal knights that he did not covet the office, and would himself vote for his competitor. Believing him, they joyfully made him great-prior. His tone now altered. " The mantle is done, now put the hood on it. You have made me great-prior, and whether you will or not I will be great-master also." The astounded knights instantly chose him.

If this account be true, the mode of election at this time must have differed very considerably from that which we have described above out of the statutes of the order. This election, moreover, took place in France, where, in 1297, Molay, we are told, held the fourth son of the king at the baptismal font.

One feeble attempt, the last military exploit of the Templars, was made by the Christians to acquire once more a footing on the continent of Asia during the mastership of Molay. In 1300, the Mongol chief Gazan came to the aid of the king of Armenia, against the Turks. As it was the policy of the Tartars, who had not as yet embraced Islam, to stir up enemies to the Mohammedans, Gazan, after over-running the country as far as Damascus, sent an embassy to the Pope, Boniface VIII., inviting the Christians, particularly the three military orders, to come and take possession of the Holy Land. The Templars, Hospitallers, and Henry, king of Cyprus, forthwith manned seven galleys and five smaller vessels. Almeric de Lusignan, Lord of Tyre, and the Masters of the two orders, landed at Tortosa, and endeavoured to maintain that islet against the Egyptian sultan, but were forced to yield to numbers. The Templars fought gallantly to no purpose, and a few of them, who defended a tower into which they had thrown themselves, surrendered, and were carried prisoners to Egypt.

The Hospitallers, in the year 1306, renewed their attacks on the isle of Rhodes, where they finally succeeded in expelling the Turks, and planting the standard of their order. The Teutonic knights transferred the sphere of their warfare to Russia, and the adjacent country, whose inhabitants were still heathens. The Templars meantime remained inactive in Cyprus, and seem even to have been meditating a retreat to Europe.

France was at this time governed by Philip the Fair, son of St. Louis. Philip, who had come to the throne at the early age of seventeen years, had been educated by Giles de Colonna, afterwards archbishop of Bourges, a man distinguished for his learning and for the boldness of his opinions. One of his favourite maxims was, "that Jesus Christ had not given any temporal dominion to his church, and that the king of France has his authority from God alone." Such principles having been early instilled into his mind, the young monarch was not likely to be a very dutiful son of the Church, and the character of Boniface VIII., who, without possessing the talents or the virtues of a Gregory or an Innocent, attempted to stretch the papal pretensions to their greatest extent,

soon roused him to resistance. In the plenitude
of his fancied authority, the pope issued a bull, forbidding the clergy to give any subsidies to lay-powers
without permission from Rome. Philip, in return,
issued an order prohibiting the exportation of gold,
silver, or merchandize from France, thereby cutting
off a great source of papal revenue. In the course of
the dispute, Boniface maintained that princes were
subject to him in temporals also. Philip's reply was,
—" Philip, by the grace of God, king of the French, to
Boniface, acting as supreme pontiff, little or no health.
Let your extreme folly know, that in temporals we
are not subject to any one." Shortly afterwards he
publicly burned a bull of the pope, and proclaimed
the deed by sound of trumpet in Paris. Boniface,
raving with indignation, summoned the French clergy
to Rome, to deliberate on the means of preserving
the liberties of the Church. Philip convoked a national assembly to Paris, in which, for the first time,
there appeared deputies of the third estate, who readily expressed their resolution to stand by their
monarch in defence of his rights, and the clergy willingly denied the temporal jurisdiction of the pontiff.
Several prelates and abbots having obeyed the summons of the pope, the king seized on their tem-
poralities. The pope menaced with deprivation all
those who had not attended, and, in his famous bull
of *Unam sanctam*, asserted that every human being
was subject to the Roman pontiff. Another bull
declared that every person, be his rank what it might,
was bound to appear personally when summoned to
Rome. Philip forbade the publication of these bulls ;
and the states general being again convoked appealed to a council against the pope. Commissaries
were sent through France to procure the adhesion of
the clergy to this act, which was given in some cases
voluntarily. in others obtained by means of a little
wholesome rigour. The king, his wife, and his son,

pledged themselves to stand by those who adhered to the resistance made by France to papal usurpation. Boniface next excommunicated the king, who intercepted the bull, and prevented its publication. The pope finally offered the crown of France to the emperor Albert of Austria. Matters were now come to an extremity, and Philip ventured on one of the boldest acts that have ever been attempted in the Christian world.

Philip had afforded an asylum at his court to some members of the Colonna family, the personal enemies of the pope. His chancellor and fast adherent was William de Nogaret, who had been his agent in the affair of appealing to a general council, by presenting to the states general a charge of simony, magic, and the usual real or imaginary crimes of the day against the pontiff. This man, and some of the Italian exiles, attended by a body of 300 horse, set out for Italy, and took up his abode at a castle between Florence and Sienna, under pretext of its being a convenient situation for carrying on negociations with Rome. The pope was meantime residing at Anagni, his native town. Nogaret having, by a liberal distribution of money, acquired a sufficient number of partisans, appeared before the gate of Anagni early on the morning of the 7th September, 1303. The gate was opened by a traitor, and the French and their partisans ran through the streets, crying *Live the king of France, die Boniface.* They entered the palace without opposition; the French ran here and there in search of plunder, and Sciarra Colonna and his Italians alone came in presence of the pope. Boniface, who was now eighty-six years of age, was clad in his pontifical vestments, and on his knees before the altar, in expectation of death. At the sight of him the conspirators, whose intention had been to slay him, stopped short, filled with involuntary awe, and did not dare to lay a hand upon him. During three days they kept him a prisoner; on the fourth the people of the town rose and expelled them, and released the pontiff. Boniface returned to Rome; but rage at the humiliation which he had undergone deranged his intellect, and in one of his paroxysms he dashed his head against the wall of his chamber, and died in consequence of the injury which he received*.

Benedict XI., the successor of Boniface, absolved Philip, and his ministers and subjects, from the sentence of excommunication. As he felt his power, he was proceeding to more vigorous measures to avenge the insulted dignity of the holy see, when he died of poison, administered, as a contemporary historian asserts, by the agents of Philip. During ten months the conclave were unable to agree on his successor among the Italian cardinals. It was then proposed by the partisans of the king of France, that one party in the conclave should name three ultramontane prelates, from among whom the other party should select one. The choice fell on Bertrand de Gotte, archbishop of Bordeaux, who had many serious causes of enmity to Philip and his brother Charles of Valois. Philip's friend, the cardinal of Prato, instantly sent off a courier with the news, advising the king to acquiesce in the election as soon as he had secured him to his interest. Philip set out for Gascony, and had a private interview with the pontiff elect, in an abbey in the midst of a forest near St. Jean d'Angély. Having sworn mutual secresy, the king told the prelate that it was in his power to make him pope on condition of his granting him six favours. He showed him his proofs, and the ambitious Gascon, falling at his feet, promised everything. The six favours demanded by Philip were a perfect reconciliation with the Church; admission to the communion for him-

* Sismondi Républiques Italiennes, iv. p. 143.

self and friends; the tithes of the clergy of France for five years, to defray the expenses of his war in Flanders; the persecution and destruction of the memory of Pope Boniface; the conferring the dignity of cardinal on James and Peter Colonna. "The sixth favour," said he, "is great and secret, and I reserve the asking of it for a suitable time and place." The prelate swore on the host, and gave his brother and two of his nephews as hostages. The king then sent orders to the cardinal of Prato, to elect the archbishop of Bordeaux, who took the name of Clement V.

Whether urged by the vanity of shining in the eyes of his countrymen, or by dread of the tyranny exercised by the cardinals over his predecessors, or, what seems more probable, in compliance with the wishes of Philip, or in consequence of impediments thrown by that monarch in the way of his departure, Clement, to the dismay of all Christendom, instead of repairing to Rome, summoned the cardinals to Lyons for his coronation. They reluctantly obeyed, and he was crowned in that city on the 17th December, 1305, the king, his brother, and his principal nobles, assisting at the ceremony. Clement forthwith created twelve new cardinals, all creatures of Philip, whose most devoted slave the pope showed himself to be on all occasions. His promises to him were most punctually fulfilled, with the exception of that respecting the memory of Boniface, which the cardinal of Prato proved to Philip it would be highly impolitic and dangerous to perform; but Clement cheerfully authorised him to seize, on the festival of St. Madelaine, all the Jews in his kingdom, to banish them, and confiscate their property in the name of religion.

What the sixth and secret grace which Philip required was is unknown. Many conjectures have been made to little purpose. It is not at all improbable that the king had at the time no definite object in view, and that, like the fabled grant of Neptune to Theseus, it was to be claimed whenever an occasion of sufficient importance should present itself.

Such as we have described them were Philip and the sovereign pontiff; the one able, daring, rapacious, ambitious, and unprincipled; the other mean, submissive, and little scrupulous. As it was the object of Philip to depress the papal power, and make it subservient to his ambition, he must naturally have desired to deprive it of support. The Templars, therefore, who had been on all occasions the staunch partizans of the papacy, must on this account alone have been objects of his aversion ; they had, moreover, loudly exclaimed against his repeated adulteration of the coin, by which they sustained so much injury ; and they were very urgent in their demands for repayment of the money which they had lent him on the occasion of the marriage of his daughter Isabella with the son of the king of England. Their wealth was great ; their possessions in France were most extensive ; they were connected with the noblest families in the realm ; they were consequently, now that they seemed to have given up all idea of making any farther efforts in the East, likely to prove a serious obstacle in the way of the establishment of the absolute power of the crown. They were finally very generally disliked on account of their excessive pride and arrogance, and it was to be expected that in an attack on their power and privileges the popular favour would be with the king. These motives will, we apprehend, sufficiently account for Philip's anxiety to give a check to the order, beyond which, as it would appear, his plans did not at first extend. We cannot venture to say when this project first entered the mind of king Philip; whether he had the Hospitallers also in view, and whether he impelled the pope to invite the Masters of the two orders to France.

As the rivalry and ill-feeling between the two orders had long been regarded as one of the principal causes of the little success of the Christians in the East, the idea of uniting them had been conceived, and Gregory X. and St. Louis had striven, but in vain, at the council at Lyons, to effect it. Pope Boniface VIII. had also been anxious to bring this project to bear, and Clement now resolved to attempt it. On the 6th June, 1306, only six months after his coronation, he wrote to the Masters of the two orders to the following effect;—The kings of Armenia and Cyprus were calling on him for aid; he therefore wished to confer with them, who knew the country well, and were so much interested in it, as to what were best to be done, and desired that they would come to him as secretly as possible, and with a very small train, as they would find plenty of their knights on this side of the sea; he directed them to provide for the defence of Limisso during their absence.

The Master of the Hospital, William de Villaret, was, when the letter arrived, engaged in the attack on Rhodes, and, therefore, could not obey the summons. But De Molay, the Master of the Temple, having confided Limisso and the direction of the order to the marshal, embarked with sixty of his most distinguished knights, taking with him the treasure of the order, consisting of 150,000 florins of gold, and so much silver, that the whole formed the lading of twelve horses. When they arrived in France, he proceeded to Paris, where the king received him with the greatest marks of favour and distinction, and he deposited the treasure in the Temple of that city. Shortly afterwards he set out for Poitiers, where he had an interview with Clement, who consulted him on the affairs of the East. On the subject of a new crusade, Molay gave it as his opinion that nothing but a simultaneous effort of all the Christian powers

would be of any avail. He objected to the union of
the orders on the following grounds, which were,
on the whole, sufficiently frivolous. He said, 1st.
That what is new is not always the best; that the
orders, as they were, had done good service in Palestine, and, in short, used the good old argument of
anti-reformists, *It works well.* 2dly. That as the
orders were spiritual as well as temporal, and many
a one had entered them for the weal of his soul, it
might not be a matter of indifference to such to leave
the one which he had selected and enter another.
3dly. There might be discord, as each order would
want its own wealth and influence, and seek to gain
the mastery for its own rules and discipline. 4thly. The
Templars were generous of their goods, while the
Hospitallers were only anxious to accumulate—a difference which might produce dissension. 5thly. As
the Templars received more gifts and support from
the laity than the Hospitallers, they would be the
losers, or at least be envied by their associates.
6thly. There would probably be some disputing between the superiors about the appointment to the dignities in the new order. He however candidly
acknowledged, that the new order would be stronger
than the old one, and so more zealous to combat the
infidels, and that many commanderies might be suppressed, and some saving effected thereby. Having
thus delivered his sentiments, Molay took leave of
the pope, and returned to Paris. Vague rumours of
serious charges made, or to be made, against the
order now beginning to prevail, Molay, accompanied
by Rimbaud de Caron, preceptor of Outre-mer.
Jeffrey de Goneville, preceptor of Aquitaine, and
Hugh de Perando, preceptor of France, repaired once
more to Poitiers, about April, 1307, to justify himself and the order in the eyes of the pope. Clement,
we are told, informed them of the serious charges of

the commission of various crimes which had been made against them; but they gave him such explanations as appeared to content him, and returned to Paris, satisfied that they had removed all doubts from his mind.

The following was the way in which the charges were made against the Templars.

There was lying in prison, at Paris or Toulouse, for some crime, a man named Squin de Flexian, a native of Beziers, who had been formerly a Templar, and prior of Mantfaucon, but had been put out of the order for heresy and other offences. His companion in captivity was a Florentine, named Noffo Dei—" a man (says Villani) full of all iniquity." These two began to plan how they might best extricate themselves from their present hopeless state; and, as it would appear, aware of the king's dislike to the Templars, and hating them for having punished him for his crimes, Squin de Flexian resolved to accuse them of the most monstrous offences, and thus obtain his liberation. Accordingly, calling for the governor of the prison, he told him that he had a discovery to make to the king, which would be more for his advantage than the acquisition of a new kingdom, but that he would only reveal it to the king in person. Squin was immediately conveyed to Paris, and brought before the king, to whom he declared the crimes of the order; and some of the Templars were seized and examined by order of Philip.

Another account says that Squin Flexian and Noffo Dei, who were both degraded Templars, had been actively engaged in an insurrection of the people some time before, from which the king was obliged to take shelter in the Temple. They had been taken, and were lying in prison without any hope of their lives, when they hit on the plan of accusing their former associates. They were both set at liberty; but

Squin was afterwards hanged, and Noffo Dei beheaded, as was said with little probability, by the Templars.

It is also said, that, about the same time, Cardinal Cantilupo, the pope's chamberlain, who had been in connexion with the Templars from his eleventh year, made some discoveries respecting it to his master.

The charges made by Squin Flexian against the order were as follows :—

1. Each Templar, on his admission, was sworn never to quit the order; and to further its interests, by right or by wrong.

2. The heads of the order are in secret alliance with the Saracens; and have more Mahommedan infidelity than Christian faith; in proof of which, they make every novice spit and trample on the cross of Christ, and blaspheme his faith in various ways.

3. The heads of the order are heretical, cruel, and sacrilegious men. Whenever any novice, on discovering the iniquity of the order, attempts to quit it, they put him to death, and bury him privately by night. They teach the women who are pregnant by them how to procure abortion, and secretly murder the new-born babes.

4. The Templars are infected with all the errors of the Fraticelli; they despise the pope and the authority of the Church; they contemn the sacraments, especially those of penance and confession. They feign compliance with the rites of the Church merely to escape detection.

5. The superiors are addicted to the most infamous excesses of debauchery; to which, if any one expresses his repugnance, he is punished by perpetual captivity.

6. The temple-houses are the receptacles of every crime and abomination that can be committed.

7. The order labours to put the Holy Land into the hands of the Saracens; and favours them more than the Christians.

8. The installation of the Master takes place in secret, and few of the younger brethren are present at it; whence there is a strong suspicion that he denies the Christian faith or promises, or does something contrary to right.

9. Many statutes of the order are unlawful, profane, and contrary to the Christian religion; the members are, therefore, forbidden, under pain of perpetual confinement, to reveal them to any one.

10. No vice or crime committed for the honour or benefit of the order is held to be a sin.

Such were the charges brought against the order by the degraded prior of Montfaucon—charges in general absurd, or founded on gross exaggeration of some of the rules of the society. Others, still more incredible, were subsequently brought forward in the course of the examinations of witnesses.

Philip and his ministers, having now what they regarded as a plausible case against the Templars, prepared their measures in secret; and on the 12th September, 1307, sealed letters were sent to all the governors and royal officers throughout France, with orders to arm themselves on the 12th of the following month; and in the night to open the letters and act according to the instructions contained therein. The appointed day arrived; and, on the morning of Friday, the 13th October, nearly all the Templars throughout France saw themselves captives in the hands of their enemies. So well had Philip taken his measures, that his meditated victims were without suspicion; and, on the very eve of his arrest, Molay was chosen by the treacherous monarch to be one of the four pall-bearers at the funeral of the Princess Catherine, wife of the Count of Valois.

The directions sent by the king to his officers had been to seize the persons and the goods of the Templars : to interrogate, torture, and obtain confessions from them; to promise pardon to those who confessed; and to menace those who denied.

On the day of the arrest of the Master and his knights, the king took possession of the Temple at Paris; and the Master and the preceptors of Aquitaine, France, and beyond sea, were sent prisoners to Corbeil. The following day the doctors of the University of Paris and several canons assembled with the royal ministers in the church of Notre Dame, and William de Nogaret, the chancellor, stated to them that the knights had been proceeded against on account of their heresies. On the 15th the University met in the Temple; and some of the heads of the order, particularly the Master, were examined, and are said to have made some confessions of the guilt of the order for the last forty years.

The king now published an act of accusation, conceived in no moderate or gentle terms. He calls the accused in it devouring wolves, a perfidious and idolatrous society, whose deeds, whose very words alone, are enough to pollute the earth and infect the air, &c. &c. The inhabitants of Paris were then assembled in the royal gardens; and the king's agents spoke, and some monks preached to them against the accused.

Philip, in his hostility to the order, would be content with nothing short of its utter ruin. Almost immediately after his *coup d'état* of the 13th October, he despatched a priest, named Bernard Peletus, to his son-in-law, Edward II., king of England, inviting him to follow his example. Edward wrote, on the 30th of the same month, to say that the charges made against the Templars by Philip and his agent appeared to him, his barons, and his prelates, to be incredible; and that he would, therefore, summon the senechal of Agen, whence this rumour had proceeded, to inform him thereupon, before proceeding any farther.

s

Clement had been at first offended at the hasty and arbitrary proceedings of the king of France against the Templars; but Philip easily managed to appease him; and on the 22d November the pope wrote to the king of England, assuring him that the Master of the Temple had spontaneously confessed that the brethren, on their admission, denied Christ; and that several of the brethren in different parts of France had acknowledged the idolatry and other crimes laid to the charge of the order; and that a knight of the highest and most honourable character, whom he had himself examined, had confessed the denial of Jesus Christ to be a part of the ceremony of admission. He therefore calls on the king to arrest all the Templars within his realms, and to place their lands and goods in safe custody, till their guilt or innocence should be ascertained.

Edward, in a letter, dated November 26, inquired particularly of the senechal of Agen, in Guienne, respecting the charges against the Templars. On the 4th December he wrote to the kings of Portugal, Castile, Aragon, and Sicily, telling them of what he had heard, and adding that he had given no credit to it; and begging of them not to hearken to these rumours. On the 10th, evidently before he had received the bull, he wrote to the pope, stating his disbelief of what he had heard, and praying of his holiness to institute an inquiry. But when the papal bull, so strongly asserting the guilt of the order, arrived, the good-hearted king did not venture to refuse compliance with it; and he issued a writ on the 15th December, appointing the morn of Wednesday after Epiphany, in the following month, for seizing the Templars and their property, but directing them to be treated with all gentleness. Similar orders were forwarded to Scotland, Wales, and Ireland, on the 20th; and on the 26th he wrote to assure the pope that his mandates would be speedily obeyed. The arrests took place accordingly; and the Templars and their property were thus seized in the two countries in which they were most powerful*.

The reluctance of the king of England and his parliament to proceed to any harsh measures against the Templars affords some presumption in their favour, and would incline us to believe that, had Philip been actuated by a similar love of justice, the order would not have been so cruelly treated in France. But Philip had resolved on the destruction of the society, and his privy councillors and favourites were not men who would seek to check him in his career of blood and spoliation. These men were William Imbert, his confessor, a Dominican monk, one of an order inured in Languedoc to blood, and deeply versed in all inquisitorial arts and practices; William Nogaret, his chancellor, the violator of the sanctity of the head of the church; William Plasian, who had shared in that daring deed, and afterwards sworn, in an assembly of the peers and prelates of France, that Boniface was an atheist and a sorcerer, and had a familiar demon. The whole order of the Dominicans also went heart and hand in the pious work of detecting and punishing the heretics. We must constantly bear in mind that the charges made against the Templars, if they may not all be classed under the term heresy, were all such as the Church was in the habit of making against those whom she persecuted as public heretics. And in this, Philip and his advisers acted wisely in their generation; for treason, or any other political charge, would have sounded dull and inefficient in the ears of the people, in comparison with the formidable word *heresy*.

---

* The arrests were made in England in the same secret and sudden manner as in France. Rymer iii. 34, 43.

Philip le Bel.

Chapter X.

Examination of the captive Knights—Different kinds of Tor-
ture—Causes of Confession—What Confessions were made
—Templars brought before the Pope—Their Declarations—
Papal Commission—Molay brought before it—Ponsard de
Gisi—Defenders of the Order—Act of Accusation—Heads
of Defence—Witnesses against the Order—Fifty-four Tem
plars committed to the flames at Paris—Remarkable words of
Aymeric de Villars-le-Duc—Templars burnt in other Places
—Further Examinations—The Head worshipped by the
Templars—John de Pollincourt—Peter de la Palu.

THE charge of conducting the inquiry against the
society was committed by Philip, without asking or
waiting for the Pope's approbation, to Imbert, who
lost no time in proceeding to action. He wrote to
all the inquisitors of his order, directing them to
proceed against the Templars, as he had already
done himself; and, in case of ascertaining the truth of
the charges, to communicate it to the Minorite Friars,
or some other order, that the people might take no
offence at the procedure ; and to send the declarations
as soon as possible to the king and himself. They
were to use no cruelty towards the prisoners ; but, if
necessary, they might employ the torture. On the
19th October, six days after their seizure, Imbert
commenced his examinations at the Temple of Paris.
One hundred and forty prisoners were examined;
when, by promises and by the aid of the torture, confessions in abundance were procured. Thirty-six of
the knights expired under the gentle method em

ployed to extract the truth from them.   The zealous
Imbert then proceeded to Bayeux, Metz, Toul, and
Verdun ; in all which places examinations were held
and confessions extorted in the same way.   It was,
however, carefully stated in each deposition, that the
witness had spoken without any constraint.

As our readers fortunately cannot be supposed
familiarly acquainted with the mild and gentle modes
employed by the brethren of St. Dominic, for elicit-
ing the truth, we will present a slight sketch of some
of them, that they may be able to form some idea of
the value of rack-extorted testimony.

Sometimes the patient was stripped naked, his
hands were tied behind his back, heavy weights were
fastened to his feet, and the cord which confined his
hands passed over a pulley.   At a given signal he
was hoisted into the air, where he hung suspended
by his arms, which were thus drawn out of their
natural position : then suddenly the cord would be
let run, but checked before the patient reached the
ground, and thus a tremendous shock given to his
frame.   Another mode of torture was to fasten the
feet of the patient on an instrument, which prevented
his drawing them back; they were then rubbed with
some unctious substance, and set before a flaming
fire ; a board was occasionally placed between his
feet and the fire, and withdrawn again, in order to
increase his pain by intervals of cessation.   The
heel of the patient was at times enclosed in an iron
heel, which could be tightened at pleasure, and thus
caused excruciating pain.   What was regarded as a
very gentle mode, and only indulged to those who
had not strength to undergo the preceding tortures,
was to place round sticks between their fingers, and
compress them till the bones of the fingers were
cracked.   The teeth of the Templars were occasionally drawn, their feet roasted, weights suspended

from all parts of their bodies; and thus they gave their testimony without constraint!

What is understood as testimony or confession, by inquisitors, is an affirmative answer to such questions as they ask. They usually assume the guilt of the accused; and no witnesses for the defence are heard. It is useless to prove the absurdity and unreasonableness of the charges; for that would be impugning the sense and judgment of those who gave ear to them; and promises are always held out that, if full and free confession is made, the criminal will be gently dealt with. The accused is, moreover, always confined in a solitary cell; he has none to console and cheer him; he feels abandoned by the whole world; conscious innocence is of no avail; his only hope is in the mercy of his judge. The Templars, we must recollect, were seized towards the commencement of winter; and at that season a dungeon of the middle ages must have been cheerless beyond description. They were barely allowed the necessaries of life; they were stripped of the habit of the order, and denied the consolations of religion, for they were treated as heretics; and they were shown a real or pretended letter of their Master, in which he confessed the crimes of the order, and exhorted them to do the same. Enthusiasts in religion or politics are supported by the consciousness of rectitude, and bear up against privations or torture in firm reliance on the favour of the Divinity, or the praise and esteem of a grateful and admiring posterity. But the great majority of the Templars were far from being such characters; they were illiterate knights, who had long lived in luxury and indulged in arrogance; they knew themselves to be objects of dislike to many, and felt that their power was gone. Need we then be surprised that, beguiled by the hopes held out, numbers of them readily acknowledged all the charges made against their order? and must we not so much the more admire the constancy of those who, unseduced by flattering hopes, and undismayed by menaces and torture, yielded up their breath rather than confess a falsehood?

At Paris the knights who confessed acknowledged the denial of Christ (this was the point which the inquisitors were most anxious to establish), but in an uncertain, contradictory manner, as what was said on one examination was retracted on another, or was enlarged or diminished. It was also confessed that an idol was adored in their chapters. At Nîmes, in November, 1307, forty-five knights confessed the guilt of the order. They afterwards retracted; but in 1311 the torture made them revert to their original declaration. At Troyes two knights confessed every-thing that was required of them. At Pont de l'Arche seven confessed. These and six others were again examined at Caen; they terminated their declarations by imploring the mercy of the Church, and entreating with tears to be spared the torture. Those examined at Carcassonne all deposed to the worship of the image; but some of them afterwards retracted that admission, and died maintaining the innocence of the order. Six Templars at Bigorre * and seven at Cahors confessed; but several of them afterwards retracted.

Philip and his creatures were at this stage of their career, when the pope began to testify some little dissatisfaction at the irregularity of the pro-ceedings. The king instantly wrote to upbraid him

---

* In the church of the romantic hamlet of Gavarnic, a few leagues from Barèges, on the road to Spain, in the heart of the Hautes Pyrénées, are shown twelve skulls, which are said to have been those of Templars who were beheaded in that place. The tradition is, in all probability, incorrect; but the Templars had possessions in Bigorre.

with his lukewarmness in the cause of religion. He stated that the bishops, who were his (the king's) helpers in the government of the Church, were the fittest persons to carry on the business, on account of their local knowledge; and added that neither he nor they could comply with the desires of the pope: "he acted," he said, "as the servant of God, and must render to God his account." Clement could not venture to impede the pious labours of such a zealous servant of the Lord; he cancelled the bull which he had prepared on the subject, only requiring that each bishop's inquisitors should be confirmed by a provincial council, and that the examination of the heads of the order should be reserved for himself. Philip then condescended to offer to put the captives into the hands of the papal judges, and to devote the goods of the order to the profit of the Holy Land. The clergy declined taking charge of the knights, and the king and pope managed the property of the order in common.

In the beginning of the year 1308, we are told *, the Master of the Templars, the preceptor of Cyprus, the visiter of France, and the great-priors of Aquitaine and Normandy, were brought before the pope at Chinon, where they voluntarily, and without the application of any torture, confessed the truth of the enormities laid to the charge of the order. They abjured their errors, and the cardinals implored the king in their favour.

M. Raynouard †, we know not on what authority, positively denies that the Master and his companions were ever brought before the pope. He says that, in the month of August following, they were on their way to Poitiers, in order to be examined by the pontiff

* This is mentioned in a private letter from Clement to Philip, of the 30th December, 1308.
† Monumens Historiques, &c. p. 46.

in person; but that, under pretext of some of them being sick, they were detained at Chinon, instead of being brought on to Poitiers, where the pope remained, and were finally conducted back to Paris without having seen him. He does not give the date of this occurrence, but it it would seem to have been in the following autumn.

The proceedings against the Templars were so manifestly contrary to the interest of the pope, that Philip deemed it necessary to keep a strict eye over him. Having, in May, 1308, convoked an assembly of the states at Tours, and obtained from them a declaration of his right to punish notorious heretics without asking the consent of the pope, and in which he was called upon to act with rigour against the Templars, he proceeded with it himself to Poitiers, and presented it to Clement. During the negociations which took place at that time, the pope attempted to make his escape to Bordeaux, but his baggage and his treasures were stopped by the king's orders at the gate of the town, and Clement remained in effect a prisoner.

While the supreme pontiff was thus in his power, Philip, who still remained at Poitiers, by way of removing all his scruples, had, on the 29th and 30th June, and 1st July, seventy-two of the Templars, who had confessed, brought before Clement and examined. As was to be expected, the greater part repeated their former declarations of the impiety, idolatry, and licentiousness of the order. From these depositions it appears clearly that the torture had been employed to extract the former confessions.

Pierre de Broel said that he had been stripped and put to the torture, but that he had said neither more nor less on that account. He added that those who tortured him were all drunk.

Guillaume de Haymes had not been tortured, but

he had been kept a month in solitary confinement on bread and water before he made any confession.

Gerard de St. Martial, who confessed to having denied Christ, and spitten *beside* the cross, said that he had been cruelly tortured, being at first ashamed to acknowledge these facts, although they were true.

Deodat Jafet had been tortured, but it was the inspiration of God and the blessed Virgin Mary, and not the rack, which had made him confess. He acknowledged every crime imputed to the order. Speaking of the idol, he said, " I was alone in a chamber with the person who received me : he drew out of a box a head, or idol, which appeared to me to have three faces, and said, *Thou shouldst adore it as thy Saviour and that of the order of the Temple.* We then bent our two knees, and I cried, *Blessed be he who will save my soul,* and I worshipped it." Yet Jafet afterwards retracted this deposition, and stood forth as one of the defenders of the order.

Iter de Rochefort, though he said he had confessed, had been tortured repeatedly, with a view to extracting more from him. He declared that, having been received in the unlawful way, he had confessed himself to the patriarch of Jerusalem, who had wept bitterly at hearing of such wickedness. As Raynouard very justly observes, the patriarch, who could hardly be a friend to the Templars, was not very likely to content himself with shedding a few useless tears had the knowledge of such a heresy come to his ears.

Pierre de Conders had confessed at the sight of the rack.

Raymond de Stéphani had been severely tortured at Carcassonne. Being asked why he did not then tell the truth, he replied, " Because I did not recollect it ; but I prayed the senechal to allow me to

confer with my companions, and when I had deliberated with them I recollected."

Who can give credit to depositions like these,
most of which were subsequently revoked? Yet it
was by these that the pope declared himself to be
perfectly satisfied of the guilt of the order, and justified the rigorous measures which he authorized
against it. Philip, we are to observe, was all this
time at Poitiers: the prisoners were examined before
the cardinals, and only those who had not retracted
their former rack-extorted confessions were produced
in the large concourse of nobles, clergy, and people
assembled on this occasion*.

Clement and Philip now arranged the convocation
of an œcumenic council at Vienne, to pronounce the
abolition of the order. The pope also appointed a
commission to take at Paris a juridical information
against it; and, on the 1st August, he authorised the
bishops and his delegates to proceed in their inquiries.
On the 12th August, by the bull *Faciens misericordiam*,
after asserting the guilt of the order, he called upon
all princes and prelates throughout the Christian
world to assist him in making inquiry into this affair.

The commission appointed by the pope was composed of the archbishop of Narbonne, the bishops of
Bayeux, Mende, and Limoges; Matthew of Naples,
archdeacon of Rouen, notary of the Holy See; John
of Mantua, archdeacon of Trent; John of Montlaur,
archdeacon of Maguelone; and William Agelin, pro-
vost of Aix, which last was prevented by business
from giving attendance. They entered on their
functions on the 7th August, 1309, and ordered that
the brethren of the Temple should be cited before
them on the first day of business after the festival of

* Raynouard, p. 253.

St. Martin, in November. The citations were to be published in presence of the people and clergy in the cathedrals, churches, and schools, in the principal houses of the order, and in the prisons in which the knights were confined. No one appearing, new citations were issued; and at length the Bishop of Paris was called on by the commission to go himself to the prison where the Master and the heads of the order were confined, and notify it to them. Having done so, he caused the same notification to be made throughout his diocese. The following circumstance, which occurred at this time, would seem to indicate that impediments were thrown in the way of those who were disposed to defend the order by the royal ministers. The commissioners were informed that the governor of the Chatelet had arrested and imprisoned some persons who were presumed to have come to defend the order. The governor being summoned before them, declared that, by order of the ministers, he had arrested seven persons who were denounced as being Templars in a lay habit, who had come to Paris with money in order to procure advocates and defenders for the accused. He acknowledged that he had put them to the torture, but said that he did not believe them to be Templars.

On Wednesday, Nov. 26, the commission sat, and Molay, the Master of the Temple, was brought before it. He was asked if he would defend the order, or speak for himself. He replied by expressing his surprise that the Church should proceed with such precipitation in this case, when the sentence relative to the Emperor Frederic had been suspended for thirty-two years. Though he had neither knowledge nor talent sufficient to defend the order, he should consider himself vile in his own eyes, and in those of others, if he hesitated to do so; but being the prisoner of the king and the pope, and without money, he asked for aid and counsel.

The commissioners desired him to reflect on his offer, and to consider the confessions respecting himself and the order which he had made. They agreed, however, to give him time ; and, that he might not be ignorant of what was alleged against him, had the documents containing their powers read to him in the vulgar language.

During the reading of the letters which recited his confession made to the cardinals at Chinon, he crossed himself repeatedly, and gave other signs of indignation and surprise, and said, that, were it not for the respect due to the envoys of the pope, he should express himself differently. They said they were not come there to receive challenges. He replied that he spoke not of cartels, he only wished they acted in this case as the Saracens and Tartars did, who cut off the head and cut the body in two of those who were found to be guilty.

Two circumstances are worthy of note in this examination ; one, that William Plasian was present at it, and, as the commissioners expressly declared, without being invited by them ; the other, that the confessions, which were imputed to Molay, and which he evidently intimated to be false, were inserted in the bull *Faciens misericordiam,* which bears the date of the 12th August, although the festival of the Assumption, that is the 16th of August, is given as the day on which they were made *. It was there declared that the heads of the order had confessed and been absolved ; yet here we find the

* Raynouard, 61. This circumstance was first remarked by Fleury, *Hist. Eccles.*, lib. xci. Yet it seems hardly credible hat the pope and his secretaries could have made so gross a mistake.

Master treated as a heretic who was still unreconciled.

The following day (Nov. 27), Ponsard de Gisi, prior of Payens, appeared before the commission. On being asked if he would defend the order, he replied, " Yes; the imputations cast on us of denying Christ, of spitting on the cross, of authorising infamous crimes, and all such accusations, are false If I, myself, or other knights, have made confessions before the bishop of Paris, or elsewhere, we have betrayed the truth—we have yielded to fear, to danger, to violence. We were tortured by Flexien de Beziers, prior of Montfaucon, and the monk William Robert, our enemies. Several of the prisoners had agreed among themselves to make these confessions, in order to escape death, and because thirty-six knights had died at Paris, and a great number in other places, under the torture. As for me, I am ready to defend the order in my own name, and in the names of those who will make common cause with me, if I am assigned out of the goods of the order as much as will defray the needful expense. I require to be granted the counsel of Raynaud of Orleans and of Peter of Bologna, priests of the order." He was asked if he had been tortured. He replied that he had, three months before he made his confession.

Next day the Master was brought up again. He demanded to be brought before the pope, appealed to the valour and charity of the Templars, and their zeal in adorning churches, in proof of their piety, and made an orthodox confession of his own faith. Nogaret, who was present, then observed, that it was related in the chronicles of St. Denis that the Master of the order had done homage to Saladin; and that the sultan had ascribed their ill fortune to their secret vices and impiety. Molay declared that he had never heard of such calumnies; and gave an instance of the prudence and good faith of a former Master, when himself and some other young men wanted him to break a truce. Molay concluded by praying the chancellor and the commissioners to procure him the favour of hearing mass, and being attended by his chaplains.

Orders having been given that all the Templars who were desirous to undertake the defence of the order should be conveyed to Paris, they were brought thither strongly guarded. The commission then renewed its sittings. As the prisoners were successively brought before it, they, with few exceptions, declared their readiness to defend their order—*till death*, cried some; *till the end*, cried others; *because I wish to save my soul*, added one. Bertrand de St. Paul declared that he never did, and never would, confess the guilt of the order, because it was not true; and that he believed that God would work a miracle if the body of Christ was administered to those who confessed and those who denied. Seven of those who had been examined before the pope, and had confessed, now declared that they had lied, and revoked what they then said. John de Valgellé maintained that he had made no confession on that occasion. " I was tortured so much, and held so long before a burning fire," said Bernard de Vado, " that the flesh of my heels was burnt, and these two bones (which he showed) came off."

In the course of these examinations, a Templar, named Laurent de Beaune, showed a letter with the seals of Philip de Voet and John Jainville, the persons set by the pope and king over the prisoners, addressed to the Templars confined at Sens, inviting them to confess what was required, and declaring that the pope had given orders that those who did not persevere in their confessions should be committed to the flames. Philip de Voet, on being interrogated, said that he did not believe that he had sent that letter; his seal had often lain in the hands of his secretary; he had always advised the prisoners to speak the truth. Jainville was not examined, neither was John Carpini, the bearer of the letter. De Beaune was one of the first afterwards committed to the flames; the supposition is natural, that the letter was a stratagem of the king and his ministers.

The Master having been again brought before the commissioners, and having renewed his demand of being sent to the pope, they promised to write to the pope on the subject, but there is no proof of their having done so.

On the 28th March all the Templars who had expressed their willingness to defend the order were assembled in the garden of the bishop's palace. Their number was 546. The Master was not among them. The articles of accusation were then read over to them in Latin; the commissioners ordered that they should be read again to them in the vulgar tongue, but the knights all cried out that it was enough, they did not desire that such abominations, which were false and not to be named, should be repeated in the vulgar language. Again, they complained of the deprivation of their religious habits and the sacraments of the church, and desired that the Master and the heads of the order should be called thither also. But this reasonable request was not complied with. In vain the Master demanded to be brought before the pope; in vain the knights required to be permitted to enjoy the presence of their chief. Neither the one nor the other suited the interest or the designs of the king.

The number of the Templars in Paris soon amounted to near 900. The commissioners were desirous that they should appoint agents to manage their defence; but this they declined to do, some alleging that they could not do so without the consent of their chief, others insisting on defending the order in person. At length, after a great deal of argument and deliberation, seventy-five Templars were chosen to draw up the defence of the order; and the priests of the order, Raynaud de Pruino and Peter of Bologna, and the knights, William de Chambonnet and Bertrand de Sartiges, were appointed to be present at the deposition of the witnesses.

The act of accusation against the Templars, drawn up in the name of the pope, ran thus. At the time of their reception they were made to deny God, Christ, the Virgin, &c.; in particular to declare that Christ was not the true God, but a false prophet, who had been crucified for his own crimes, and not for the redemption of the world. They spat and trampled on the cross, especially on Good Friday. They worshipped a cat which sometimes appeared in their chapters. Their priests, when celebrating mass, did not pronounce the words of consecration. They believed that their Master could absolve them from their sins. They were told at their reception that they might abandon themselves to all kinds of licentiousness. They had idols in all their provinces, some with three faces, some with one. They worshipped these idols in their chapters, believed that they could save them, regarded them as the givers of wealth to the order, and of fertility to the earth; they touched them with cords which they afterwards tied round their own bodies. Those who at the time of their reception would not comply with these practices were put to death or imprisoned. All this, it was stated, took place *according to the statutes of the order;* it was a general and ancient custom, and there was no other mode of reception. The act of accusation stated farther that the Templars stopped at no means of enriching the order *.

The Templars, in their reply, asserted that all these imputations were false, and that if any of them had confessed them, they had done so under terror and violence, thirty-six having expired by torture at Paris and several others elsewhere. The forms of law had been violated with respect to them; to obtain from them false depositions letters of the king had been shown them declaring that the order had been condemned irrevocably, and offering life, liberty, and pensions, to those who would depose falsely. "All these facts, said they, are so public and so notorious that there are no means or pretexts for disavowing them." The heads of accusation were nothing but falsehoods and absurdities, and the bull contained nothing but horrible, detestable, and iniquitous falsehoods. Their order was pure, and if their statutes were consulted they would be found to be the same for all Templars and for all countries. Their belief was that of the Church; parents brought their children, brothers each other, uncles their nephews, into the order, because it was pure and holy. When in captivity to the infidels, the Templars died sooner than renounce their religion. They declared their readiness to defend their innocence in every way, and against every person except the pope and the king, demanded to be brought personally before the general council, required that those who had quitted the order and deposed against it should be

* All these crimes had been acknowledged by various members of the order. Yet what can be more improbable than the worship of the cat for instance? This charge, by the way, had already been made against the sect of the Cathari, who were said to have derived their name *a catta:*—rather their name gave origin to the invention.

kept in close custody till their truth or falsehood should be ascertained, and that no layman should be present to intimidate the accused when under examination.   The knights, they maintained, had been struck with such terror, that the false confessions made by some were less matter of surprise than the courage of those who maintained the truth was of admiration.   Inquire, said they, of those who were present at the last moments of the knights who died in prison ; let their confessions be revealed, and it will be seen if the accusations are true.   Is it not strange, asked they in conclusion, that more credit should be given to the lies of those who yielded to tortures or to promises than to the asseverations of those who, in defence of the truth, have died with the palm of martyrdom—of the sound majority of those knights who have suffered and still suffer so much for conscience' sake?

On the 11th April, 1310, the hearing of the witnesses against the order commenced.   Only twenty-one were produced, two of whom did not belong to the order, the others being principally those who had persisted in their declarations before the pope. As might be expected, all the crimes laid to the charge of the order in the papal bull were again deposed to by these men ; but the commission had only got as far as the examination of the thirteenth witness when the impatience of the king manifested itself in a barbarous and illegal act, which had apparently long been meditated.

The Archbishop of Sens, whose suffragan the Bishop of Paris was, had died about Easter, 1309, and the pope had reserved the nomination to himself. Philip wrote to him requiring of him to nominate Philip de Marigny, Bishop of Cambray, brother to Enquerrand, his prime minister, alleging that his youth was no just impediment, and that his acts would prove how much he was beyond his age. The pope, though very reluctant, was obliged to consent, and in April, 1310, Marigny was installed. No time was now lost in proceeding to operation. On Sunday, May 10, the four defenders of the order learned that the provincial council of Sens was convoked at Paris in order to proceed against the knights individually. They took alarm, and applied to the commission, which, though it did not sit on Sundays, assembled, and Peter of Bologna informed them of what he had heard. He begged that they would suffer him to read an appeal which he had drawn up. This they declined doing, but said that, if he had any defence of the order to give in, they would receive it. He forthwith laid down a written paper, stating the danger which the prisoners were in dread of, appealing to the holy see, and entreating the commission to stop the proceedings of the archbishop and his suffragans. The defenders of the order then retired, and the further consideration of the affair was put off till after vespers, when they re-appeared and gave in an address to the Archbishop of Sens, containing an appeal to the pope. The commissioners, however, declined interfering for the present.

It is to be noticed that the defenders of the order prayed on this occasion of the commission to nominate one or more of its notaries to draw up their act of defence, because they could find no notary who would act for them, owing probably to fear of the royal displeasure, or to the want of funds by the accused.

On Monday and Tuesday two more of the witnesses were heard. One of them named Humbert de Puy declared that, having refused to acknowledge the crimes laid to the charge of the order, he had been tortured three times and kept for thirty-six weeks on bread and water in the bottom of an inected tower, by order of John de Jainville.

While thus engaged, the commissioners learned
to their dismay that the council was about to commit
to the flames fifty-four of the knights who had stepped forth as the defenders of the order. They
instantly sent one of their notaries and one of the
keepers of the prison of the Templars to entreat the
archbishop to act with caution, as there were strong
reasons for doubting the truth of the charges; and
representing that the witnesses were so terrified at
what they had heard of the intentions of the council,
that they were incapable of giving their evidence;
that moreover the Templars had delivered in an
appeal to the pope.

The archbishop, who was paying the price of his
elevation to a hard creditor, was not to be stopped
by these considerations. He was making short work
of the business. On the Monday he had a number
of those who had undertaken the defence of the order
brought before the council, and he interrogated them
once more himself. Those of them who, having confessed, had afterwards retracted, and now persisted
in their retractation, were declared to be *relapsed
heretics*, and were delivered over to the secular arm
and condemned to the flames; those who had not
confessed, and would not, were sentenced to imprisonment as *unreconciled* Templars; those who persisted
in their confession of the enormities laid to the charge
of the order were set at liberty, and called *reconciled*
Templars.

The next morning the fifty-four Templars who
had been declared relapsed were taken from their
prison, placed in carts, and conducted to the place
of execution, where they beheld the piles prepared,
and the executioners standing with flaming torches
in their hands. An envoy from the court was present, who proclaimed liberty and the royal favour for
those who would even then retract their declarations

and confess the guilt of the order. The friends and relatives of the unhappy victims crowded round them, with tears and prayers, imploring of them to make the required acknowledgment and save their lives. In vain. These gallant knights, who, yielding to the anguish of torture, and worn down by solitude and privations, had confessed to the truth of the most absurd charges, now that they beheld the certain limit of their sufferings, disdained to purchase by falsehood a prolongation of life to be spent in infamy and contempt. With one voice they re-asserted their own innocence and that of their order. They called on God, the Virgin, and all the saints to aid and support them, raised the hymn of death, and expired amidst the tears and commiseration of the by-standers.

Felons convicted on the clearest evidence will, as is well known, die asserting their innocence ; but this is when they have no hope of escape remaining. Here life and liberty were offered, and the victims were implored by those whom they most loved to accept of them. May we not then assert that the men who resisted all solicitations were sincere and spoke the truth, and were supported by their confidence of being received as martyrs by that God whom they devoutly adored according to the doctrines of their church ?

On Wednesday, Aymeric de Villars-le-Duc, aged about fifty years, was brought before the commissioners. He was quite pallid, and seemed terrified beyond measure. On the articles to which he was to depose being explained to him, he asseverated in the strongest manner his resolution to speak the truth ; then striking his breast with his clenched hands, he bent his knees, and stretching his hands towards the altar, spake these memorable words :—

" I persist in maintaining that the errors imputed to the Templars are absolutely false, though I have confessed some of them myself, overcome by the tortures which G. de Marcillac and Hugh de Celle, the king's knights, ordered to be inflicted on me. I have seen the fifty-four knights led in carts to be committed to the flames because they would not make the confessions which were required of them. I have heard that they were burnt; and I doubt if I could, like them, have had the noble constancy to brave the terrors of the pile. I believe that, if I were threatened with it, I should depose on oath before the commission, and before any other persons who should interrogate me, that these same errors imputed to the order are true. *I would kill God himself if it was required of me.*"

He then earnestly implored the commissioners and the notaries who were present not to reveal to the king's officers, and to the keepers of the Templars, the words which had escaped him, lest they should deliver him also to the flames.

Ought not these simple honest words, the very accents of truth, to prevail with us against all the confessions procured by torture, or by promises or threats, and satisfy us as to their value?

The commissioners, whose conduct throughout the whole affair was regulated by humanity and justice, declared that the evening before one of the witnesses had come to them and implored of them to keep his deposition secret, on account of the danger which he ran if it should be known; and, judging that in their present state of terror it would not be just to hear the witnesses, they deliberated on proroguing their session to a future period.

We thus see that even the papal commission could not protect against the king such of the witnesses as were honest and bold enough to maintain the innocence of the order. Strict justice was therefore out of the question, Philip *would* have the order guilty of the most incredible crimes, and death awaited the witness who did not depose as he wished. Meantime his agents were busily engaged in tampering with the prisoners; and by threats and promises they prevailed on forty-four of them to give up their design of defending the order.

On the 21st May the commissioners met, in the absence of the Archbishop of Narbonne and the Archdeacon of Trent, and, declaring their labours suspended for the present, adjourned to the 3d November.

In the interval the conduct of the council of Sens had been imitated in other provinces. The Archbishop of Rheims held a council at Senlis, by whose sentence nine Templars were committed to the flames. Another council was held at Pont-de-l'Arche by the Archbishop of Rouen, and several knights were burnt. The Bishop of Carcassonne presided at a council which delivered many victims to the secular arm. On the 18th August the Archbishop of Sens held a second council, and burned four knights. Thibault, Duke of Lorraine, the close friend of King Philip, put many Templars to death, and seized the property of the order.

On the 3d November three of the papal commissioners met at Paris : they asked if any one wished to defend the order of the Templars. No one appearing they adjourned to the 27th December. On resuming their sittings they called on William de Chambonnet and Bertrand de Sartiges to give their presence at the hearing of the witnesses. These knights required the presence of Raynaud de Pruino and Peter of Bologna, but were informed that these priests had solemnly and voluntarily renounced the defence of the order, and revoked their retractations ; that the latter had escaped from his prison and fled, and that the former could not be admitted to defend the order

T

as he had been degraded at the council of Sens The knights reiterated their refusal and retired. The commissioners then proceeded in their labours without them, and continued the examination of witnesses till the 26th May, 1311.

The whole number of persons examined before the commision amounted to 231, for the far greater part serving-brethren. Of these about two-thirds acknowledged the truth of the principal charges against the order. The denial of Christ and spitting on the cross were very generally confessed, but many said they had spitten *beside* it, not *on* it, and also that they had denied God with their lips, not with their hearts.

With respect to the head which the Templars were said to worship, as it was of some importance to prove this offence, in order to make out the charge of heresy, it was testified to by a few. Some said it was like that of a man with a long white beard, others that it was like that of a woman, and that it was said to be the head of one of the 11,000 virgins. One witness gave the following account of it, which he said he had had from a secular knight at Limisso, in Cyprus.

A certain nobleman was passionately in love with a maiden. Being unable, however, to overcome her repugnance to him, he took her body, when she was dead, out of her grave, and cut off her head, and while thus engaged he heard a voice crying—*Keep it safe, whatever looks on it will be destroyed.* He did as desired, and made the first trial of it on the Grissons, an Arab tribe, which dwelt in Cyprus and the neighbouring country, and whenever he uncovered the head and turned it towards any of their towns, its walls instantly fell down. He next embarked with the head for Constantinople, being resolved to destroy that city also. On the way his nurse, out of curiosity, opened the box which contained the head. Instantly there came on a terrific storm, the ship went to pieces, and nearly all who were on board perished. The very fish vanished from that part of the sea.

Another of the witnesses had heard the same story. The common tradition of the East, he said, was, that in old times, before the two spiritual orders of knighthood were founded, a head used to rise in a certain whirlpool named Setalia, the appearance of which was very dangerous for the ships which happened to be near it. We are to suppose, though it does not appear that the witnesses said so, that the Templars had contrived to get possession of this formidable head.

We are to observe that the witnesses who thus deposed had been picked and culled in all parts of France, by the king's officers, out of those who had confessed before the different prelates and provincial councils, and who were, by threats and promises, engaged to persist in what they had said. The terror they were under was visible in their countenances, their words, and their actions. Many of them began by saying that they would not vary from what they had deposed before such a bishop or such a council; yet even among these some were bold enough to revoke their confessions, declaring that they had been drawn from them by torture, and asserted the innocence of the order. Others retracted their confessions when brought before the commissioners, but shortly afterwards, having probably in the interval been well menaced or tortured by the king's officers, returned and retracted their retractation.

The case of John de Pollencourt, the thirty-seventh witness, is a remarkable instance. He began in the usual way, by declaring that he would persist in his confession made before the Bishop of Amiens, touching the denial of Christ, &c. The commissioners, observing his paleness and agitation, told him to tell the truth and save his soul, and not to persist in his confession if it had not been sincere, assuring him that neither they nor their notaries would reveal any thing that he said. After a pause he replied:—

" I declare then, on peril of my soul, and on the oath which I have taken, that, at the time of my reception, I neither denied God nor spat upon the cross, nor committed any of the indecencies of which we are accused, and was not required so to do. It is true that I have made confessions before the inquisitors; but it was through the fear of death, and because Giles de Rotangi had, with tears, said to me, and many others who were with me in prison at Montreuil, that we should pay for it with our lives, if we did not assist by our confessions to destroy the order. I yielded, and afterwards I wished to confess myself to the Bishop of Amiens; he referred me to a Minorite friar; I accused myself of this falsehood, and obtained absolution, on condition that I would make no more false depositions in this affair. I tell you the truth; I persist in attesting it before you; come what may of it, I prefer my soul to my body."

Nothing can bear more plainly the character of truth than this declaration; yet three days afterwards the witness came back, revoked it all, spoke of the cat which used to appear in the chapters, and said that, if the order had not been abolished, he would have quitted it. Had he not been well menaced and tortured in the *interim* ?

The examination of Peter de la Palu, a bachelor in theology of the order of the preachers, the 201st witness, brought from him these remarkable words: " I have been present at the examination of several Templars, some of whom confessed many of the things contained in the said articles, and some others totally denied them; and for many reasons it appeared to me that greater credit was to be given to those who denied than to those who confessed."

CHAPTER XI.

Examinations in England—Germany—Spain—Italy—Naples
and Provence—Sicily—Cyprus—Meeting of the Council of
Vienne—Suppression of the order—Fate of its Members—
Death of Molay.

THE time fixed for the meeting of the council at
Vienne was now at hand, in which the fate of the
order was to be decided. Before we proceed to
narrate its acts we will briefly state the result of the
examinations of the Templars in other countries.

The pope sent, as his judges, to England, Dieu-
donné, abbot of Lagny, and Sicard de Vaux, canon
of Narbonne; and the examinations commenced at
York, London, Lincoln, and other places, on the
25th November, 1309. The inquiry continued till
the council held in London in 1311; the number of
Templars examined was two hundred and twenty-
eight; that of the witnesses against the order was
seventy-two, almost all Carmelites, Minorites, Dominicans, and Augustinians, the natural foes of the
order. The Templars were treated with great mildness; and in England, Ireland, and Scotland, they
were unanimous and constant in their assertion of
the innocence of the order. The evidence against
the order was almost all hearsay: its nature will be
shown by the following specimens.

John de Goderal, a Minorite, had *heard* that
Robert de Raxat, a Templar, had once gone about
a meadow crying "Wo, wo is me! that ever I
was born. I have been forced to deny God, and
give myself up to the devil."

T 3

A Templar had said to William de Berney, in the presence of several respectable people, at the funeral of the parish-priest of Duxworth, near Cambridge, that a man has no more a soul, after death, than a dog.

John De Eure, a secular knight, said that he once invited the prior William de Fenne to dine with him. After dinner the prior took from his bosom a book, and gave it to the knight's lady to read. She found on a paper which was fastened into the book the following words, " Christ was not the Son of God, nor born of a virgin, but conceived by Mary, the wife of Joseph, in the same way as all other men. Christ was not a true but a false prophet, and was crucified for his own crimes and not for the redemption of mankind, &c." The lady showed this paper to her husband, who spoke to the prior, who only laughed at it ; but, being brought before a court of justice, he confessed the truth, excusing himself on the grounds of his being illiterate and ignorant of what the book contained.

Robert of Oteringham, a Minorite, said, " One evening my prior did not appear at table, as relics were come from Palestine which he wished to show the brethren. About midnight I heard a confused noise in the chapel ; I got up, and, looking through the keyhole, saw that it was lighted. In the morning I asked a brother who was the saint in whose honour they had celebrated the festival during the night? He turned pale with terror, thinking I had seen something, and said " Ask me not ; and if you value your life say nothing of it before the superiors."

Another witness said that the son of a Templar had peeped through the slits of the door into the chapter-room, and seen a new member put to death for hesitating to deny Christ. Long afterwards, being asked by his father to become a Templar, he refused, telling what he had seen : his father instantly slew him.

John of Gertia, a Minorite, was told by a woman named Agnes Lovecote, who said she had it from Exvalethus, prior in London, that when in one of the chapters a brother had refused to spit on the cross, they suspended him in a well and covered it up. This witness also deposed to some other enormities which he said he had heard of from the same woman, herself speaking from hearsay.

In June, 1310, the pope wrote to King Edward, blaming his lenity and calling on him to employ the torture in order to elicit the truth. The council of London, after a long discussion, ordered it to be employed, but so as not to mutilate the limbs or cause an incurable wound or violent effusion of blood. The knights persisted in asserting their innocence.

In Germany the different prelates examined the Templars in their respective dioceses. Nothing was elicited. At Mentz the order was pronounced innocent. The Wildgraf Frederic, preceptor on the Rhine, offered to undergo the ordeal of glowing iron. He had known the Master intimately in the East, and believed him to be as good a Christian as any man.

The Templars in the Spanish peninsula were examined, and witnesses heard for and against them in Castile, Leon, Aragon, and Portugal, and nothing was proved against them. The council of Tarragona in Aragon, after applying the torture, pronounced the order free from the stain of heresy. At the council of Medina del Campo in Leon, one witness said that he had heard that, when some Minorites visited the preceptor at Villalpando, they found him reading a little book, which he instantly locked up in three boxes, saying, " This book might fall into hands where it may be very dangerous to the order."

The influence of the pope may be supposed to have been stronger in Italy than in the countries above mentioned, and accordingly we find that declarations similar to those made in France were given there. Yet it was at Florence that the adoration of the idols, the cat, &c., was most fully acknowledged. In the patrimony of St. Peter some confessions to the same effect were made; but at Bologna, Cesena, and Ancona, nothing transpired. Nine Templars maintained the innocence of the order before the council of Ravenna. It was debated whether the torture should be employed. Two Dominican inquisitors were for it, the remainder of the council declared against it. It was decreed that the innocent should be absolved, the guilty punished according to law. *Those who had revoked the confessions made under torture, or through fear of it, were to be regarded as innocent*—a very different rule from that acted on by King Philip.

Charles II. of Anjou, the relation of King Philip, and the enemy of the Templars, who were on the side of Frederick, king of Sicily, had the Templars seized and examined in Provence and Naples. Those examined in Provence were all serving-brethren, and some of them testified to the impiety and idolatry of the order. Two Templars were examined at Brindisi, in the kingdom of Naples, in June, 1310; one had denied the cross in Cyprus, he said, six years after he had entered the order; the other had trampled on the cross at the time of his reception. He, as well as others, had bowed down and worshipped a grey cat in the chapters.

In Sicily six Templars, the only ones who were arrested, deposed against the order. One of them said he had been received in the unlawful way in

Catalonia, where, as we have just seen, the innocence of the order was fully recognized. His evidence was full of absurdity. He said the cat had
not appeared for a long time in the chapters but
that the ancient statutes of Damietta said that it
used to appear and be worshipped.

In Cyprus 110 witnesses were examined; 75
belonged to the order and maintained its innocence; the testimony of the remainder was also in
favour of it.

We thus find that, in every place beyond the
sphere of the influence of the king of France and
his creature the pope, the innocence of the order was
maintained and acknowledged; and undoubtedly the
same would have been the case in France if the
proceedings against it had been regulated by justice
and the love of truth.

The time appointed for the meeting of the general
council was now arrived. On the 1st October, 1311,
the pope came to Vienne, which is a short distance
from the city of Lyons, and found there 114
bishops, besides several other prelates, already assembled. On the 13th, the anniversary of the arrest
of the Templars four years before, the council commenced its sittings in the cathedral. The pope, in
his opening speech, stated the grounds of its having
been convoked, namely, the process against the Templars, the support of the Holy Land, the reformation
of the Church. The bishops of Soissons, Mende,
Leon, and Aquila, who had been appointed to draw
up a report of the result of the different examinations respecting the order, read it before the assembled fathers, who then once more invited any Templars who wished to defend the order to appear.

Though the order was now broken up and
persecuted, and numbers of its ablest members dead
or languishing in dungeons with their superiors, yet

nine knights had the courage to come forward in defence of their order, and present themselves before the council as the representatives of from 1500 to 2000 Templars, who were still dwelling or rather lurking in Lyons and its vicinity. The pope was not present when they appeared, but his letter of the 11th November shows how he acted when he heard that defenders of the order had presented themselves. Clement had these brave knights arrested and thrown into prison, and, in real or affected terror at the number of Templars at large, he took additional precautions for the security of his person, and counselled the king to do the same.

To the honour of the assembled fathers, they refused to sanction this flagrant act of injustice. The prelates of Spain, Germany, Denmark, England, Ireland, and Scotland, without exception; the Italians, all but one; the French, with the exception of the archbishops of Rheims, Sens, and Rouen, declared, but in vain, for admitting the Templars and hearing their defence. Instead of complying with this demand of justice and humanity, Clement suddenly put an end to the session. The winter passed away in arguments and negociations.

Philip, whose practice it was always to look after his affairs himself, deeming his presence necessary at Vienne, set out for that place, where he arrived early in February, accompanied by his three sons, his brother, and several nobles and men-at-arms. The effect of his presence was soon perceptible; the pope assembled the cardinals and several other prelates in a secret consistory, and abolished the order, by his sole authority, on the 22nd March, 1313.

The second session of the council was opened on the 3rd April, with great solemnity; the king of France, his sons, and his brother, gave their presence at it, and the royal guards appeared for honour, for protection, or for intimidation. The pope read his bull of abolition. All present listened in silence. No one ventured to raise his voice in the cause of justice. The wealthy and powerful order of the knights of the Temple was suppressed. On the 2d May the bull was published, and the order as such ceased to exist.

The order being suppressed, persecution became needless, and it consequently ceased in a great measure. The king and the pope converted to their own use the moveable property of the order in France. Its other possessions were, sorely against the will of the king, assigned to the order of the Hospitallers, who were, however, obliged to pay such large fines to the king and pope as completely impoverishe l them. This extended to all countries, except the Spanish peninsula and Majorca. The property of the Templars in Aragon was given to the order of Our Lady of Montesa, which was founded in 1317. Its destination was to combat the Moors; its habit was similar to that of the Templars; and it might, therefore, be almost called the same order. Diniz, the able and enlightened king of Portugal, did not suppress the order, whose innocence his prelates had recognised. To yield a show of obedience to the papal will, he made it change its name, and the great-prior of the Templars in Portugal became the master of the Order of Christ, which has continued to the present times.

With respect to the remaining Templars, who were in prison, it was ordered in council that those who should be found guiltless should be set at liberty, and maintained out of the property of the order; that the guilty, if they confessed and lamented their offences, should be treated with mildness; if they did not, dealt with according to the ecclesiastical law, and kept in custody in the former temple-houses and in the convents. Those who had escaped were, if they did not appear within a year before the council or their diocesan, to be excommunicated.

Most of the knights were immediately set at liberty; but the property of the order was all gone, and no means of support remained for them: they were, therefore, reduced to the greatest distress, and many of them obliged to submit to the most menial employment in order to gain a livelihood. A great number were received into the order of St. John, on the same footing as they had stood on in their own order—a strong proof that the guilt of the order of the Templars was not, by any means, regarded as proved. Gradually, as the members died off, or merged into other orders, the name of the Templars fell into oblivion, or was only recollected with pity for their unmerited fate.

While the noble order over which he had presided was thus suppressed, its members scattered, its property bestowed on others, the Master, James de Molay, with his three companions, the great-prior of Normandy, Hugh de Peyraud, visiter of France, and Guy, brother to the Dauphin of Auvergne, still languished in prison. Molay had there but one attendant, his cook; the allowance made to him was barely sufficient to procure him common necessaries, and life had now lost all its value in his eyes. The pope at length determined to inform the captives of the fate destined for them.

A papal commission, composed of the bishop of Alba and two other cardinals, proceeded to Paris, not to hear the prisoners, but, taking their guilt for proved, to pronounce their sentence. To give all publicity to this act, probably in accordance with the desire of the king, a stage was erected in front of the church of Notre Dame, on which the three commissioners, with the archbishop of Sens and several other prelates, took their places, on the 18th March, 1314. An immense concourse of people stood around. The four noble prisoners were conducted from their dungeons, and led up on the stage. The cardinal of Alba read out their former confessions, and pronounced the sentence of perpetual imprisonment. He was then proceeding to expose the guilt of the order, when the Master interrupted him, and thus spoke, taking all the spectators to witness :—

" It is just that, in so terrible a day, and in the last moments of my life, I should discover all the iniquity of falsehood, and make the truth to triumph. I declare, then, in the face of heaven and earth, and acknowledge, though to my eternal shame, that I have committed the greatest of crimes ; but it has been the acknowledging of those which have been so foully charged on the order. I attest, and truth obliges me to attest, that it is innocent. I made the contrary declaration only to suspend the excessive pains of torture, and to mollify those who made me endure them. I know the punishments which have been inflicted on all the knights who had the courage to revoke a similar confession ; but the dreadful spectacle which is presented to me is not able to make me confirm one lie by another. The life offered me on such infamous terms. I abandon without regret."

Molay was followed by Guy in his assertion of the innocence of the order ; the other two remained silent. The commissioners were confounded, and stopped. The intelligence was conveyed to the king, who, instantly calling his council together, without any spiritual person being present, condemned the two knights to the flames.

A pile was erected on that point of the islet in the Seine where afterwards was erected the statue of Henry IV., and the following day Molay and his

companion were brought forth and placed upon it.
They still persisted in their assertion of the innocence of the order.   The flames were first applied to
their feet, then to their more vital parts.   The fetid
smell of their burning flesh infected the surrounding
air, and added to their torments; yet still they per-
severed in their declarations.   At length death terminated their misery.   The spectators shed tears at
the view of their constancy, and during the night
their ashes were gathered up to be preserved as
relics.

Portrait of last Grand Master.

It is mentioned as a tradition, by some historians,
that Molay, ere he expired, summoned Clement to
appear within forty days before the Supreme Judge,

and Philip to the same tribunal within the space of a year. The pontiff actually *did* die of a cholic on the night of the 19th of the following month, and, the church in which his body was laid taking fire, the corpse was half consumed. The king, before the year had elapsed, died of a fall from his horse. Most probably it was these events which gave rise to the tradition, which testifies the general belief of the innocence of the Templars. It was also remarked that all the active persecutors of the order perished by premature or violent deaths.

It remains to discuss the two following points :— Did the religio-military order of the Knights Templars hold a secret doctrine subversive of religion and morality? Has the order been continued down to our own days?

We have seen what the evidence against the Templars was, and it is very plain that such evidence would not be admitted in any modern court of justice. It was either hearsay, or given by persons utterly unworthy of credit, or wrung from the accused by agony and torture. The articles themselves are absurd and contradictory. Are we to believe that the same men had adopted the pure deism of the Mahommedans, and were guilty of a species of idolatry* almost too gross for the lowest superstition? But when did this corruption commence among the Templars? Were those whom St. Bernard praised as models of Christian zeal and piety, and whom the whole Christian world admired and revered, engaged in a secret conspiracy against religion and government? Yes, boldly replies Hammer, the two humble and pious knights who founded the order were the pupils and secret allies of

* Almost every charge brought against the Templars had been previously made against the Albigenses, with how much truth every one is aware.

the Mahommedan Ismaelites. This was going too far for Wilike, and he thinks that the guilt of introducing the secret doctrine lies on the chaplains; for he could discern that the doctrines of gnosticism, which the Templars are supposed to have held, were beyond the comprehension of illiterate knights, who, though they could fight and pray, were but ill qualified to enter into the mazes of mystic metaphysics. According, therefore, to one party, the whole order was corrupt from top to bottom; according to another, the secrets were confined to a few, and, contrary to all analogy, the heads of the order were frequently in ignorance of them. Neither offer any thing like evidence in support of their assumption.

The real guilt of the Templars was their wealth and their pride*: the last alienated the people from them, the former excited the cupidity of the king of France. Far be it from us to maintain that the morals of the Templars were purer than those of the other religious orders. With such ample means as they possessed of indulging all their appetites and passions, it would be contrary to all experience to suppose that they always restrained them, and we will even concede that some of their members were obnoxious to charges of deism, impiety, breaches of their religious vows, and gross licentiousness. We only deny that such were the rules of the order. Had they not been so devoted as they were to the Holy See they would perhaps have come down to us

---

* Our readers will call to mind the well-known anecdote of King Richard I. When admonished by the zealous Fulk, of Neuilly, to get rid of his three favourite daughters, pride, avarice, and voluptuousness,—"You counsel well," said the king, "and I hereby dispose of the first to the Templars, of the second to the Benedictines, and of the third to my prelates '

as unsullied as the knights of St. John*; but they sided with Pope Boniface against Philip the Fair, and a subservient pontiff sacrificed to his own avarice and personal ambition the most devoted adherents of the court of Rome †.

We make little doubt that any one who coolly and candidly considers the preceding account of the manner in which the order was suppressed will readily concede that the guilt of its members was anything but proved. It behoves their modern impugners to furnish some stronger proofs than any they have as yet brought forward. The chief adversary of the Templars at the present day is a writer whose veracity and love of justice are beyond suspicion, and who has earned for himself enduring fame by his labours in the field of oriental literature, but in whose mind, as his most partial friends must allow, learning and imagination are apt to over-balance judgment and philosophy ‡. He has been replied to by Raynouard, Münter, and other able advocates of the knights.

We now come to the question of the continuance of the order to the present day. That it has in some sort been transmitted to our times is a matter of no

* Similar charges are said to have been brought against the Hospitallers in the year 1238, but without effect. There was no Philip the Fair at that time in France.

† Clement, in a bull dated but four days after that of the suppression, acknowledged that the whole of the evidence against the order amounted only to suspicion!

‡ We mean the illustrious Jos. von Hammer, whose essay on the subject is to be found in the sixth volume of the Mines de l'Orient, where it will be seen that he regards Sir W. Scott, in his Ivanhoe, as a competent witness against the Templars, on account of his *correct and faithful* pictures of the manners and opinions of the middle ages. We apprehend that people are beginning now to entertain somewhat different ideas on the subject of our great romancer's fidelity, of which the present pages present some instances.

doubt; for, as we have just seen, the king of Portugal formed the Order of Christ out of the Templars in his dominions. But our readers are no doubt aware that the freemasons assert a connexion with the Templars, and that there is a society calling themselves Templars, whose chief seat is at Paris, and whose branches extend into England and other countries. The account which they give of themselves is as follows :—

James de Molay, in the year 1314, in anticipation of his speedy martyrdom, appointed Johannes Marcus Lormenius to be his successor in his dignity. This appointment was made by a regular well-authenticated charter, bearing the signatures of the various chiefs of the order, and it is still preserved at Paris, together with the statutes, archives, banners, &c., of the soldiery of the Temple. There has been an unbroken succession of grand-masters down to the present times, among whom are to be found some of the most illustrious names in France. Bertrand du Guesclin was grand-master for a number of years; the dignity was sustained by several of the Montmorencies; and during the last century the heads of the society were princes of the different branches of the house of Bourbon. Bernard Raymond Fabré Palaprat is its head at present, at least was so a few years ago *.

This is no doubt a very plausible circumstantial account; but, on applying the Ithuriel spear of criticism to it, various ugly shapes resembling falsehood start up. Thus Molay, we are told, appointed his successor in 1314. He was put to death on the

* See Manuel des Templiers. As this book is only sold to members of the society, we have been unable to obtain a copy of it. Our account has been derived from Mills's History of Chivalry. That this writer should have believed it implicitly is, we apprehend, no proof of its truth.

18th March of that year, and the order had been abolished nearly a year before. Why then did he delay so long, and why was he become so apprehensive of martyrdom at that time, especially when, as is well known, there was then no intention of putting him to death? Again, where were the chiefs of the society at that time? How many of them were living? and how could they manage to assemble in the dungeon of Molay and execute a formal instrument! Moreover, was it not repugnant to the rules and customs of the Templars for a Master to appoint his successor? These are a few of the objections which we think may be justly made; and, on the whole, we feel strongly disposed to reject the whole story.

As to the freemasons, we incline to think that it was the accidental circumstance of the name of the Templars which has led them to claim a descent from that order; and it is possible that, if the same fate had fallen on the knights of St. John, the claim had never been set up. We are very far from denying that at the time of the suppression of the order of the Temple there was a secret doctrine in existence, and that the overthrow of the papal power, with its idolatry, superstition, and impiety, was the object aimed at by those who held it, and that freemasonry may possibly be that doctrine under another name*. But we are perfectly convinced that no proof of any weight has been given of the Templars' participation in that doctrine, and that all probability is on the other side. We regard them, in fine, whatever their sins may have been, as martyrs—martyrs to the cupidity, blood-thirstiness, and ambition of the king of France.

* This has, we think, been fully proved by Sr. Rossetti. It must not be concealed that this writer strongly asserts that the Templars were a branch of this society.

THE

SECRET TRIBUNALS OF WESTPHALIA*,

CHAPTER I.

Introduction—The Original Westphalia—Conquest of the Saxons by Charlemagne — His Regulations — Dukes of Saxony—State of Germany—Henry the Lion—His Outlawry—Consequences of it—Origin of German Towns—Origin of the Fehm-gerichte, or Secret Tribunals—Theories of their Origin—Origin of their Name—Synonymous Terms.

WE are now arrived at an association remarkable in itself, but which has been, by the magic arts of romancers, especially of the great archimage of the north, enveloped in darkness, mystery, and awe, far beyond the degree in which such a poetical investiture can be bestowed upon it by the calm inquirer after truth. The gloom of midnight will rise to the mind of many a reader at the name of the Secret

* Dr. Berck has, in his elaborate work on this subject (*Geschichte der Westphälischen Femgerichte*, Bremen, 1815), collected, we believe, nearly all the information that is now attainable. This work has been our principal guide; for, though we have read some others, we cannot say that we have derived any important information from them. As the subject is in its historical form entirely new in English literature, we have, at the hazard of appearing occasionally dry, traced with some minuteness the construction and mode of procedure of these celebrated courts.

Tribunals of Westphalia: a dimly lighted cavern beneath the walls of some castle, or peradventure Swiss *hostelrie*, wherein sit black-robed judges in solemn silence, will be present to his imagination, and he is prepared with breathless anxiety to peruse the details of deeds without a name *.

We fear that we cannot promise the full gratification of these high-wrought expectations. Extraordinary as the Secret Tribunals really were, we can only view them as an instance of that compensating principle which may be discerned in the moral as well as in the natural empire of the Deity; for, during the most turbulent and lawless period of the history of Germany, almost the sole check on crime, in a large portion of that country, was the salutary terror of these Fehm-Gerichte, or Secret Tribunals. And those readers who have taken their notions of them only from works of fiction will learn with surprise that no courts of justice at the time exceeded, or perhaps we might say equalled, them in the equity of their proceedings.

Unfortunately their history is involved in much obscurity, and we cannot, as in the case of the two preceding societies, clearly trace this association from its first formation to the time when it became evanescent and faded from the view. While it flourished, the dread and the fear of it weighed too heavily on the minds of men to allow them to venture to pry into its mysteries. Certain and instantaneous death was the portion of the stranger who was seen at any place where a tribunal was sitting, or who dared so

* The romantic accounts of the Secret Tribunals will be found in Sir W. Scott's translation of Goëthe's Götz von Berlichingen, and in his House of Aspen and Anne of Geierstein. From various passages in Sir W. Scott's biographical and other essays, it is plain that he believed such to be the true character of the Secret Tribunals.

much as to look into the books which contained the laws and ordinances of the society. Death was also the portion of any member of the society who revealed its secrets; and so strongly did this terror, or a principle of honour, operate, that, as Æneas Sylvius (afterwards Pope Pius II.), the secretary of the Emperor Frederick III., assures us, though the number of the members usually exceeded 100,000, no motive had ever induced a single one to be faithless to his trust. Still, however, sufficient materials are to be found for satisfying all reasonable curiosity on the subject.

To ascertain the exact and legal sphere of the operation of this formidable jurisdiction, and to point out its most probable origin, are necessary preliminaries to an account of its constitution and its proceedings. We shall therefore commence with the consideration of these points.

Westphalia, then, was the birth-place of this institution, and over Westphalia · alone did it exercise authority. But the Westphalia of the middle ages did not exactly correspond with that of the later times. In a general sense it comprehended the country between the Rhine and the Weser; its southern boundary was the mountains of Hesse; its northern, the district of Friesland, which at that time extended from Holland to Sleswig. In the records and law-books of the middle ages, this land bears the mystic appellation of the *red earth*, a name derived, as one writer thinks, from the *gules*, or red, which was the colour of the field in the ducal shield of Saxony; another regards it as synonymous with the *bloody earth;* and a third hints that it may owe its origin to the *red* colour of the soil in some districts of Westphalia.

This land formed a large portion of the country of the Saxons, who, after a gallant resistance of thirty yeais, were forced to submit to the sway of Charlemagne, and to embrace the religion of their conqueror. The Saxons had hitherto lived in a state of rude independence, and their dukes and princes possessed little or no civil power, being merely the presidents in their assemblies and their leaders in war. Charlemagne thought it advisable to abolish this dignity altogether, and he extended to the country of the Saxons the French system of counts and counties. Each count was merely a royal officer who exercised in the district over which he was placed the civil and military authority. The *missi dominici* or *regii* were despatched from the court to hold their visitations in Saxony, as well as in the other dominions of Charles, and at these persons of all classes might appear and prefer their complaints to the representative of the king, if they thought themselves aggrieved by the count or any of the inferior officers.

In the reign of Louis the German, the excellent institutions of Charlemagne had begun to fall into desuetude; anarchy and violence had greatly increased. The incursions of the Northmen had become most formidable, and the Vends *·also gave great disturbance to Germany. The Saxon land being the part most immediately exposed to invasion, the emperor resolved to revive the ancient dignity of dukes, and to place the district under one head, who might direct the energies of the whole people against the invaders. The duke was a royal lieutenant, like the counts, only differing from them in the extent of the district over which he exercised authority. The first duke of Saxony was Count Ludolf, the founder of Gandersheim; on his death the dignity was conferred on his son Bruno, who, being

* The Vends (*Wenden*) were a portion of the Slavonian race who dwelt along the south coast of the Baltic.

slain in the bloody battle of Ebsdorf fought against the Northmen, was succeeded by his younger brother Otto, the father of Henry the Fowler.

On the failure of the German branch of the Carlo-vingians, the different nations which composed the Germanic body appointed Conrad the Franconian to be their supreme head; for a new enemy, the Mag-yars, or Hungarians, now harassed the empire, and energy was demanded from its chief. Of this Con-rad himself was so convinced, that, when dying, after a short reign, he recommended to the choice of the electors, not his own brother, but Henry the Fowler, Duke of Saxony, who had, in his conflicts with the Vends and the Northmen, given the strongest proofs of his talents and valour. Henry was chosen, and the measures adopted by him during his reign, and the defeat of the Hungarians, justified the act of his elevation.

On the death of Henry, his son Otto, afterwards justly styled the Great, was unanimously chosen to succeed him in the imperial dignity. Otto conferred the Duchy of Saxony on Herman Billung. From their constant warfare with the Vends and the Northmen, the Saxons were now esteemed the most valiant nation in Germany, and they were naturally the most favoured by the emperors of the house of Saxony. This line ending with Henry II. in 1024, the sceptre passed to that of Franconia, under which and the succeeding line of Suabia, owing to the contests with the popes about investitures and to various other causes, the imperial power greatly declined in Germany; anarchy and feuds prevailed to an alarming extent; the castles of the nobles became dens of robbers; and law and justice were nowhere to be found.

The most remarkable event of this disastrous period, and one closely connected with our subject, is the outlawry of Henry the Lion, Duke of Saxony and Bavaria. Magnus, the last of the Billungs of Saxony, died, leaving only two daughters, of whom the eldest was married to Henry the Black, Duke of Bavaria, who consequently had, according to the maxims of that age, a right to the Duchy of Saxony; but the Emperor Henry V. refused to admit his claim, and conferred it on Lothaire of Supplinburg. As, however, Henry the Black's son, Henry the Proud, was married to the only daughter of Lothaire, and this prince succeeded Henry V. in the empire, Henry found no difficulty in obtaining the Duchy of Saxony from his father-in-law, who also endeavoured to have him chosen his successor in the imperial dignity. But the other princes were jealous of him, and on the death of Lothaire they hastily elected Conrad of Suabia, who, under the pretext that no duke should possess two duchies, called on Henry to resign either Saxony or Bavaria. On his refusal, Conrad, in conjunction with the princes of the empire, pronounced them both forfeited, and conferred Bavaria on the Margraf of Austria, and Saxony on Albert the Bear, the son of the second daughter of Duke Magnus of Saxony.

Saxony was, however, afterwards restored by Conrad to Henry the Lion, son of Henry the Proud, and Conrad's successor, Frederick Barbarossa, gave him again Bavaria. Henry had himself carried his arms from the Elbe to the Baltic, and conquered a considerable territory from the Vends, which he regarded as his own peculiar principality. He was now master of the greater part of Germany, and it was quite evident that he must either obtain the imperial dignity or fall. His pride and his severity made him many enemies ; but as he had no child but a daughter, who was married to a cousin of the emperor, his power was regarded without much apprehension. It was, however, the ambition of Henry to be the father of a race of heroes, and, after the fashion of those times, he divorced his wife and espoused Matilda, daughter of Henry II. of England, by whom he had four sons. Owing to this and other circumstances all friendly feeling ceased between Henry and the emperor, whom, however, he accompanied on the expedition to Italy, which terminated in the battle of Legnano. But he suddenly drew off his forces and quitted the imperial army on the way, and Frederick, imputing the ill success which he met with in a great measure to the conduct of the Duke of Saxony, was, on his return to Germany, in a mood to lend a ready ear to any charges against him. These did not fail soon to pour in : the Saxon clergy, over whom he had arrogated a right of investiture, appeared as his principal accusers. Their charges, which were partly true, partly false, were listened to by Frederick and the princes of the empire, and the downfall of Henry was resolved upon. He was thrice summoned, but in vain, to appear and answer the charges made against him. He was summoned a fourth time, but to as little purpose; the sentence of outlawry was then formally pronounced at Würtzburg. He denied the legality of the sentence, and attempted to oppose its execution; several counts stood by him in his resistance ; but he was forced to submit and sue for grace at Erfurt. The emperor pardoned him and permitted him to retain his allodial property on condition of his leaving Germany for three years. He was deprived of all his imperial fiefs, which were immediately bestowed upon others.

In the division of the spoil of Henry the Lion Saxony was cut up into pieces ; a large portion of it went to the Archbishop of Cologne; and Bernhard of Anhalt, son of Albert the Bear, obtained a considerable part of the remainder ; the supremacy over Holstein, Mecklenburg, and Pomerania, ceased ; and Lübeck became a free imperial city. All the archbishops, bishops, counts, and barons, seized as much as they could, and became immediate vassals of the empire. Neither Bernhard nor the Archbishop of Cologne was able completely to establish his power over the portion assigned him, and lawless violence everywhere prevailed. " There was no king in Israel, and every one did that which was right in his own eyes," is the language of the Chronicler *.

We here again meet an instance of the compensatory principle which prevails in the arrangements of Providence. It was the period of turbulence and anarchy succeeding the outlawry of Henry the Lion which gave an impulse to the building or enlarging of towns in the north of Germany. The free Germans, as described by Tacitus, scorned to be pent up within walls and ditches; and their descendants in Saxony would seem to have inherited their sentiments, for there were no towns in that country till the time of Henry the Fowler. As a security against the Northmen, the Slaves, and the Magyars, this monarch caused pieces of land to be enclosed by earthen walls and ditches, within which was collected a third part of the produce of the surrounding country, and in which he made every ninth man of the population fix his residence. The courts of justice were held in these places to give them consequence ; and, their strength augmenting with their population, they became towns capable of resisting the attacks of the enemy, and of giving shelter and defence to the people of the open country. Other towns, such as Münster, Osnabrück (*Osnaburgh*), Paderborn, and Minden, grew up gradually, from the desire of the

* Arnold of Lübeck, Chronica Slavorum, l. iii. c. 1., apud Leibnitz Scriptores Rerum Brunsvicarum, t. ii. p. 653.

people to dwell close to abbeys, churches, and episcopal residences, whence they might obtain succour
in time of temporal or spiritual need, and derive
protection from the reverence shown to the church.
A third class of towns owed their origin to the stormy
period of which we now write; for the people of the
open country, the victims of oppression and tyranny,
fled to where they might, in return for their obedience, meet with some degree of protection, and
erected their houses at the foot of the castle of some
powerful nobleman. These towns gradually increased
in power, with the favour of the emperors, who, like
other monarchs, viewing in them allies against the
excessive power of the church and the nobility, gladly
bestowed on them extensive privileges; and from
these originated the celebrated Hanseatic League, to
which almost every town of any importance in Westphalia belonged, either mediately or immediately.

But the growth of cities, and the prosperity and
the better system of social regulation which they
presented, were not the only beneficial effects which
resulted from the overthrow of the power of Henry
the Lion. There is every reason to conclude that it
was at this period that the Fehm-gerichte, or Secret
Tribunals, were instituted in Westphalia; at least,
the earliest document in which there is any clear and
express mention of them is dated in the year 1267.
This is an instrument by which Engelbert, Count of
the Mark, frees one Gervin of Kinkenrode from the
feudal obligations for his inheritance of Broke, which
was in the county of Mark; and it is declared to have
been executed at a place named Berle, the court
being presided over by Bernhard of Henedorp, and
the *Fehmenotes* being present. By the Fehmenotes
were at all times understood the initiated in the secrets
of the Westphalian tribunals; so that we have here
a clear and decisive proof of the existence of these

tribunals at that time. In another document, dated 1280, the Fehmenotes again appear as witnesses, and after this time the mention of them becomes frequent.

We thus find that, in little more than half a century after the outlawry of Henry the Lion, the Fehmgerichte were in operation in Westphalia; and there is not the slightest allusion to them before that date, or any proof, at all convincing, to be produced in favour of their having been an earlier institution. Are we not, therefore, justified in adopting the opinion of those who place their origin in the first half of the thirteenth century, and ascribe it to the anarchy and confusion consequent on the removal of the power which had hitherto kept within bounds the excesses of the nobles and the people? And is it a conjecture altogether devoid of probability that some courageous and upright men may have formed a secret determination to apply a violent remedy to the intolerable evils which afflicted the country, and to have adopted those expedients for preserving the public peace, out of which gradually grew the Secret Tribunals? or that some powerful prince of the country, acting from purely selfish motives, devised the plan of the society, and appointed his judges to make the first essay of it *?

Still it must be confessed that the origin of the Fehm-gerichte is involved in the same degree of obscurity which hangs over that of the Hanseatic league and so many other institutions of the middle ages; and little hopes can be entertained of this obscurity ever being totally dispelled. Conjecture will, therefore, ever have free scope of the subject; and the opinion which we have just expressed ourselves as inclined to adopt is only one of nine which have been already advanced on it. Four of these carry

* Berck, pp. 259, 260.

back the origin of the Fehm-gerichte to the time of
Charlemagne, making them to have been either directly instituted by that great prince, or to have gradually grown out of some of his other institutions
for the better governing of his states. A fifth places
their origin in the latter half of the eleventh century,
and regards them as an invention of the Westpha-
ian clergy for forwarding the views of the popes in
their attempt to arrive at dominion over all temporal
princes. A sixth ascribes the institution to St. Engelbert, Archbishop of Cologne, to whom the Emperor Frederic II. committed the administration of
affairs in Germany during his own absence in Sicily,
and who was distinguished for his zeal in the persecution of heretics. He modelled it, the advocates of
this opinion say, on that of the Inquisition, which had
lately been established. The seventh and eighth
theories are undeserving of notice. On the others
we shall make a few remarks.

The first writers who mention the Fehm-gerichte
are Henry of Hervorden, a Dominican, who wrote
against them in the reign of the Emperor Charles IV.,
about the middle of the fourteenth century; and
Æneas Sylvius, the secretary of Frederic III., a century later. These writers are among those who refer
the origin of the Fehm-gerichte to Charlemagne, and
such was evidently the current opinion of the time—
an opinion studiously disseminated by the members
of the society, who sought to give it consequence in
the eyes of the emperor and people, by associating it
with the memory of the illustrious monarch of the
West. There is, however, neither external testimony
nor internal probability to support that opinion.
Eginhart, the secretary and biographer of Charlemagne, and all the other contemporary writers, are
silent on the subject ; the valuable fragments of the
ancient Saxon laws collected in the twelfth century

make not the slightest allusion to these courts; and, in fine, their spirit and mode of procedure are utterly at variance with the Carlovingian institutions.   As to the hypothesis which makes Archbishop Engelbert the author of the Fehm-gerichte, it is entirely unsupported by external evidence, and has nothing in its favour but the coincidence, in point of time, of Engelbert's administration with the first account which we have of this jurisdiction, and the similarity which it bore in the secrecy of its proceedings to that of the Holy Inquisition—a resemblance easy to be accounted for, without any necessity for having recourse to the supposition of the one being borrowed from the other.

We can therefore only say with certainty that, in the middle of the thirteenth century, the Fehm-gerichte were existing and in operation in the country which we have described as the Westphalia of the middle ages.   To this we may add that this jurisdiction extended over the whole of that country, and was originally confined to it, all the courts in other parts of Germany, which bore a resemblance to the Westphalian Fehm-gerichte, being of a different character and nature *.

It remains, before proceeding to a description of these tribunals, to give some account of the origin of their name.   And here again we find ourselves involved in as much difficulty and uncertainty as when inquiring into the origin of the society itself.

Almost every word in the German and cognate languages, which bears the slightest resemblance to the word *Fehm* †, has been given by some writer or other as

---

* See Berck, l. i. c. 5, 6, 7.

† Spelt also *Fem, Fäm, Vem, Vehm*.   In German *f* and *v* are pronounced alike, as also are *ä* and *e*.   The words from which *Fahm* has been derived are *Fahne*, a standard; *Femen*, to skin; *Fehde*, feud; *Vemi* (i. e. væ mihi), wo is me; *Ve* or *Vaem*, which Dreyer says signifies, in the northern languages,

its true etymon. It is unnecessary, in the present sketch of the history of the Fehm-gerichte, to discuss the merits of each of the claimants: we shall content ourselves with remarking that, among those which appear to have most probability in their favour, is the Latin *Fama*, which was first proposed by Leibnitz. At the time when we have most reason for supposing these tribunals to have been instituted the Germans were familiar with the language of the civil and canonical laws; the Fehm-gerichte departed from the original maxim of German law, which was—*no accuser, no judge*, and, in imitation of those foreign laws*, proceeded on *common fame*, and without any formal accusation against persons suspected of crime or of evil courses. Moreover, various tribunals, not in Westphalia, which proceeded in the same manner, on common report, were also called Fehm-gerichte, which may therefore be interpreted Fame-tribunals, or such as did not, according to the old German rule, require a formal accusation, but proceeded to the investigation of the truth of any charge which common fame or general report made against any person—a dangerous mode of proceeding, no doubt, and one liable to the greatest abuse, but which the lawless state of•Germany at that period, and the consequent impunity which great criminals would else have enjoyed, from the fear of them, which would have kept back accusers and witnesses, perhaps abundantly justified. It is proper to observe, however, that *fem* appears to be an old German word, signify-

holy; *Vitte* (old German), prudence; *Vette*, punishment; the *Fimmiha* of the Salic law; Swedish *Fem*, Islandic *Fimm*, five, such being erroneously supposed to be the number of judges in a Fehm, or court. Finally, Mözer deduces it from *Fahm*, which he says is employed in Austria and some other countries for *Rahm*, cream.

* Common fame was a sufficient ground of arraignment in England, also, in the Anglo-Saxon period.

ing condemnation ; and it is far from being unlikely, after all, that the Fehm-gerichte may mean merely the tribunals of condemnation—in other words, courts for the punishment of crime, or what we should call criminal courts.

The Fehm-gerichte was not the only name which these tribunals bore; they were also called *Fehm-ding*, the word *ding* * being, in the middle ages, equivalent to *gericht*, or tribunal. They were also called the Westphalian tribunals, as they could only be holden in the *Red Land*, or Westphalia, and only Westphalians were amenable to their jurisdiction. They were further styled free-seats (*Frei-stühle, stühl* also being the same as *gericht*), free-tribunals, &c., as only freemen were subject to them. A Frei-gericht, however, was not a convertible term with a Westphalian Fehm-gericht ; the former was the genus, the latter the species. They are in the records also named Secret Tribunals, (*Heimliche Gerichte*), and Silent Tribunals (*Stillgerichte*), from the secrecy of their proceedings ; Forbidden Tribunals (*Verbotene Gerichte*), the reason of which name is not very clear ; Carolinian Tribunals, as having been, as was believed, instituted by Charles the Great ; also the Free Bann, which last word was equivalent to *jurisdiction*. A Fehm-gericht was also termed a *Heimliche Acht*, and a *Heimliche beschlossene Acht* (secret and secret-closed tribunal); *acht* also being the same as *gericht*, or tribunal.

* In the northern languages, *Ting ;* hence the *Store Ting* (in our journals usually written *Storthing*), i. e. *Great Ting*, or Parliament of Norway.

Chapter II.

The Tribunal-Lord—The Count—The Schöppen—The Messengers—The Public Court—The Secret Tribunal—Extent
of its Jurisdiction—Places of holding the Courts—Time of
holding them—Proceedings in them—Process where the
criminal was caught in the fact—Inquisitorial Process.

HAVING traced the origin of the Fehm-gerichte and
their various appellations, as far as the existing documents and other evidences admit, we are now to
describe the constitution and procedure of these
celebrated tribunals, and to ascertain who were the
persons that composed them ; whence their authority
was derived ; and over what classes of persons their
jurisdiction extended.

Even in the periods of greatest anarchy in Germany,
the emperor was regarded as the fountain of all
judicial power and authority, more particularly where
it extended to the right of inflicting capital punishment.   The Fehm-gerichte, therefore, regarded the
emperor as their head, from whom they derived all
the power which they possessed, and acknowledged
his right to control and modify their constitution
and decisions.   These rights of the emperors we
shall, in the sequel, describe at length.

Between the emperor and the Westphalian tribunal-lords (*Stuhlherren*), as they were styled, that is,
lay and ecclesiastical territorial lords, there was no
intermediate authority until the fourteenth century,
when the Archbishop of Cologne was made the im-

perial lieutenant in Westphalia. Each tribunal-lord
had his peculiar district, within which he had the power
of erecting tribunals, and beyond which his authority did not extend. He either presided in person in
his court, or he appointed a count (*Freigraf*) to supply his place. The rights of a stuhlherr * had some
resemblance to those of the owner of an advowson
in this country. He had merely the power of nomi-
nating either himself or another person as count; the
right to inflict capital punishment was to be conferred
by the emperor or his deputy. To this end, when a
tribunal-lord presented a count for investiture, he
was obliged to certify on oath that the person so
presented was truly and honestly, both by father and
mother, born on Westphalian soil ; that he stood in
no ill repute ; that he knew of no open crime he had
committed ; and that he believed him to be perfectly
well qualified to preside over the county.

The count, on being appointed, was to swear that
he would judge truly and justly, according to the law
and the regulations of the emperor Charles and the
closed tribunal; that he would be obedient to the emperor or king, and his lieutenant; and that he would
repair, at least once in each year, to the general
chapter which was to be held on the Westphalian
land, and give an account of his conduct, &c.

The income of the free-count arose from fees and
a share in fines; he had also a fixed allowance in
money or in kind from the stuhlherr. Each free-
schöppe who was admitted made him a present, *to
repair*, as the laws express it, *his countly hat.* If
the person admitted was a knight, this fee was a
mark of gold ; if not, a mark of silver. Every one
of the initiated who cleared himself by oath from

---

* *Stuhlherr* is *tribunal-lord,* or, literally, *lord of the seat* (of
judgment); *stuhl* (*Anglice,* stool) being a seat, or chair.

any charge paid the count a cross-penny. He had a share of all the fines imposed in his court, and a fee on citations, &c.

There was in general but one count to each tribunal; but instances occur of there being as many as seven or eight. The count presided in the court, and the citations of the accused proceeded from him.

Next to the count were the assessors or (*Schöppen*)*. These formed the main body and strength of the society. They were nominated by the count with the approbation of the tribunal-lord. Two persons, who were already in the society, were obliged to vouch on oath for the fitness of the candidate to be admitted. It was necessary that he should be a German by birth; born in wedlock of free parents; of the Christian religion; neither excommunicate nor outlawed; not involved in any Fehm-gericht process; a member of no spiritual order, &c.

These schöppen were divided into two classes, the knightly, and the simple, respectable assessors; for, as the maxim that every man should be judged by his peers prevailed universally during the middle ages, it was necessary to conform to it also in the Fehm-tribunals.

Previous to their admission to a knowledge of the secrets of the society, the schöppen were named Ignorant; when they had been initiated they were called Knowing (*Wissende*) or Fehmenotes. It was only these last who were admitted to the secret-

---

* This word, which cannot be adequately translated, is the low-Latin *Scabini*, the French *Echevins*. We shall take the liberty of using it throughout. The schöppen were called frei-(*free*) schöppen, as the count was called *frei-graf*, the court *frei-stuhl*, on account of the jurisdiction of the tribunals being confined to freemen.

tribunal. The initiation of a schöppe was attended with a good deal of ceremony. He appeared bare-headed before the assembled tribunal, and was there questioned respecting his qualifications. Then, kneeling down, with the thumb and forefinger of his right hand on a naked sword and a halter, he pronounced the following oath after the count :—

" I promise, on the holy marriage, that I will, from henceforth, aid, keep, and conceal the holy Fehms, from wife and child, from father and mother, from sister and brother, from fire and wind, from all that the sun shines on and the rain covers, from all that is between sky and ground, especially from the man who knows the law, and will bring before this free tribunal, under which I sit, all that belongs to the secret jurisdiction of the emperor, whether I know it to be true myself, or have heard it from trustworthy people, whatever requires correction or punishment, whatever is Fehm-free (*i. e.* a crime committed in the county), that it may be judged, or, with the consent of the accuser, be put off in grace ; and will not cease so to do, for love or for fear, for gold or for silver, or for precious stones; and will strengthen this tribunal and jurisdiction with all my five senses and power ; and that I do not take on me this office for any other cause than for the sake of right and justice ; moreover, that I will ever further and honour this free tribunal more than any other free tribunals ; and what I thus promise will I stedfastly and firmly keep, so help me God and his Holy Gospel."

He was further obliged to swear that he would ever, to the best of his ability, enlarge the holy empire ; and that he would undertake nothing with unrighteous hand against the land and people of the stuhlherr.

The count then inquired of the officers of the

court (the *Frohnboten*) if the candidate had gone
through all the formalities requisite to reception, and
when that officer had answered in the affirmative, the
count revealed to the aspirant the secrets of the tribunal, and communicated to him the secret sign by
which the initiated knew one another. What this
sign was is utterly unknown : some say that when
they met at table they used to turn the point of
their knife to themselves, and the haft away from
them.   Others take the letters S S G G, which were
found in an old MS. at Herford, to have been the
sign, and interpret them *Stock Stein, Gras Grein.*
These are, however, the most arbitrary conjectures,
without a shadow of proof.   The count then was
bound to enter the name of the new member in his
register, and henceforth he was one of the powerful
body of the initiated.

Princes and nobles were anxious to have their
chancellors and ministers, corporate towns to have
their magistrates, among the initiated. Many princes
sought to be themselves members of this formidable
association, and we are assured that in the fourteenth
and fifteenth centuries (which are the only ones of
which we have any particular accounts) the number
of the initiated exceeded 100,000.

The duty of the initiated was to go through the
country to serve citations and to trace out and de-
nounce evil-doers; or, if they caught them in the
fact, to execute instant justice upon them. They
were also the count's assessors when the tribunal
sat.   For that purpose seven at least were required
to be present, all belonging to the county in which
the court was held; those belonging to other
counties might attend, but they could not act as
assessors ; they only formed a part of the bystanders
of the court.   Of these there were frequently some
hundreds present.

All the initiated of every degree might go on foot and on horseback through the country, for daring was the man who would presume to injure them, as certain death was his inevitable lot. A dreadful punishment also awaited any one of them who should forget his vow and reveal the secrets of the society; he was to be seized, a cloth bound over his eyes, his hands tied behind his back, a halter put about his neck; he was to be thrown upon his belly, his tongue pulled out behind by the nape of his neck, and he was then to be hung seven feet higher than any other felon. It is doubtful, however, if there ever was a necessity for inflicting this punishment, for Æneas Sylvius, who wrote at the time when the society had degenerated, assures us that no member had ever been induced, by any motives whatever, to betray its secrets ; and he describes the initiated as grave men and lovers of right and justice. Similar language is employed concerning them by other writers of the time.

Besides the count and the assessors, there were required, for the due holding a Fehm-court, the officers named *Frohnboten**, or serjeants, or messengers, and a clerk to enter the decisions in what was called the blood-book (*Liber sanguinis*). These were, of course, initiated, or they could not be present. It was required that the messengers should be freemen belonging to the county, and have all the qualifications of the simple schöppen. Their duty was to attend on the court when sitting, and to take care that the ignorant, against whom there was any charge, were duly cited†.

* *Frohnbote* is interpreted a *Holy Messenger*, or a *Servant of God.*

† When a person was admitted into the society he paid, besides the fee to the count already mentioned, to each schöppe

The count was to hold two kinds of courts, the one public, named the Open or Public Court *(Offenbare Ding)*, to which every freeman had access; the other private, called the Secret Tribunal (*Heimliche Acht*), at which no one who was not initiated could venture to appear.

The former court was held at stated periods, and at least three times in each year. It was announced fourteen days previously by the messengers *(Frohnboten)*, and every householder in the county, whether initiated or not, free or servile, was bound under a penalty of four heavy shillings, to appear at it and declare on oath what crimes he knew to have been committed in the county.

When the count held the Secret Court, the clergy, who had received the tonsure and ordination, women and children, Jews and Heathens *, and, as it would appear, the higher nobility, were exempted from its jurisdiction. The clergy were exempted, probably, from prudential motives, as it was not deemed safe to irritate the members of so powerful a body, by encroaching on their privileges; they might, however, voluntarily subject themselves to the Fehmgerichte if they were desirous of partaking of the advantages of initiation. Women and children were exempt on account of their sex and age, and the period of infancy was extended, in the citations, to fourteen, eighteen, and sometimes twenty years of age. Jews, Heathens, and such like, were exempted on account of their unworthiness. The higher nobility were exempted (if such was really the case) in compliance with the maxim of German law that

who was assisting there, and to each frohnbote, four livres Tournois.

* The natives of Prussia were still heathens at that time.

each person should be judged by his peers, as it was scarcely possible that in any county there could be found a count and seven assessors of equal rank with accused persons of that class.

In their original constitution the Fehm-gerichte, agreeably to the derivation of the name from *Fem*, condemnation, were purely criminal courts, and had no jurisdiction in civil matters. They took cognizance of all offences against the Christian faith, the holy gospel, the holy ten commandments, the public peace, and private honour—a category, however, which might easily be made to include almost every transgression and crime that could be committed. We accordingly find in the laws of the Fehm-gerichte, sacrilege, robbery, rape, murder, apostacy, treason, perjury, coining, &c., &c., enumerated; and the courts, by an astute interpretation of the law, eventually managed to make matters which had not even the most remote appearance of criminality *Fehm-bar*, or within their jurisdiction.

But all exceptions were disregarded in cases of contumacy, or of a person being taken in the actual commission of an offence. When a person, after being duly cited, even in a civil case, did not appear to answer the charge against him, he was outlawed, and his offence became *fehmbar*; every judge was then authorized to seize the accused, whether he belonged to his county or not; the whole force of the initiated was now directed against him, and escape was hardly possible. Here it was that the superior power of the Fehm-gerichte exhibited itself. Other courts could outlaw as well as they, but no other had the same means of putting its sentences into execution. The only remedy which remained for the accused was to offer to appear and defend his cause, or to sue to the emperor for protection. In cases where a person was caught *flagranti delicto*, the Westphalian

x 3

tribunals were competent to proceed to instant punishment.

Those who derive their knowledge of the Fehm-gerichte from plays and romances are apt to imagine that they were always held in subterranean chambers, or in the deepest recesses of impenetrable forests, while night, by pouring her deepest gloom over them, added to their awfulness and solemnity. Here, as elsewhere, we must, however reluctantly, lend our aid to dispel the illusions of fiction. They were *not* held either in woods or in vaults, and rarely even under a roof. There is only *one* recorded instance of a Fehm-gericht being held under ground, viz., at Heinberg, under the house of John Menkin. At Paderborn indeed it was held in the town-house; there was also one held in the castle of Wulften. But the situation most frequently selected for holding a court was some place under the blue canopy of heaven, for the free German still retained the predilection of his ancestors for open space and expansion. Thus at Nordkirchen and Südkirchen (*north and south church*) the court was held in the churchyard; at Dortmund, in the market-place close by the town-house. But the favourite place for holding these courts was the neighbourhood of trees, as in the olden time: and we read of the tribunal at Arensberg in the orchard; of another under the hawthorn; of a third under the pear-tree; of a fourth under the linden, and so on. We also find the courts denominated simply from the trees by which they were held, such as the tribunal at the elder, that at the broad oak, &c.

The idea of their being held at night is also utterly devoid of proof, no mention of any such practice being found in any of the remaining documents. It is much more analogous to Germanic usage to infer that, as the Public Court, and the German courts in general, were held in the morning, soon after the break of day, such was also the rule with the Secret Court.

When an affair was brought before a Fehm-court, the first point to be determined was whether it was a matter of Fehm-jurisdiction. Should such prove to be the case, the accused was summoned to appear and answer the charge before the Public Court. All sorts of persons, Jews and Heathens included, might be summoned before this court, at which the uninitiated schöppen also gave attendance, and which was as public as any court in Germany. If the accused did not appear, or appeared and could not clear himself, the affair was transferred to the Secret Court. Civil matters also, which on account of a denial of satisfaction were brought before the Fehm-court, were, in like manner, in cases of extreme contumacy, transferred thither.

The Fehm-tribunals had three different modes of procedure, namely, that in case of the criminal being taken in the fact, the inquisitorial, and the purely accusatorial.

Two things were requisite in the first case; the criminal must be taken in the fact, and there must be three schöppen, at least, present to punish him. With respect to the first particular, the legal language of Saxony gave great extent to the term *taken in the fact*. It applied not merely to him who was seized in the instant of his committing the crime, but to him who was caught as he was running away. In cases of murder, those who were found with weapons in their hands were considered as taken in the fact; as also, in case of theft, was a person who had the key of any place in which stolen articles were found, unless he could prove that they came there without his consent or knowledge. The Fehm-law enumerated three tokens or proofs of guilt in these cases; the Habende Hand (*Having Hand*), or having the proof in his hand; the Blickende Schein (*looking appearance*), such as the wound in the body of one who was slain; and the Gichtige Mund (*faltering mouth*), or confession of the criminal. Still, under all these circumstances, it was necessary that he should be taken immediately; for if he succeeded in making his escape, and was caught again, as he was not this time taken in the fact, he must be proceeded against before the tribunal with all the requisite formalities.

The second condition was, that there should be at least three initiated persons together, to entitle them to seize, try, and execute a person taken in the fact. These then were at the same time judges, accusers, witnesses, and executioners. We shall in the sequel describe their mode of procedure. It is a matter of uncertainty whether the rule of trial by peers was observed on these occasions: what is called the Arensberg Reformation of the Fehm-law positively asserts, that, in case of a person being taken *flagranti delicto*, birth formed no exemption, and the noble was to be tried like the commoner. The cases, however, in which three of the initiated happened to come on a criminal in the commission of the fact must have been of extremely rare occurrence.

When a crime had been committed, and the criminal had not been taken in the fact, there remained two ways of proceeding against him, namely, the *inquisitorial* and the *accusatorial* processes. It depended on circumstances which of these should be adopted. In the case, however, of his being initiated, it was imperative that he should be proceeded against accusatorially.

Supposing the former course to have been chosen, —which was usually done when the criminal had been taken in the fact, but had contrived to escape, or when he was a man whom common fame charged openly and distinctly with a crime,—he was not cited to appear before the court or vouchsafed a hearing. He was usually denounced by one of the initiated; the court then examined into the evidence of his guilt, and if it was found sufficient he was outlawed, or, as it was called, *forfehmed* *, and his name was inscribed in the blood-book. A sentence was immediately drawn out, in which all princes, lords, nobles, towns, every person, in short, especially the initiated, were called upon to lend their aid to justice. This sentence, of course, could originally have extended only to Westphalia; but the Fehm-courts gradually enlarged their claims; their pretensions were favoured by the emperors, who regarded them as a support to their authority; and it was soon required that their sentence should be obeyed all over the empire, as emanating from the imperial power.

Unhappy now was he who was *forfehmed*; the whole body of the initiated, that is 100,000 persons, were in pursuit of him. If those who met him were sufficient in number, they seized him at once; if they felt themselves too weak, they called on their brethren to aid, and every one of the society was bound, when thus called on by three or four of the initiated, who averred to him on oath that the man was *forfehmed*, to help to take him. As soon as they had seized the criminal they proceeded without a moment's delay to execution; they hung him on a tree by the road-side and not on a gallows, intimating thereby that they were entitled to exercise their office in the king's name anywhere they pleased, and without any regard to territorial jurisdiction. The halter which they employed was, agreeably to the usage of the middle ages, a *withy*; and they are said to have had so much practice, and to have arrived at such expert-

---

* In German *Verfehmt*. We have ventured to coin the word in the text. The English *for* answers to the German *ver; vergessen* is *forget; verloren* is *forlorn*.

ness in this business, that the word *Fehmen* at last began to signify simply *to hang*, as *execution* has come to do in English. It is more probable, however, that this, or something very near it, was the original signification of the word from which the tribunals took their name. Should the malefactor resist, his captors were authorised to knock him down and kill him. In this case they bound the dead body to a tree, and stuck their knives beside it, to intimate that he had not been slain by robbers, but had been executed in the name of the emperor.

Were the person who was *forfehmed* uninitiated, he had no means whatever of knowing his danger till the halter was actually about his neck; for the severe penalty which awaited any one who divulged the secrets of the Fehm-courts was such as utterly to preclude the chance of a friendly hint or warning to be on his guard. Should he, however, by any casualty, such, for instance, as making his escape from those who attempted to seize him, become aware of how he stood, he might, if he thought he could clear himself, seek the protection and aid of the Stuhlherr, or of the emperor.

If any one knowingly associated with or entertained a person who was *forfehmed*, he became involved in his danger. It was necessary, however, to prove that he had done so knowingly—a point which was to be determined by the emperor, or by the judge of the district in which the accused resided. This rule originally had extended only to Westphalia, but the Fehm-judges afterwards assumed a right of punishing in any part of the empire the person who entertained one who was *forfehmed*.

Nothing can appear more harsh and unjust than this mode of procedure to those who would apply the ideas and maxims of the present to former times. But violent evils require violent remedies; and the disorganized state of Europe in general, and of Germany in particular, during the middle ages, was such as almost to exceed our conception. Might it not then be argued that we ought to regard as a benefit, rather than as an evil, any institution which set some bounds to injustice and violence, by infusing into the bosom of the evil-doer a salutary fear of the consequences? When a man committed a crime he knew that there was a tribunal to judge it from which his power, however great it might be, would not avail to protect him; he knew not who were the initiated, or at what moment he might fall into their hands; his very brother might be the person who had denounced him; his intimate associates might be those who would seize and execute him. So strongly was the necessity of such a power felt in general, that several cities, such as Nuremberg, Cologne, Strasburg, and others, applied for and obtained permission from the emperors, to proceed to pass sentence of death on evil-doers even unheard, when the evidence of common fame against them was satisfactory to the majority of the town council. Several counts also obtained similar privileges, so that there were, as we may see, Fehm courts in other places besides Westphalia, but they were far inferior to those in power, not having a numerous body of schöppen at their devotion.

It is finally to be observed that it was only when the crimes were of great magnitude, and the voice of fame loud and constant, that the inquisitorial process could be properly adopted. In cases of a minor nature the accused had a right to be heard in his own behalf. Here then the inquisitorial process had its limit: if report was not sufficiently strong and overpowering, and the matter was still dubious, the offender was to be proceeded against accusatorially. If he was one of the initiated, such was his undoubted right and privilege in all cases.

CHAPTER III.

Accusatorial process—Persons liable to it—Mode of citation—
Mode of procedure—Right of appeal.

As we have stated above, the first inquiry when a
matter was brought before a Fehm-court was, did it
come within its jurisdiction, and, on its being found
to do so, the accused was summoned before the Public
Court, and when he did not appear, or could not
clear himself, the cause was transferred to the Secret
Court. We shall now consider the whole procedure
specially.

The summons was at the expense of the accuser;
it was to be written on good new parchment, without any erasures, and sealed with at least seven seals,
to wit, those of the count and of six assessors. The
seals of the different courts were different. The
summonses varied according to whether the accused
was a free-count, a free-schöppe, or one of the ignorant and uninitiated, a community, a noth-schöppe, or
a mere vagabond. In all cases they were to be
served by schöppen. They were to have on them
the name of the count, of the accuser, and of the accused, the charge, and the place where the court was
to be holden. The stuhlherr was also to be previously informed of it.

For a good and legal service it was requisite that
two schöppen should either serve the accused personally or leave the summons openly or clandestinely
at his residence, or at the place where he had taken
refuge. If he did not appear to answer the charge

within six weeks and three days, he was again summoned by four persons. Six weeks was the least erm set for appearing to this summons, and it was requisite that a piece of imperial coin should be given with it. Should he still neglect appearing, he was summoned for the third and last time by six schöppen and a count, and the term set was six weeks and three days as before.

If the accused was not merely initiated but also a count, he was treated with corresponding respect. The first summons was served by seven schöppen, the second by fourteen and four counts, and the third by twenty-one and six counts.

The uninitiated, whether bond or free, did not share in the preceding advantages. The summons was served on themselves, or at their residence, by a messenger, and only once. There is some doubt as to the period set for their appearance, but it seems to have been in general the ordinary one of six weeks and three days.

The summons of a town or community was usually addressed to all the male inhabitants. In general some of them were specially named in it ; the Arensberg Reformation directed that the names of at least thirty persons should be inserted. The term was six weeks and three days, and those who served the summons were required to be *true and upright* schöppen.

The noth-schöppe, that is, the person who had surreptitiously become possessed of the secrets of the society, was summoned but once. The usual time was allowed him for appearing to the charge.

Should the accused be a mere vagabond, one who had no fixed residence, the course adopted was to send, six weeks and three days before the day the court was to sit, and post up four summonses at a cross-road which faced the four cardinal points, placing a piece of imperial money with each. This was esteemed good and valid service, and if the accused did not appear the court proceeded to act upon it.

Notwithstanding the privileges which the members of the society enjoyed, and the precautions which were employed to ensure their safety, and moreover the deadly vengeance likely to be taken on any one who should aggrieve them, we are not to suppose the service of a summons to appear before a Fehm-court to have been absolutely free from danger. The tyrannic and self-willed noble, when in his own strong castle, and surrounded by his dependents, might not scruple to inflict summary chastisement on the audacious men who presumed to summon him to answer for his crimes before a tribunal; the magistrates of a town also might indignantly spurn at the citation to appear before a Fehm-court, and treat its messengers as offenders. To provide against these cases it was determined that it should be considered good service when the summons was affixed by night to the gate of a town or castle, to the door of the house of the accused, or to the nearest alms-house. The schöppen employed were then to desire the watchman, or some person who was going by, to inform the accused of the summons being there, and they were to take away with them a chip cut from the gate or door, as a proof of the service for the court.

If the accused was resolved to obey the summons, he had only to repair on the appointed day to the place where the court was to be held, the summons being his protection. Those who would persuade us that the Fehm-courts were held by night in secret places say that the mode appointed for the accused to meet the court was for him to repair three-quarters of an hour before midnight to the next cross-roads, where a schöppe was always waiting for him, who bound his eyes and led him to where the court was sitting. This, however, is all mere fiction; for the place where the court was to be held was expressly mentioned in every summons.

The Fehm-courts (like the German courts in general) were holden on a Tuesday*. If on this day the accused, or his attorney, appeared at the appointed place, and no court was holden, the summons abated or lost its force; the same was the case when admission was refused to him and his suite, a circumstance which sometimes occurred. But should he not appear to the first summons, he was fined the first time thirty shillings, the second time sixty, the third time he was *forfehmed*. The court had however the power of granting a further respite of six weeks and three days previous to passing this last severe sentence. This term of grace was called the King's Dag, or the Emperor Charles's Day of Grace.

The plea of necessary and unavoidable absence was, however, admitted in all cases, and the Fehm-law distinctly recognised four legal impediments to appearance, namely, imprisonment, sickness, the service of God (that is, pilgrimage), and the public service. The law also justly added the following cases :— inability to cross a river for want of a bridge or a boat, or on account of a storm ; the loss of his horse when the accused was riding to the court, so that he could not arrive in time ; absence from the country on knightly, mercantile, or other honest occasions ; and lastly, the service of his lord or master. In short, any just excuse was admitted. As long as the impediment continued in operation all proceedings against the accused were void. If the impediment arose from his being in prison, or in the public service, or that of his master, he was to notify the same by letter sealed with his seal, or else by his own oath

* In German, *Dienstag*, probably *Dinstag*, i. e. *Court-day.*

Y 2

and those of two or three other persons. The other impediments above enumerated were to be sworn to by himself alone.

If the accused neglected answering the two first summonses, but appeared to the third, he was required to pay the two fines for non-appearance; but if he declared himself too poor to pay them, he was obliged to place his two fore-fingers on the naked sword which lay before the court, and swear, *by the death which God endured on the cross*, that such was the case. It was then remitted to him, and the court proceeded to his trial.

When a Fehm-court sat the count presided; before him lay on the table a naked sword and a withy-halter; the former, says the law, signifying the cross on which Christ suffered and the rigour of the court, the latter denoting the punishment of evil-doers, whereby the wrath of God is appeased. On his right and left stood the clerks of the court, the assessors, and the audience. All were bare-headed, to signify, says the law, that they would proceed openly and fairly, punish men only for the crimes which they had committed, and *cover no right with unright.* They were also to have their hands uncovered to signify that they would do nothing covertly and underhand. They were to have short cloaks on their shoulders, significatory of the warm love which they should have for justice; *for as the cloak covers all the other clothes and the body, so should their love cover justice.* They were to wear neither weapons nor harness, that no one might feel any fear of them, and to indicate that they were under the peace of the emperor, king, or empire. Finally, they were to be free from wrath and sober, that drunkenness might not lead them to pass unrighteous judgment, *for drunkenness causes much wickedness.*

If one who was not initiated was detected in the

assembly, his process was a brief one. He was seized without any ceremony, his hands and feet were tied together, and he was hung on the next tree. Should a noth-schöppe be caught in the assembly, a halter of oaken twigs was put about his neck, and he was thrown for nine days into a dark dungeon, at the end of which time he was brought to trial, and, if he failed in clearing himself, he was proceeded with according to law, that is, was hanged.

The business of the day commenced, as in German courts in general, by the count asking of the messengers if it was the day and time for holding a court under the royal authority. An affirmative answer being given, the count then asked how many assessors should there be on the tribunal, and how the seat should be filled. When these questions were answered, he proclaimed the holding of the court.

Each party was permitted to bring with him as many as thirty friends to act as witnesses and compurgators. Lest, however, they might attempt to impede the course of justice, they were required to appear unarmed. Each party had, moreover, the right of being represented by his attorney. The person so employed must be initiated; he must also be the peer of the party, and if he had been engaged on either side he could not, during any stage of the action, be employed on the other, even with the permission of the party which had just engaged him. When he presented himself before the court, his credentials were carefully examined, and if found strictly conformable to what the law had enjoined, they were declared valid. It was necessary that they should have been written on good, new, and sound parchment, without blot or erasure, and be sealed by the seals of at least two frei-schöppen.

The attorney of a prince of the empire appeared

with a green cross in his right hand, and a golden
penny of the empire in his left.   He was also to have
a glove on his right hand.   If there were two attor-
neys, they were both to bear crosses and pence. The
attorney of a simple prince bore a silver penny. The
old law, which loves to give a reason for every thing,
says, " Bv the cross they intimate that the prince
whom they represent will, in case he should be found
guilty, amend his conduct according to the direction
of the faith which Jesus Christ preached, and be
constant and true to the holy Christian faith, and
obedient to the holy empire and justice."

All the preliminaries being arranged, the trial
commenced by the charge against him being made
known to the accused, who was called upon for his
defence.   If he did not wish to defend himself in
person, he was permitted to employ an advocate
whom he might have brought with him.   If it was a
civil suit, he might, however, stay the proceedings at
once by giving good security for his satisfying the
claims of the plaintiff, in which case he was allowed
the usual grace of six weeks and three days.   He
might also except to the competence of the court, or
to the legality of the summons, or to anything else
which would, if defective, annul the proceedings.

If the accused did not appear, the regular course
was for the prosecutor to *overswear* him ; that is,
himself to swear by the saints to the truth of what
he had stated, and six true and genuine frei-schöppen to swear that they believed him to have spoken
the truth.

The older Fehm-law made a great distinction
between the initiated and the ignorant, and one very
much to the advantage of the former. The accused,
if initiated, was allowed to clear himself from the
charge by laying his two fore-fingers on the naked
sword, and swearing by the saints " that he was

innocent of the things and the deed which the court had mentioned to him, and which the accuser charged him with, so help him God and all the saints." He then threw a cross-penny (Kreutzer?) to the court and went his way, no one being permitted to let or hinder him. But if he was one of the uninitiated, he was not permitted to clear himself in this manner, and the truth of the fact was determined by the evidence given.

It is plain, however, that such a regulation as this could properly only belong to the time when none but persons of irreproachable character were initiated. As the institution degenerated, this distinction was gradually lost sight of, and facts were determined by evidence without any regard to the rank of the accused.

The accuser could prevent the accused from clearing himself thus easily, by offering himself and six compurgators to swear to the truth of his charge. If the accused wanted to outweigh this evidence, he was obliged to come forward with thirteen or twenty compurgators and swear to his innocence. If he could bring the last number he was acquitted, for the law did not allow it to be exceeded; but if he had but thirteen, the accuser might then overpower him by bringing forward twenty to vouch for his veracity.

If the accuser had convicted the accused, he forthwith prayed the count to grant him a just sentence. The count never took on himself the office of finding the verdict; he always directed one of the assessors to perform it. If the assessor thought the matter too difficult for his judgment, he averred on oath that such was the case, and the court then gave the duty to another, who might free himself from the responsibility in the same manner. Should none of the

assessors be able to come to a decision, the matter
was put off till the next court-day.

But if the assessor undertook the finding of the
verdict, it lay with himself whether he should do so
alone, or retire to take the opinion of the other assessors and the by-standers. To give the verdict due
force it must be found sitting, otherwise it might be
objected to. Whether or not the assessor was bound
to decide according to the majority of voices is uncertain. When the verdict had been found the assessor appeared with his colleagues before the tribunal,
and delivered it to the count, who then passed sentence. What the penalties were for different offences
was a secret known only to the initiated; but, if they
were of a capital nature, the halter, as was intimated
by the one which lay before the count, was the instrument of punishment.

Should the accused not have appeared, and been
in consequence outlawed, he was *forfehmed* by the
following awful curse: it was declared that " he
should be excluded from the public peace, from
all liberties and rights, and the highest *un-peace*,
un-grace, and halter be appointed for him; that
he should be cut off from all communication with
any Christian people, and be cursed so that he
might wither in his body, and neither become any
more verdant, nor increase in any manner; that his
wife should be held to be a widow, and his children
orphans; that he should be without honour and
without right, and given up to any one; that his
neck should be left to the ravens, his body to all
beasts, to the birds of the air and the fishes in the
water; but his soul should be commended to God,"
&c. &c.

If he continued a year and a day under the sentence of outlawry, all his goods then fell to the

emperor or king. A prince, town, or community, that incurred the sentence of outlawry, lost thereby at once all liberties, privileges, and graces.

Should the sentence passed be a capital one, the count flung the halter over his head out of the inclosure of the tribunal, the schöppen spat on it, and the name of the condemned was entered in the bloodbook. If the criminal was present he was instantly seized, and, according to the custom of the middle ages, when, as in the East, no disgrace was attached to the office of executioner, the task of executing him was committed to the youngest schöppe present, who forthwith hung him from the nearest tree. The quality of the criminal was duly attended to; for if he was initiated he was hung seven feet higher than any other, as being esteemed a greater criminal. If the accused was not present, all the schöppen were, as we have already described, set in pursuit of him, and wherever they caught him they hanged him without any further ceremony.

The sentence was kept a profound secret from the uninitiated. A copy of it, drawn up in the usual form, and sealed with seven seals, was given to the accuser.

We thus see that the proceedings in the Fehmcourts were strictly consonant to justice, and even leaned to the side of mercy. But this was not all: the right of appeal was also secured to the accused in case the schöppen who consulted about the verdict did not agree, or that the witnesses did not correspond in their evidence; or, finally, if the verdict found was considered unjust or unsuitable; which last case afforded a most ample field of appeal, for it must have been very rarely that a sentence did not appear unjust or over-severe to the party who was condemned. It was, however, necessary that the appeal should be made on publication of the sen-

tence, or at least before the court broke up. The
parties were allowed to retire for a few minutes, to
consult with their friends who had accompanied them.
If they did not then say that they would appeal, the
sentence was declared absolute, and they were forbidden, under heavy penalties, to oppose it in any
other court. If they did resolve to appeal, both
parties were obliged to give security. *de lite prose-
quenda*. Should either party, being poor or a
stranger, be unable to give security, his oath was
held to be sufficient, that, as the law humanely and
justly expresses it, " the stranger or the poor man
may be able to seek his right in the Holy Roman
Empire as well as the native or the rich man."

The appeal lay to the general chapter of the *Secret
closed Tribunal of the Imperial Chamber*, which usually, if not constantly, sat at Dortmund; or it lay to
the emperor, or king, as the supreme head of these
tribunals. In case of the monarch being initiated,
he could examine into the cause himself; otherwise
he was obliged to commit the inquiry to such of his
councillors as were initiated, or to initiated commissioners, and that only on Westphalian soil. Of this
species of appeal there are numerous instances.
Finally, the appeal might be made to the imperial
lieutenant, who then inquired into the matter himself, with the aid of some initiated schöppen, or
brought it before the general chapter of which he
was president. There was no appeal to the emperor
from his sentence, or from that of the chapter.

There were, besides the right of appeal, other
means of averting the execution of the sentence of
a Fehm-court. Such was what was called *replacing
in the former state*, of which, however, it was only
the initiated who could avail himself. Setnence
having been passed on a person who had not appeared, he might voluntarily and personally repair to

where the secret tribunal was sitting, and sue for this favour. He was to appear before the court which had passed the sentence, accompanied by two frei-schöppen, with a halter about his neck, with white gloves on him, and his hands folded, with an imperial coin and a green cross in them. He and his companions were then to fall down on their knees, and pray for him to be placed in the condition which he was in before the proceedings commenced against him. There was also what was called the complaint of nullity, in case the prescribed form of the proceedings had been violated. Some other means shall presently be noticed.

Chapter IV.

The General Chapter—Rights of the Emperor—Of his Lieutenant—Of the Stuhlherrn, or Tribunal-Lords.

To complete the sketch of the Fehm-tribunals and
their proceedings, we must state the rights and
powers of the general chapter and of the emperor,
his lieutenant, and the tribunal-lords.

The general chapter was a general assembly of
the Westphalian tribunal-lords, counts, and schöppen,
summoned once a-year by the emperor or his lieutenant. Every count was bound by oath to appear
at it. It could only be holden in Westphalia, and
almost exclusively at Dortmund or Arensberg. No
one could appear at it who was not initiated, not
even the emperor himself. The president was the
emperor, if present and initiated, otherwise the lieutenant or his substitute.

The business of the general chapter was to inquire into the conduct and proceedings of the different Fehm-courts. The counts were therefore to
give an account of all their proceedings during the
past year; to furnish a list of the names of the schöppen who had been admitted, as well as of the suits
which had been commenced, with the names of the
accusers, the accused, the *forfehmed*, &c. Such
counts as had neglected their duty were deposed by
the general chapter.

The general chapter was, as we have above observed, a court of appeal from all the Fehm-tribunals.
In matters of great importance the decrees of the

lower courts were, to give them greater weight, confirmed by the general chapter. It was finally at the general chapter that all regulations, laws, and reformations, concerning the Fehm-law and courts, were made.

The emperor, even when the imperial authority was at the lowest, was regarded in Germany as the fountain of judicial authority. The right of passing capital sentence in particular was considered to emanate either mediately or immediately from him. The Fehm-courts were conspicuous for their readiness to acknowledge him as the source of their authority, and all their decrees were pronounced in his name.

As superior lord and judge of all the counts and tribunals, the emperor had a right of inspection and reformation over them. He could summon and preside in a general chapter; he might enter any court; and the presiding count was obliged to give way and allow him to preside in his stead. He had the power to make new schöppen, provided he did so on Westphalian soil. Every schöppe was moreover bound to give a true answer to the emperor when he asked whether such a one was *forfehmed* or not, and in what court. He could also depose disobedient counts, but only in Westphalia.

The emperor could even withdraw a cause out of the hands of the tribunals. The right of appeal to him has been already noticed; but, besides this, he had a power of forbidding the count to proceed in the cause when the accused offered himself to him *for honour and right;* and it was at his own risk then that the count proceeded any further in the business. The emperor could also grant a safe-conduct to any person who might apply for it under apprehension of having been *forfehmed*, which safe-conduct the schöppen dared not violate. Even when a person had been *forfehmed*, the emperor could save him by issuing his command to stay execution of the sentence for a hundred years, six weeks, and a day.

It is plain, that, to be able to exercise these rights, the emperor must be himself *initiated*, for otherwise he could not, for instance, appear where a court was sitting, make alterations in laws with which, if *ignorant*, he must necessarily be unacquainted, or extend mercy when he could not know who was *forfehmed* or not. In the laws establishing the rights of the emperor it was therefore always inserted, *provided he be initiated*, and the acts of uninitiated emperors were by the Fehm-courts frequently declared invalid. The emperor had, therefore, his choice of setting a substitute over the Fehm-courts, or of being himself initiated. The latter course was naturally preferred, and each emperor, at his coronation at Aix-la-Chapelle, was initiated by the hereditary Count of Dortmund. Though Aix-la-Chapelle was not in Westphalia, the law sanctioned this departure from the general rule that frei-schöppen should only be made in that country.

The emperor's lieutenant, who was almost always the Archbishop of Cologne, had the right of confirming such counts as were presented to him by the Tribunal-lords, and of investing them with the powers of life and death. He could also summon general chapters, and preside and exercise the other imperial rights in them. He might decide, with the aid of some schöppen, in cases of appeal to him, without bringing the affair before the general chapter; and he had the power of making schöppen at any tribunal in Westphalia, which proves that, like the emperor, he had free access to them all. Hence it is clear that he also must have been initiated.

The dignity and pre-eminence of the Archbisho

of Cologne, when this office had been conferred on
him, caused a good deal of envy and jealousy among
the lords of Westphalia, who had been hitherto his
equals, and who considered themselves equally entitled to it with him. They never let slip an occasion
of showing their feelings, and they always had their
counts invested by the emperor, and not by the archbishop; nay, there are not wanting instances of their
having such counts as he had invested confirmed
and re-invested by the emperor.

There now remain only the Tribunal-Lords (*Stuhlherrn*) to be considered.

The Tribunal-lord was the lord of the district in
which there was a Fehm-tribunal. He might himself, if initiated, become the count of it, having previously obtained the power of life and death from the
emperor, or his lieutenant ; or, if he did not choose to
do so, he might, as we have already seen, present a
count to be invested, for whose conduct he was held
responsible ; and, if the count appointed by him
misconducted himself, the Stuhl-herr was liable to a
forfeiture of his rights. He was, in consequence,
permitted to exercise a right of inspection over the
Fehm-courts in his territory ; no schöppé could be
made, no cause brought into the court, not even
a summons issued, without his approbation. There
even lay a kind of appeal to him from the sentence of the count; and he could also, like the
emperor, withdraw certain persons and causes from
his jurisdiction. But as his power did not extend
beyond his own tertitory, the count might refer those
causes in which he wished, but was prohibited, to
proceed, to the courts in other territories ; he might
also, if he apprehended opposition from the Tribunal-
lord, require him (if initiated) to be present at the
proceedings.

The Tribunal-lord, if uninitiated, could, like the

emperor in the same case, exercise these powers only by initiated deputies.

The great advantage which resulted from the right of having Fehm-tribunals induced the high lords, both spiritual and temporal, to be very anxious to become possessed of this species of territorial property, and in consequence nearly all the lords in Westphalia had Fehm-tribunals. Even towns, such as Dortmund, Soëst, Münster, and Osnabrück, had these tribunals, either within their walls, or in their districts, or their neighbourhood, for it would not have been good policy in them to suffer this sort of *Status in Statu*, to be independent of their authority.

CHAPTER V.

Fehm-courts at Celle—At Brunswick—Tribunal of the Know
ing in the Tyrol—The Castle of Baden—African Purrahs.

WE have now gone through the constitution and
modes of procedure of the Fehm-tribunals of Westphalia, as far as the imperfect notices of them which
have reached the present age permit. It remains to
trace their history down to the last vestiges of them
which appear. A matter of some curiosity should,
however, be previously touched on, namely, how far
they were peculiar to Westphalia, and what institutions resembling them may be elsewhere found.

Fehm-tribunals were, in fact, as we have already
observed, not peculiar to Westphalia. In a MS. life
of Duke Julius of Celle, by Francis Algermann*, of
the year 1608, we read the following description of
a Fehm-court, which the author remembered to have
seen holden at Celle in his youth :—

" When the Fehm-law† was to be put in operation, all the inhabitants of the district who were above
twelve years of age were obliged to appear, without
fail, on a heath or some large open place, and sit
down on the ground. Some tables were then set
in the middle of the assembly, at which the prince,
his councillors, and bailiffs, took their seats. The
Secret Judges then reported the delinquents and the
offences ; and they went round with a white wand

* Berck, p. 231, from Spittler's History of Hanover.
† *Vimricht*, i. e. *Fehm-law*, the German word, of which the
author presently gives a childish etymology.

and smote the offenders on the legs. Whoever then
had a bad conscience, and knew himself to be guilty
of a capital offence, was permitted to stand up and
to quit the country within a day and a night. He
might even wait till he got the second blow. But if
he was struck the third time, the executioner was at
hand, a pastor gave him the sacrament, and away
with him to the nearest tree.

"But if a person was struck but once or twice,
that was a paternal warning to him to amend his life
thenceforward. Hence it was called *Jus Veniæ*, because there was grace in it, which has been corrupted
and made *Vim-richt*."

There were similar courts, we are told, at places
named Wölpe and Rotenwald. Here the custom
was for the Secret Judges, when they knew of any
one having committed an offence which fell within
the Fehm-jurisdiction, to give him a private friendly
warning. To this end they set, during the night, a
mark on his door, and at drinking-parties they
managed to have the can sent past him. If these
warnings took no effect the court was held.

According to an ancient law-book, the Fehm-
court at Brunswick was thus regulated and holden.
Certain of the most prudent and respectable citizens,
named *Fehmenotes*, had the secret duty of watching
the conduct of their fellow-citizens and giving information of it to the council. Had so many offences
been committed that it seemed time to hold a Fehm-
court, a day was appointed for that purpose. Some
members of the council from the different districts
of the town met at midnight in St. Martin's churchyard, and then called all the council together. All
the gates and entrances of the town were closed;
all corners and bridges, and the boats both above and
below the town, were guarded. The Fehm-clerk was
then directed to begin his office, and the Fehme-

notes were desired to give their informations to him to be put into legal form if the time should prove sufficient.

At daybreak it was notified to the citizens that the council had resolved that the Fehm-court should be holden on this day, and they were directed to repair to the market-place as soon as the tocsin sounded.

When the bell had tolled three times all who had assembled accompanied the council, through the gate of St. Peter, out of the town to what was called the Fehm-ditch. Here they separated; the council took their station on the space between the ditch and the town-gate, the citizens stood at the other side of the ditch. The Fehmenotes now mingled themselves among the townsmen, inquired after such offences as were not yet come to their knowledge, and communicated whatever information they obtained, and also their former discoveries (if they had not had time to do so in the night) to the clerk, to be put by him into proper form and laid before the council.

The clerk having delivered his protocol to the council, they examined it and ascertained which of the offences contained in it were to be brought before a Fehm-court, and which not; for matters under the value of four shillings did not belong to it. The council then handed the protocol back to the clerk, who went with it to the Fehm-court, which now took its seat in presence of a deputation of the council.

Those on whom theft had been committed were first brought forward and asked if they knew the thief. If they replied in the negative, they were obliged to swear by the saints to the truth of their answer; if they named an individual, and that it was the first charge against him, he was permitted to clear himself by oath; but if there was a second charge against him, his own oath was not sufficient,

and he was obliged to bring six compurgators to
swear along with him. Should there be a third
charge, his only course was to clear himself by the
ordeal. He was forthwith to wash his hand in water,
and to take in it a piece of glowing-hot iron, which
the beadles and executioners had always in readiness on the left of the tribunal, and to carry it a
distance of nine feet. The Fehm-count, according
to ancient custom, chose whom he would to find the
verdict. The council could dissolve the court whenever they pleased. Such causes as had not come on,
or were put off on account of sickness, or any other
just impediment, were, on such occasions, noted and
reserved for another session.

It is evident, however, that this municipal court,
of which the chief object was the punishment of
theft, the grand offence of the middle ages, though
called a Fehm-court, was widely different from those
of the same name in Westphalia.

The Tribunal of the Knowing (*Gericht der Wis-
senden*), in Tyrol, has also been erroneously supposed
to be the same with the Westphalian courts. The
mode of procedure in this was for the accuser to lay
his finger on the head of the accused, and swear that
he knew him to be an infamous person, while six
reputable people, laying their fingers on the arm of
the accuser, swore that they knew him to have sworn
truly and honestly. This was considered sufficient
evidence against any person, and the court proceeded
to judgment on it.

The ideal Fehm-court beneath the castle of Baden
must not be passed over without notice, as it seems
to be the model after which our popular novelist described his Fehm-tribunal in Switzerland ! A female
writer in Germany* informs us that beneath the

* Friederika Brun. Episoden aus Reisen durch das Süd-
liche Deutschland, &c.

castle of Baden the vaults extend to a considerable distance in labyrinthine windings, and were in former times appropriated to the secret mysteries of a Fehm-tribunal. Those who were brought before this awful tribunal were not conducted into the castle-vaults in the usual way; they were lowered into the gloomy abyss by a cord in a basket, and restored to the light, if so fortunate as to be acquitted, in the same manner; so that they never could, however inclined, discover where they had been. The ordinary entrance led through a long dark passage, which was closed by a door of a single stone as large as a tombstone. This door revolved on invisible hinges, and fitted so exactly, that when it was shut the person who was inside could not distinguish it from the adjoining stones, or tell where it was that he had entered. It could only be opened on the outside by a secret spring. Proceeding along this passage you reached the torture-room, where you saw hooks in the wall, thumb-screws, and every species of instruments of torture. A door on the left opened into a recess, the place of the *Maiden's Kiss*. When any person who had been condemned was led hither, a stone gave way under his feet, and he fell into the arms of the Maiden, who, like the wife of Nabis, crushed him to death in her arms, which were thick set with spikes. Proceeding on farther, after passing through several doors, you came to the vault of the Tribunal. This was a long spacious quadrangle hung round with black. At the upper end was a niche in which were an altar and crucifix. In this place the chief judge sat; his assessors had their seats on wooden benches along the walls.

We need not to observe how totally different from the proceedings of a genuine Fehm-tribunal is all this. That there are vaults under the castle of Baden is certain, and the description above given is possibly

correct. But the Fehm-court which was held in
them is the mere coinage of the lady's brain, and
utterly unlike any thing real, unless it be the Holy
Office, whose secret proceedings never could vie in
justice or humanity with those of the Westphalian
Fehm-courts. It is, moreover, not confirmed by any
document, or even by the tradition of the place, and
would be undeserving of notice were it not for the
reason assigned above.

The similarity between the Fehm-courts and the
Inquisition has been often observed. In the secrecy
of their proceedings, and the great number of agents
which they had at their devotion, they resemble each
other; but the Holy Office had nothing to correspond
to the public and repeated citations of the Fehm-
courts, the fair trial given to the accused, the leaning
towards mercy of the judges, and the right of appeal
which was secured.

The most remarkable resemblance to the Fehm-
tribunals is (or was) to be found among the negroes
on the west coast of Africa, as they are described by
a French traveller*. These are the Purrahs of the
Foollahs, who dwell between Sierra Leone river and
Cape Monte.

There are five tribes of this people, who form a
confederation, at the head of which is a union of warriors, which is called a Purrah. Each tribe has its
own separate Purrah, and each Purrah has its chiefs
and its tribunal, which is, in a more restricted sense,
also called a Purrah. The general Purrah of the
confederation is formed from the Purrahs of the five
tribes.

To be a member of the inferior Purrahs, a man
must be thirty years of age; no one under fifty can
have a seat in the general Purrah. The candidate

---

* Golberry, Voyage en Afrique, t. i. p. 114, and seq.

for admission into an inferior Purrah has to undergo
a most severe course of probation, in which all the
elements are employed to try him. Before he is permitted to enter on this course, such of his relatives
as are already members are obliged to pledge themselves for his fitness, and to swear to take his life if
ever he should betray the secrets of the society. Having passed through the ordeal, he is admitted into
the society and sworn to secrecy and obedience. If
he is unmindful of his oath, he becomes the child of
death. When he least expects it a warrior in disguise makes his appearance and says, "The great
Purrah sends thee death." Every one present de-
parts ; no one ventures to make any opposition, and
the victim falls.

The subordinate Purrahs punish all crimes committed within their district, and take care that their
sentences are duly executed. They also settle disputes and quarrels between the leading families.

It is only on extraordinary occasions that the great
Purrah meets. It then decides on the punishment
of traitors and those who had resisted its decrees.
Frequently too it has to interfere to put an end to
wars between the tribes. When it has met on this
account it gives information to the belligerents,
directing them to abstain from hostilities, and menac-
ing death if a drop more of blood should be spilt. It
then inquires into the causes of the war, and con-
demns the tribe which is found to have been the
aggressor to a four days' plundering. The warriors
to whom the execution of this sentence is committed
must, however, be selected from a neutral district.
They arm and disguise themselves, put horrible-
looking vizards on their faces, and with pitch-torches
in their hands set out by night from the place of
assembly. Making no delay, they reach the devoted
district before the break of day, and in parties of

from forty to sixty men, they fall unexpectedly on the devoted tribe, and, with fearful cries, making known the sentence of the great Purrah, proceed to put it into execution. The booty is then divided : one half is given to the injured tribe, the other falls to the great Purrah, who bestow one half of their share on the warriors who executed their sentence.

Even a single family, if its power should appear to be increasing so fast as to put the society in fear for its independence, is condemned to a plundering by the Purrah. It was thus, though under more specious pretexts, that the Athenian democracy sought to reduce the power of their great citizens by condemning them to build ships, give theatrical exhibitions, and otherwise spend their fortunes.

Nothing can exceed the dread which the Purran inspires. The people speak of it with terror and awe, and look upon the members of it as enchanters who are in compact with the devil. The Purrah itself is solicitous to diffuse this notion as much as possible, esteeming it a good mean for increasing its power and influence. The number of its members is estimated at upwards of 6000, who recognise each other by certain words and signs. Its laws and secrets are, notwithstanding the great number of the members, most religiously concealed from the knowledge of the uninitiated.

Chapter VI.

The Emperor Lewis the Bavarian—Charles IV.—Wenceslaus
—Rupertian Reformation—Encroachments of the Fehm-
courts—Case of Nickel Weller and the town of Görlitz—
Of the City of Dantzig—Of Hans David and the Teutonic
Knights—Other instances of the presumption of the Free-
counts—Citation of the Emperor Frederic III.—Case of the
Count of Teckenburg.

THE history of the Fehm-gerichte, previous to the
fifteenth century, offers but few events to detain at-
attention. The Emperor Lewis the Bavarian appears to have exerted his authority on several occasions in granting privileges in Westphalia according,
as it is expressly stated, to the Fehm-law. His successor, the luxurious Charles IV., acted with the same
caprice respecting the Fehm-tribunals as he did in
every thing else, granting privileges and revoking
them just as it seemed to accord with his interest at
the moment. This monarch attempted also to extend the Fehm-system beyond Westphalia, deeming
it perhaps a good mean for bringing all Germany
under the authority of his patrimonial kingdom of
Bohemia. He therefore gave permission to the
Bishop of Hildesheim to erect two Free-tribunals
out of Westphalia. On the representations of the
Archbishop of Cologne and the lords of Westphalia,
however, he afterwards abolished them.

Wenceslaus, the son of Charles, acted with his usual
folly in the case of the Fehm-tribunals; he is said,
as he could keep nothing secret, to have blabbed their

z

private sign, and he took on him to make frei-schöppen, contrary to the law, out of Westphalia. These
schöppen of the emperor's making did not, however,
meet with much respect from the genuine ones, as
the answer given to the Emperor Rupert by the
Westphalian tribunals evinces. On his asking how
they acted with regard to such schöppen, their reply
was, " We ask them at what court they were made
schöppen. Should it appear that they were made
schöppen at courts which had no right so to do, we
hang them, in case of their being met in Westphalia,
on the instant, without any mercy." Wenceslaus, little
as he cared about Germany in general, occasionally
employed the Fehm-courts for the furtherance of his
plans, and, in the year 1389, he had Count Henry of
Wernengerode tried and hanged for treason by
Westphalian schöppen. The reign of Wenceslaus is
particularly distinguished by its being the period in
which the Archbishop of Cologne arrived at the important office of lieutenant of the emperor over all
the Westphalian tribunals.

The reign of Rupert was, with respect to the
Westphalian Fehm-courts, chiefly remarkable by the
reformation of them named from him. This reformation, which is the earliest publicly-accredited source
from which a knowledge of the Fehm-law can be
derived, was made in the year 1404. It is a collection of decisions by which the rights and privileges
of a king of the Romans are ascertained with respect
to these tribunals.

The Rupertian reformation, and the establishment
of the office of lieutenant in the person of the Archbishop of Cologne, which was completed by either
Rupert or his successor Sigismund, form together an
epoch in the history of the Fehm-gerichte. Hitherto
Westphalia alone was the scene of their operations,
and their authority was of evident advantage to the

empire. Their power had now attained its zenith; confidence in their strength led them to abuse it ; and, during the century which elapsed between the Rupertian reformation and the establishment of the Perpetual Public Peace and the Imperial Chamber by the Emperor Maximilian, we shall have to contemplate chiefly their abuses and assumptions.

The right of citation was what was chiefly abused by the Free-courts. Now that they were so formally acknowledged to act under the imperial authority, they began to regard Westphalia as too narrow a theatre for the display of their activity and their power. As imperial commissioners, they maintained that their jurisdiction extended to every place which acknowledged that of the emperor's, and there was hardly a corner of Germany free from the visits of their messengers; nay, even beyond the limits of the empire men trembled at their citations.

It was chiefly the towns which were harassed by these citations, which were frequently issued at the instance of persons whom they had punished or expelled for their misdeeds. Their power and consequence did not protect even the greatest: we find, during the fifteenth century, some of the principal cities of the empire summoned before the tribunals of Westphalian counts. Thus in the records of those times we read of citations served on Bremen, Lübeck, Augsburg, Nuremberg, Erfurt, Görlitz, and Dantzig. Even Prussia and Livonia, then belonging to the order of the Teutonic knights, were annoyed by their interference.

One of the most remarkable cases which this period presents is that of the uneasiness caused to the town of Görlitz by means of one of its inhabitants named Nickel Weller. This man, who was a Westphalian schöppe, was accused of having disinterred an unchristened child, and of having made a candle of the bone of its arm, which he had filled with the wax of an Easter-taper and with incense, and of having employed it in a barn in presence of his mother, his wife, and an old peasant, for magical purposes. As he could not deny the fact, he was, according to the law of those times, liable to be hanged; but the high-bailiff of Stein, and some other persons of consequence, interfering in his favour, the magistrates contented themselves with expelling him the town and confiscating his goods. As it afterwards proved, they would have acted more wisely had they condemned him to perpetual imprisonment.

Weller immediately repaired to Bresslau, and besought the council, the Bishop of Waradein, and the imperial chancellor, to advocate his cause. They acceded to his desire; but the magistrates of Görlitz perfectly justified their conduct. Weller, still indisposed to rest, applied to the pope, Innocent VIII., asserting that he could not to any purpose bring an accusation against the council of Görlitz within the town of the diocese of Meissen, and that he had no chance of justice there. The pope forthwith named John de' Medici and Dr. Nicholas Tauchen of Bresslau spiritual commissioners in this affair, and these desired the high-bailiff of Stein to do his best that Weller should recover his rights within the space of a month, on his taking his oath to the truth of his statements, otherwise they should be obliged themselves to take measures for that purpose.

From some unassigned cause, however, nothing came of this, and Weller once more addressed himself to the pope, with whom the Bishop of Ostia became his advocate. He was re-admitted into the bosom of the Church; but the decree of the magistracy of Görlitz still remained in force, and the new commissioners appointed by the pope even confirmed it.

Finding that he had nothing to expect from papal

interference, Weller had at last recourse to the Fehm-tribunals, and on the 3d May, 1490, John of Hul-schede, count of the tribunal at Brackel, cited the burgomasters, council, and all the lay inhabitants of Görlitz above the age of eighteen years, before his tribunal. This summons was served in rather a remarkable manner, for it was found fastened to a twig on a hedge, on a farm belonging to a man named Wenzel Emmerich, a little distance from the town.

As by the Golden Bull of the Emperor Charles IV., and moreover by a special privilege granted by Sigismund, Görlitz was exempted from all foreign jurisdiction, the magistracy informed Vladislaus, King of Bohemia, of this citation, and implored his mediation. The Bohemian monarch accordingly addressed himself to the tribunal at Brackel, but George Hackenberg, who was at that time the free-count of that court, Hulschede being dead, did not even deign to give him an answer.

Meanwhile the appointed period had elapsed without the people of Görlitz having appeared to the summons, and Weller, charging them with disobedience and contempt of court, prayed that they might be condemned in all the costs and penalties thereby incurred, and that he might be himself permitted to proceed with his complaint. To this end he estimated the losses and injuries which he had sustained at 500 Rhenish florins, and made a declaration to that effect on oath, with two joint-swearers. He was accordingly authorised by the court to indemnify himself in any manner he could at the expense of the people of Görlitz. It was farther added that, if any one should impede Weller in the prosecution of his rights, that person should *ipso facto* fall under the heavy displeasure of the empire and the pains and penalties of the tribunal at Brackel, and be moreover obliged to pay all the costs of the accuser.

On the 16th August of the same year, the count set a new peremptory term for the people of Görlitz, assuring them that, in case of disobedience, "he should be obliged, though greatly against his inclination, to pass the heaviest and most rigorous sentence on their persons, their lives, and their honour." The citation was this time found on the floor of the convent church. The council in consternation applied to the Archbishop of Cologne and to the free-count himself, to be relieved from this condition, but in vain; the count did not condescend to take any notice of their application, and when they did not appear at the set time, declared the town of Görlitz outlawed for contumacy.

It appears that Weller had, for some cause or other, brought an accusation against the city of Bresslau also; for in the published decree of outlawry against Görlitz it was included. By this act it was prohibited to every person, under penalty of similar outlawry, to harbour any inhabitant of either of these towns; to eat or drink, or hold any intercourse with them, till they had reconciled themselves to the Fehm-tribunals, and given satisfaction to the complainant. Weller himself stuck up a copy of this decree on a market-day at Leipzig; but it was instantly torn down by some of the people of Görlitz who happened to be there.

The two towns of Görlitz and Bresslau held a consultation at Liegnitz, to devise what measures it were best to adopt in order to relieve themselves from this system of persecution. They resolved that they would jointly and separately defend themselves and their proceedings by a public declaration, which should be posted up in Görlitz, Bresslau, Leipzig, and other places. They also resolved to lay their griefs before the Diet at Prague, and pray for its intercession with the Archbishop of Cologne and the Land-

graf of Hessen. They accordingly did so, and the
Diet assented to their desire ; but their good offices
were of no avail, and the answer of the landgraf
clearly showed, either that he had no authority over
his count, or that he was secretly pleased with what
he had done.

The indefatigable Weller now endeavoured to seize
some of the people of Bresslau and Görlitz, in Hein
and other places in Meissen. But they frustrated his
plans by obtaining a promise of protection and safe-
conduct from the Duke George. Weller, however,
did not desist, and when Duke Albert came from the
Netherlands to Meissen, he sought and obtained his
protection. But here again he was foiled; for, when
the high-bailiff and council of Görlitz had informed
that prince of the real state of the case, he withdrew
his countenance from him. Wearied out by this
ceaseless teasing, the towns applied, through the king
of Bohemia, to the Emperor Frederic III. for a
mandate to all the subjects of the empire, and an
inhibition to the tribunal at Brackel and all the free-
counts and schöppen. These, when obtained, they
took care to have secretly served on the council of
Dortmund and the free-count of Brackel. By these
means they appear to have put an end to their annoy-
ances for the remainder of Weller's life. But, in the
year 1502, his son and his son-in-law revived his
claims on Görlitz. Count Ernest of Hohenstein
interceded for them ; but the council adhered firmly
to their previous resolution, and declared that it was
only to their own or to higher tribunals that they
must look for relief. The matter then lay over for
ten years, when it was again stirred by one Guy of
Taubenheim, and was eventually settled by an ami-
cable arrangement.

As we have said, the Fehm-tribunals extended
their claims of jurisdiction even to the Baltic. We

find that a citizen of the town of Dantzig, named
Hans Holloger, who was a free schöppe, was cited
to appear before the tribunal of Elleringhausen,
under the hawthorn, "because he had spoken what
he ought not to have spoken about the Secret Tribunal." This might seem just enough, as he belonged
to the society; but the town-council were commanded,
under a penalty of fifty pounds of fine gold, to cast
the accused into prison till he had given security for
standing his trial.

Even the powerful order of the Teutonic Knights,
who were the masters of Prussia and Livonia, did
not escape being annoyed by the Fehm-tribunals.
How little their power availed against that formidable
jurisdiction is evinced by the answer made by the
Grand Master to the towns which sued to him for
protection. "Beloved liegemen! you have besought
us to protect you therefrom; we would cheerfully do
it knew we but ways and means thereto." And
when he wrote to Mangolt, the count of the tribunal
at Freyenhagen, warning him against summoning before him the subjects of the order, the latter haughtily
replied, "You have your rights from the empire,
and I have power to judge over all who hold of the
empire."

The following very curious case occurred in the
first half of the fifteenth century:—

A shopkeeper at Liebstadt died very much indebted to the two officers of the Teutonic order,
whose business it was to keep the small towns in
Prussia supplied with mercantile goods, and they
accordingly seized on the effects which he had left
behind him. These, however, were not sufficient to
satisfy even the demands of one of them, much less
of both, and they had made up their minds to rest
content with the loss, when, to their surprise, Hans
David, the son of the deceased, came forward with

an account against the order of such amount, that, as it was observed, if all the houses in the town were sold, and all the townsmen taxed to the utmost, the produce would not discharge the one-half of it. He however produced a document purporting to be a bond of the order. This instrument bore all the marks of falsification; it was full of erasures and insertions; among the witnesses to it, some were set down as priors who were only simple brethren of the order; there were the names of others who had never seen it; it was asserted to have been attested and verified by the tribunal at Passnar, but in the records of that court there were not the slightest traces of it; the seal of the Grand Master, which was appended to every document of any importance, was wanting   Of course payment was resisted, but Hans David was told to pursue his claim, if he pleased, before the emperor and the pope, whom the order recognised as their superiors.

As Hans David was under the protection of the king of Poland, he had recourse to that prince; but he declined interfering any farther than to apply for a safe-conduct for him that he might apply for a new inquiry. The Grand Master, on application being made to him, swore on his honour that he owed to the complainant nothing, and that the bond was a forgery; he moreover promised to answer the charge in any fit place that the complainant might select; nay, even in Prussia, and he granted him a safe-conduct as before.

It is not known what course Hans David now adopted; but nine years afterwards (1441) we find him addressing himself to the Free-tribunal at Freyenhagen, whose count, the notorious Mangolt, forthwith issued his citations, " because, as he expressed himself, the order judges with the sword and gentle murder and burning." The Grand Master, indignant at this piece of arrogance, immediately brought the matter before the assembly of the free-counts at Coblentz, who declared the proceedings null, and Mangolt liable to punishment, as the knights were spiritual persons. He moreover applied to the emperor, who, to gratify him, issued a mandate, addressed to all princes of the empire, declaring the act of Mangolt to be a piece of iniquity, and null and void.

Hans David was now cast into prison at Cologne, and, notwithstanding a prohibition of the Free-tribunal, was detained there for two years. Existing documents attest (though the fact is inexplicable) that the emperor directed the Archbishop of Cologne and the Margraf of Baden to examine anew into the affair, and to send the acts into the imperial chancery, and, finally, to set the complainant free on his oath, or on his giving bail to appear at Nuremberg. As this proceeding can only be ascribed to the influence of the Secret Tribunals, bent on annoying the order, it serves to show what their power and consequence must have been at that time.

Two years afterwards it was clearly proved at Vienna that the bond had been forged, at the desire of Hans David, by a scholar of Elbingen, named Rothofé. As the case against the former was now so plain, it might be supposed that he would be punished at once. Instead of that, the emperor referred the parties to the pope, as Hans David had struck a prior of the order, and this last was not content with the satisfaction accorded by the emperor.

The cause of the order was triumphant in Rome also, yet still Hans David found means to keep off the execution of the sentence already passed on him at Vienna. It was not till after the death of the then Grand Master that final judgment was formally delivered by Cardinal Jossi, and Hans David, his com-

rade Paul Frankleuen, and the Count Mangolt, were
condemned to perpetual silence, and to payment of the
sum of 6,000 Rhenish florins to the order, and, in case
of disobedience, they were declared to be outlawed.
All this, however, did not yet avail, and two years
afterwards Jossi was obliged to apply to the emperor
for the aid of the temporal arm for the execution of
the sentence. The chaplain of the order at Vienna
also found that Hans David had still the art to deceive many and gain them over to his cause, and he
accordingly took care to have the whole account of
his conduct posted up on the church-doors.

Still the unwearied Hans David did not rest. He
now went to the Free-tribunal at Waldeck, and had
the art to deceive the count by his false representations. He assured him that the order had offered
him no less than 15,000 florins and an annuity, if
he would let his action drop; that they would have
been extremely well content if he had escaped out
of prison at Cologne, but that he preferred justice
and truth to liberty. The order however succeeded
here again in detecting and exposing his arts, and
the count honestly confessed that he had been deceived by him. He cast him off forthwith, and Hans
David, ceasing to annoy the order, devoted himself
to astrology and conjuring for the rest of his days*.

He had, however, caused othe rder abundance of

---

* The following is one of his predictions, delivered by him,
under the name of Master Von Dolete, in the year 1457: "In
the ensuing month, September, the sun will appear like a
black dragon; cruel winds will blow, the sea will roar, and
men will be knocked to pieces by the wind. The sun will then
be turned to blood; that betokeneth war in the East and West.
A mighty emperor will die; the earth will quake, and few
men will remain alive. Wherefore secure your houses and
chambers; lay up provisions for thirty days in caverns," &c.,
&c. The arts of knaves and the language of impostors are
the same in all ages and countries

uneasiness and expense. Existing documents prove that this affair cost them no less than upwards of 1580 ducats, and 7000 florins, which must be in a great measure ascribed to the secret machinations of the Free-tribunals, anxious to depress the Teutonic Knights, who stood in their way.

In 1410 the Wild and Rhein Graf was summoned before the tribunal at Nordernau, and, in 1454, the Duke of Saxony before that at Limburg. The Elector-Palatine found it difficult, in 1448, to defend himself against a sentence passed on him by one of the Fehm-courts. Duke Henry of Bavaria found it necessary on the following occasion, actually to become a fre -schöppe in order to save himself. One Gaspar, of Torringen, had accused him before the tribunal of Waldeck of "having taken from him his hereditary office of Chief Huntsman; of having seized and beaten his huntsmen and servants, taken his hounds, battered down his castle of Torringen, and taken from his wife her property and jewels, in despite of God, honour, and ancient right." The free-count forthwith cited the duke, who applied to the emperor Sigismund, and procured an inhibition to the count. The duke found it necessary, notwithstanding, to appear before the court; but he adopted the expedient of getting himself made a frei-schöppe, and then, probably in consequence of his rank and influence, procured a sentence to be passed in accordance with his wishes. Gaspar, who was probably an injured man, appealed to the emperor, who referred the matter to the Archbishop of Cologne, and we are not informed how it ended.

But the audacity of the free-counts went so far as even to cite the head of the empire himself before their tribunals. The imperial chancery having, for just and good cause, declared several free-counts and their Tribunal-lord, Walrabe of Waldeck, to be outlawed, three free-counts had the hardihood, in 1470, to cite the emperor Frederic III., with his chancellor, the Bishop of Passau, and the assessors of the chancery-court, to appear before the free-tribunal between the gates of Wünnenberg in the diocese of Paderborn, " there to defend his person and highest honour under penalty of being held to be a disobedient emperor ; " and on his not appearing, they had the impudence to cite him again, declaring that, if he did not appear, justice should take its course. Feeble, however, as was the character of the emperor, he did not give way to such assumptions.

Even robbery and spoliation could find a defence with the Fehm-courts. Towards the end of the thirteenth century a count of Teckenburg plundered and ravaged the diocese of Münster. The bishop assembled his own people and called on his allies to aid him, and they took two castles belonging to the count and pushed him to extremity. To extricate himself he accused the bishop, and all those who were with him, before his Fehm-court, and though there were among them the Bishop of Paderborn, three counts, and several knights, the free-count had the boldness to cite them all to appear and defend their honour. The affair was eventually amicably arranged and the citation recalled.

These instances may suffice to show how far the Fehm-tribunals had departed from the original object of their institution, and how corrupt and iniquitous they were become.

Chapter VII.

Cause of the degeneracy of the Fehm-courts—Attempts at reformation—Causes of their high reputation—Case of the Duke of Würtemberg—Of Kerstian Kerkerink—Causes of the decline of the Fehm-jurisdiction.

The chief cause of the degeneracy of the Fehm-courts was the admission of improper persons into the society. Originally, as we have seen, no man was admitted to become a schöppe without producing satisfactory evidence as to the correctness of his character; but now, in the case of either count or schöppe, a sufficient sum of money availed to supersede inquiry, and the consequence was that men of the most disgraceful characters frequently presided at the tribunals and wielded the formidable powers of the society. A writer in the reign of Sigismund says, "that those who had gotten authority to hang men were hardly deserving enough to keep pigs; that they were themselves well worthy of the gallows if one cast a glance over their course of life; that they left not unobserved the mote in their brother's eye, but overlooked the beam in their own, &c." And it required no small courage in the writer thus to express himself; for, according to his own testimony, people then hardly ventured even to speak of the Secret Tribunals, so great was the awe in which they were held.

The consequence was that justice was not to be had at any tribunal which was presided over by corrupt judges, as they selected assessors, and even by-standers, of the same character with themselves, and whatever verdict they pleased was found. The tribunal-lord generally winked at their proceedings, while the right of appeal to the emperor was treated with little respect; for these monarchs had generally affairs of more immediate importance to themselves to occupy their attention. The right of exemption was also trampled on; sovereign princes were, as we have seen, cited before the tribunals; so also were the Jews. Purely civil matters were now maintained to belong to the Fehm-jurisdiction, and parties in such cases were cited before the tribunals, and *forfehmed* in case of disobedience. In short, the Fehm-jurisdiction was now become a positive evil instead of being, as heretofore, a benefit to the country.

Various attempts were doubtless made to reform the Fehm-law and tribunals, such as the Arensberg reformation, the Osnaburgh regulation, and others, but to little purpose. The system, in fact, was at variance with the spirit which was now beginning to prevail, and could not be brought to accord with it.

Before we proceed to the decline of the society, we will pause a moment to consider the causes of the great reputation and influence which it obtained and exercised during the period in which it flourished.

The first and chief cause was the advantage which it was found to be of for the maintenance of social order and tranquillity. In the very worst and most turbulent times a portion of mankind will always be found desirous of peace and justice, even independently of any private interest; another portion, feeling themselves the victims of oppression, will gladly catch at any hope of protection; even the mighty and the oppressive themselves will at times view with satisfaction any institution which may avail to shield them against power superior to their own, or which they conceive may be made the instrument of extending and strengthening their consequence. The Fehm-jurisdiction was calculated to suit all these orders of persons. The fourteenth and fifteenth centuries were the most anarchic periods of Germany; the imperial power was feeble to control; and the characters of most of the emperors were such as to render still more unavailing the little au thority which, as heads of the empire, they possessed. Sensible of their weakness, these monarchs generally favoured the Fehm-tribunals, which so freely, and even ostentatiously, recognised the imperial superiority, as long as it did not seek to control them or impede them in their proceedings. The knowledge which, if initiated, they could derive of the crimes and misdemeanors committed in the empire, and the power of directing the arms of the society against evil-doers, were also of no small importance, and they gradually became of opinion that their own existence was involved in that of the Fehm-courts. The nobles of Westphalia, in like manner, found their advantage in belonging to the society, and the office of tribunal-lord was, as we have seen, one of influence and emolument.

But it was the more helpless and oppressed classes of society, more especially the unhappy serfs, that most rejoiced in the existence of the Fehm-tribunals; for there only could they hope to meet with sure redress when aggrieved, and frequently was a cause, when other courts had been appealed to in vain, brought before the Secret Tribunal, which judged without respect of persons. The accuser had farther not to fear the vengeance of the evil-doer, or his friends and dependents; for his name was kept a profound secret if the proofs which he could furnish were sufficient to justify the inquisitorial process already described, and thus the robber-noble, or the feudal tyrant, often met his merited punishment at a time when he perhaps least dreaded it, and when he held his victim, whose cries to justice had brought it on him, in the greatest contempt; for, like the Nemesis, or the "gloom-roaming" Erinnys of antiquity, the retributive justice of the Fehm-tribunals moved to vengeance with stealthy pace, and caught its victim in the midst of his security.

A second cause was the opinion of these courts having been instituted by Charles the Great, a monarch whose memory was held in such high estimation and such just veneration during the middle ages. Emperors thought themselves bound to treat with respect the institution of him from whom they derived their authority; and the clergy themselves, exempt from its jurisdiction, were disposed to view with favour an institution established by the monarch to whom the Church was so deeply indebted, and of whose objects the punishment of heretics was one of the most prominent.

A third, and not the least important cause, was the excellent organization of the society, which enabled it to give such effect to its decrees, and to which nothing in those times presented any parallel. The veil of secrecy which enveloped all its proceedings, and the number of agents ready to execute its mandates, inspired awe; the strict inquiry which was known to be made into the character of a man before he was admitted into it gained it respect. Its sentences were, though the proofs were unknown, believed to have emanated from justice; and bad men trembled, and good men rejoiced, as they beheld the body of a criminal suspended from a tree, and the schöppe's knife stuck beside it to intimate by whom he had been judged and condemned.

The reign of the Emperor Maximilian was a period of great reform in Germany, and his establishment of the Perpetual Public Peace, and of the Imperial Chamber, joined with other measures, tended considerably to alter and improve the condition of the empire. The Fehm-tribunals should, as a matter of prudence, have endeavoured to accommodate themselves to the new order of things ; but this is a part of wisdom of which societies and corporate bodies are rarely found capable ; and, instead of relaxing in their pretensions, they even sought to extend them farther than before. Under their usual pretext—the denial of justice—they extended their citations to persons and places over which they had no jurisdiction, and thereby provoked the enmity and excited the active hostility of cities and powerful territorial lords.

The most remarkable cases which this period presents of the perversion of the rights and powers of the Fehm-tribunals are the two following :—

Duke Ulrich of Würtemberg lived unhappily with his duchess Sabina. There was at his court a young nobleman named Hans Hutten, a member of an honourable and powerful family, to whose wife the duke was more particular in his attentions than could be agreeable to a husband. The duchess, on her side, testified a particular esteem for Hans Hutten, and the intimacy between them was such as the duke could not forgive. Hutten was either so vain or so inconsiderate as to wear publicly on his finger a valuable ring which had been given to him by the duchess. This filled up the measure of the jealousy and rage of the duke, and one day, at a hunting-party in the wood of Bebling, he contrived to draw Hutten away from the rest of the train, and, taking him at unawares, ran him through with his sword; he then took off his girdle, and with it suspended him from one of the oak-trees in the wood. When the murder was discovered he did not deny it, but asserted that he was a free schöppe, and had performed the deed in obedience to a mandate of the Secret Tribunal, to which he was bound to yield obedience. This tale, however, did not satisfy the family of Hutten, and they were as little content with the proposal made by the murderer of giving them satisfaction before a Westphalian tribunal. They loudly appealed to the emperor for justice, and the masculine eloquence of Ulrich von Hutten interested the public so strongly in their favour, that the emperor found himself obliged to issue a sentence of outlawry against the Duke of Würtemberg. At length, through the mediation of Cardinal Lang, an accommodation both with the Hutten family and the duchess was effected; but the enmity of the former was not appeased, and they some time afterwards lent their aid to effect the deposition of the duke and the confiscation of his property.

It would seem that the Fehm-tribunals would have justified the assassination committed by the duke, at least that all confidence in their justice was now gone; and, at this period, even those writers who are most lavish in their praises of the schöppen of the olden time can find no language sufficiently strong to describe the iniquity of those of their own days. It was now become a common saying that the course of a Fehm-court was first to hang the accused and then to examine into the charges against him. By a solemn recess of the Diet at Triers, in 1512, it was declared "that by the Westphalian tribunals many an honest man had lost his honour, body, life, and property;" and the Archbishop of Cologne, who must have known them well, shortly afterwards asserted, among other charges, in a capitulation which he issued, that "by very many they were shunned and regarded as seminaries of villains."

The second case to which we alluded affords a still stronger proof of their degeneracy.

A man named Kerstian Kerkerink, who lived near the town of Münster, was accused, and probably with truth, of having committed repeated acts of adultery. The Free-tribunal of Münster determined to take cognizance of the affair, and they sent and had him taken out of his bed in the dead of the night. In order to prevent his making any noise and resistance, the persons who were employed assured him that he was to be brought before the tribunal of a respectable councillor of the city of Münster, and prevailed on him to put on his best clothes. They took him to a place named Beckman's-bush, where they kept him concealed while one of them conveyed intelligence of their success to the town-council.

At break of day the tribunal-lords, free-count, and schöppen, taking with them a monk and a common hangman, proceeded to Beckman's-bush, and had the prisoner summoned before them. When he appeared he prayed to be allowed to have an advocate; but this request was refused, and the court proceeded forthwith to pass sentence of death. The unfortunate man now implored for the delay of but one single day to settle his affairs and make his peace with God; but this request also was strongly refused, and it was signified to him that he must die forthwith, and that if he wished he might make his confession, to which end a confessor had been brought to the place. When the unhappy wretch sued once more for favour, it was replied to him that he should find favour and be beheaded, not hung. The monk was then called forward, to hear his confession; when that was over the executioner (who had previously been sworn never to reveal what he saw) advanced and struck off the head of the delinquent.

Meantime, information of what was going on had reached the town, and old and young came forth to witness the last act of the tragedy, or perhaps to interfere in favour of Kerkerink. But this had been foreseen and provided against; officers were set to watch all the approaches from the town till all was over, and when the people arrived they found nothing but the lifeless body of Kerkerink, which was placed in a coffin and buried in a neighbouring churchyard.

The bishop and chapter of Münster expressed great indignation at this irregular proceeding and encroachment on their rights, and it served to augment the general aversion to the Fehm-courts.

Our readers will at once perceive how much the proceedings in this case, which occurred in the year 1580, differed from those of former times. Then the accused was formally summoned, and he was allowed to have an advocate; here he was seized without knowing for what, and was hardly granted even the formality of a trial. Then the people who came, even accidentally, into the vicinity of a Fehm-court, would cross themselves and hasten away from the place, happy to escape with their lives: now they rush without apprehension to the spot where it was sitting, and the members of it fly at their approach. Finally, in severity as well as justice, the advantage was on the side of the old courts. The criminal suffered by the halter; we hear of no father confessor being present to console his last moments, and his body, instead of being deposited in consecrated earth, was left to be torn by the wild beasts and ravenous birds. The times were evidently altered!

The Fehm-tribunals were never formally abolished; but the excellent civil institutions of the Emperors Maximilian and Charles V., the consequent decrease of the turbulent and anarchic spirit, the introduction of the Roman law, the spread of the Protestant religion, and many other events of those times, conspired to give men an aversion for what now appeared to be a barbarous jurisdiction and only suited to such times as it was hoped and believed never could return. Some of the courts were abolished; exemptions and privileges against them were multiplied; they were prohibited all summary proceedings; their power gradually sank into insignificance; and, though up to the present century a shadow of them remained in some parts of Westphalia, they have long been only a subject of antiquarian curiosity as one of the most striking phenomena of the middle ages. They were only suited to a particular state of society: while that existed they were a benefit to the world; when it was gone they remained at variance with the state which succeeded, became pernicious, were hated and despised, lost all their

Seal of the Secret Tribunals.

influence and reputation, shared the fate of every thing human, whose character is instability and decay, and have left only their memorial behind them.

It is an important advance in civilization, and a great social gain, to have got rid, for all public purposes, of Secret Societies—both of their existence and of their use ; for, that, like most of the other obsolete forms into which the arrangements of society have at one time or other resolved themselves, some of these mysterious and exclusive institutions, whether for preserving knowledge or dispensing justice, served, each in its day, purposes of the highest utility, which apparently could not have been accomplished by any other existing or available contrivance, has been sufficiently shown by the expositions that have been given, in the preceding pages, of the mechanism and working of certain of the most remarkable of their number. But it has been made at least equally evident that the evils attendant upon their operation, and inherent in their nature, were also very great, and that, considered even as the suitable remedies for a most disordered condition of human affairs, they were at best only not quite so bad as the disease. They were institutions for preserving knowledge, not by promoting, but by preventing that diffusion of it which, after all, both gives to it its chief value, and, in a natural state of things, most effectually ensures its purification, as well as its increase ; and for executing justice, by trampling under foot the rights alike of the wrong-doer and of his victim. Mankind may be said to have stepped out of night into day, in having thrown off the burden and bondage of this form of the social system, and having attained to the power of pursuing knowledge in the spirit of knowledge, and justice in the spirit of justice. We have now escaped from that state of confusion and conflict in which one man's gain was necessarily another man's loss, and are fairly on our way towards that opposite state in which, in everything, as far as the constitution of this world will permit, the gain of one shall be the gain of all. This latter, to whatever degree it may be actually attainable, is the proper nope and goal of all human civilization.

THE END.

London: Printed by W. CLOWES and Sons, Stamford Street.